D1391908

The Economics of Unemployment

The Economics of Unemployment:

A Comparative Analysis of Britain and the United States

James J. Hughes

Reader in Economics
University of Kent

and

Richard Perlman

Professor of Economics
University of Wisconsin-Milwaukee

CAMBRIDGE UNIVERSITY PRESS
NEW YORK

Published by the Press Syndicate of the University of Cambridge
32 East 57th Street, New York, NY 10022, USA

© James J. Hughes and Richard Perlman, 1984

First published in Great Britain by Wheatsheaf Books Ltd 1984

First published in the USA by Cambridge University Press 1984

Printed in Great Britain

Library of Congress Cataloging in Publication Data
Hughes, James J.
    The economics of unemployment.

    1. Unemployment——Great Britain.   2. Unemployment——
United States.   I. Perlman, Richard.   II. Title.
HD5765.A6H83 1984   331.13'7941   84-7648
ISBN 0-521-26788-9
ISBN 0-521-31865-3 (pbk.)

Dedicated to
Heinz Schmidt
for his friendship and generosity over the
years to one of the authors
and to
Liviana Avello
for her long-term friendship to the other

Contents

Contents

Acknowledgements

We are indebted to several people who have read and commented upon earlier drafts of individual chapters. Richard Disney read several chapters and commented freely. Although we have not always taken his advice, we have benefited greatly from his incisive comments. In addition, we should like to record our thanks to John Addison, Ian Bain, Walter Elliot, Boris Pesek, Stanley Siebert, Jim Taylor and Tony Thirlwall. Although all of these individuals have contributed towards making this a better book than it might otherwise have been, all are exempted from any shortcomings in the final product.

James Hughes would also like to record his thanks to the British Academy and the Faculty of Social Sciences at the University of Kent, both of which provided small grants and made it possible for him to visit the US during the summer of 1982 to collaborate with Richard Perlman. Thanks are also due to Shirley Krug for undertaking some library searches.

Finally, our thanks are due to Barbara Fisher and Lois Grebe who shared the typing of the first draft. We are particularly indebted to Barbara Fisher for undertaking the second draft and all subsequent typing and retyping. Without her it is difficult to envisage that this book would ever have been finished.

Introduction

Current fashion in the academic as well as popular literature tends to minimise the importance of unemployment as a measure of weakness in the economy or misery for the unemployed. Several arguments are usually advanced in support of this view. For example, it is usually argued that compared to the past, unemployment insurance and welfare transfers soften the blow of lost earnings. Similarly, the higher proportion of married women who are now wage or salary earners means that within any family unit there is a greater probability than there used to be that female earnings will offset any loss in male earnings. Secondly, much of the increase in unemployment is said to be voluntary, reflecting the conscious choice of workers for temporary idleness while looking for better jobs. Thirdly, it is argued that the increase in unemployment in recent years does not reflect a general weakness in the economy, but rather a shift within the labour force towards demographic groups with characteristically high unemployment rates. Finally, the fact that countries can prosper (i.e. grow) while at the same time experiencing relatively high unemployment has meant that the definition of full employment (a catch-phrase for the politically and socially acceptable rate of unemployment) has been revised to take account of this.

While it might be true that for both individuals and the economy at large the significance of unemployment has changed through time, this does not imply that unemployment is costless or that increases in it are not cause for concern. Indeed, the dominant theme of this book is that, despite all the mitigating factors embedded in measurement and supported by modern theory which are given close examination herein, unemployment remains perhaps the most chronic economic problem facing the industrial economies of the UK and US, and requires an expansion in aggregate demand for its reduction.

One of the aims of the book is comparative, but since many of the facets of the problem are similar in the two countries there is never need to force a comparison. In both countries there is concern over measurement methods which are so important a determinant of the reported count that influences policy decisions. Both have similar institutions and programmes that affect the unemployment rate, and while the scope of unemployment insurance is more or less the same in the two countries, minimum wage effects are probably stronger in the US. On the other hand, special employment measures—including public employment programmes—are probably more common in the UK.

Chapter 1 analyses the methods of counting the unemployed and begins by discussing the stocks and flows that are involved. At any point unemployment is represented by the stock, but the flows into and out of this stock determine its volume. The purpose of this chapter is much more than taxonomic. Although the classification of flows into and out of employment may be of interest for its own sake, the nature of these flows is of great importance since at any point in time they determine the level of unemployment as well as explain the differential rates among labour force sub-groups, subjects to be treated in subsequent chapters. Measurement methods in the two countries are compared, as too are the actual rates of unemployment when these are adjusted to common definitions. Even in this chapter on measurement there is controversy—over who should be included, how the issue of the 'hidden unemployed' should be considered, and over the merits of an alternative measure to the unemployment rate.

Chapter 2 is on the classification of unemployment types. Unemployment needs to be disaggregated into its component parts if the correct remedial policies are to be pursued. It is argued here that reliable and accurate vacancy data are just as important as unemployment data for this disaggregation to proceed. The section on the debate over the voluntary–involuntary nature of unemployment lays the groundwork for the next two theoretical chapters.

The difficulty in Chapter 3 is to find new paths through familiar territory. Nevertheless an attempt to do just this is made. The critical macroeconomic debate revolves around the contrasting positions of monetarists and Keynesians, but as this chapter points out, the focus of the controversy lies in the definition of unemployment. Is unemployment involuntary, resulting from a weakness in aggregate demand? Or is it basically a supply-side phenomenon, dependent on the conscious choices of workers in trading off work against job search and leisure, and the inability of the labour market to clear? This chapter discusses some of the implications of this question even if it does not go on to provide a definitive answer. The arguments are compared and contrasted and applied to different economic conditions.

Chapter 4 is concerned with the relationship between inflation and unemployment. The differences between the two theories that attempt to explain the relationship—i.e. the traditional Phillips–Lipsey explanation and the natural rate hypothesis—are examined and it is suggested that unemployment can be reduced to its natural (i.e. frictional-structural) rate, with the least serious consequences for inflation, if demand is expanded against a background of monetary restraint.

The next two chapters (5–6) study the relationship between two institutions—minimum wages and unemployment benefits—and unemployment. Although the theoretical arguments that both induce unemployment are strong, minimum wages by pricing labour above its market level, and unemployment insurance by causing workers to engage in more job search and/or take more leisure, the empirical evidence does not indicate significant unemployment effects for either.

Chapter 7 details the post-war UK and US unemployment experience. The record is assessed against the declared aim in both countries to make low unemployment a governmental responsibility. The flow analysis developed in Chapter 1 serves as a framework for assigning the proximate source of unemployment in both countries. Particular attention is paid to the duration of unemployment as a contributor to the measured rate.

The analysis is continued in Chapter 8, but the emphasis here is on high-incidence groups, that is, those segments of the working population which have unemployment rates well above the average. Flow analysis helps explain the labour force factors leading to high unemployment for teenagers, women and racial minorities. It also explains the differential impact of recessions on the employability of these groups. While all three suffer heavy job losses, the unemployment rate for women and white teenagers is less adversely affected because of their withdrawal from the labour force into housework and school, respectively.

Chapter 9 studies the costs of unemployment. These are viewed from the perspective of the economy at large (i.e. lost production), the exchequer (i.e. reduction in tax receipts plus increase in transfer payments), as well as the individual. For the individual unemployed worker there are the costs of reduced earnings as well as the unmeasurable, but severe, human costs associated with lowered status and loss of self-esteem, not to mention the health problems associated with the worry and frustration of being out of work. In addition to the political instability that high unemployment causes as confidence is lost in the government that presides over it, there is a deeper latent threat to democratic institutions as confidence is lost in the system of government itself.

While Chapter 9 underlines the fact that the costs associated with unemployment are not just economic, Chapter 10 emphasises the main theme of the book, that unemployment is mainly a consequence of inadequate demand. It points to the futility of attempting to cure the condition by means other than demand stimulation. Public employment programmes drain off a little unemployment, work-sharing schemes through reduced hours can substitute short time for some at the expense of total joblessness of others, and early retirement programmes can bring about a once-and-for-all labour supply reduction, but each of these palliatives has severe limitations, and even when taken together they represent an inadequate alternative to demand stimulation. However, demand stimulation must take place against a background of incomes and manpower policy to temper inflationary pressures.

EDITORIAL NOTE

All references to billions and trillions are based upon the American usage.

1. Counting the Unemployed

INTRODUCTION

In both the UK and the US the level of unemployment and its rate are probably the most widely quoted of all economic statistics. When unemployment is high and rising, comparisons are frequently made with earlier periods, often without qualification or reference to changes in the definition of unemployment or changes in the administrative arrangements for collecting the statistics. In this chapter we discuss the definitions of unemployment that underlie its measurement in the UK and US, point to the major changes in these definitions over the post-second world war period, and indicate how these changes have affected the measured rate. We also point to the adjustments that have to be made to take account of the differences in the methods of measurement when comparisons across the two countries are made.

The measurement of any economic variable is important when it acts as a guide to policy-makers. Unemployment statistics are particularly important because they are widely regarded as an indicator of the overall performance of the economy. Thus, if the unemployment rate increases over a number of months then pressures will begin to build up for major policy changes. In a narrower labour market sense the unemployment rate is an indicator of the utilisation of labour, providing summary information about the extent to which the economy is able to provide jobs for those that want them. Finally, given that earnings losses are associated with unemployment, the unemployment rate is sometimes regarded as an indicator of economic hardship or need. For all of these reasons governments and policy-makers are sensitive to changes in the rate of unemployment.

Superficially, unemployment might appear to be a simple and straightforward concept. Either the worker has a job, in which case he is employed, or he is without a job and therefore regarded as being unemployed. However, this interpretation glosses over a number of important issues. For example, it fails to draw the distinction between being 'out of work' and being 'without a job'. An individual with no job and no attachment to the labour force will clearly regard himself as being without a job, but is unlikely to look upon himself as being out of work and, therefore, unemployed. Another individual, with a strong attachment to the labour force, will equate being without a job with being out of work. To such an individual joblessness will therefore imply unemployment. Between these two extremes, where attachment to the labour force is neither absolute nor zero, the distinction between joblessness and unemployment becomes blurred, and changes in unemployment do not simply mirror changes in employment.

A related issue to that of labour force attachment is the distinction between full-time and part-time working. The question that has to be faced is whether part-time workers are given equal weighting to full-time workers when employment and unemployment are being measured. Although from a theoretical standpoint the answer would seem obvious, in fact the distinction between full-time and part-time working might not always be so clear cut.

The same question arises in relation to differences in worker productivity. Should the unemployment of an unskilled, low-productivity worker be treated in identical fashion to that of a highly-skilled and highly-productive worker? Or should differences in productivity be taken into account when measuring unemployment? This issue is important when the unemployment rate is seen as a measure of the performance of the economy.

Before touching upon these issues we examine the level and rate of unemployment in relation to labour market stocks and flows, thereby establishing the framework within which these measurement problems will be discussed.

LABOUR MARKET STOCKS AND FLOWS

At any point in time the size and structure of the working age population (P) is given and can be subdivided between labour force (L) and non-labour force (N). All three variables, P, L and N, constitute stocks and dividing L by P gives the labour force participation rate (r), often referred to as the activity rate. Such rates can be calculated for any sub-group within the working age population. Thus at time t we have:

$$r_t = L_t/P_t,$$
or   (1)
$$L_t = r_t P_t$$

Since at any point in time L will consist of workers who are employed (E), and those who are unemployed (U), then:

$$L_t = E_t + U_t,$$
or   (2)
$$U_t = L_t - E_t$$

Substituting for L_t this can be rewritten:

$$U_t = r_t P_t - E_t$$ (3)

and changes in the stock of unemployed between two points in time, t and t – 1, will be given by:

$$U_t - U_{t-1} = (r_t P_t - r_{t-1} P_{t-1}) - (E_t - E_{t-1}) \qquad (4)$$

Changes in the unemployment stock between t and t–1 will therefore depend upon the changes in working age population and participation rate as well as the change in the stock of employment. (These points are taken up again in the discussion of high incidence groups in Chapter 8.) Only if the participation rate is constant for a population of given size will changes in the level of unemployment mirror changes in the level of employment.

Of course, any net change in the stock of unemployment, $U_t - U_{t-1}$, will result from labour market flows that take place between t and t–1. If changes in the working age population are ruled out, as they might be when month-to-month changes in unemployment are being considered, changes in unemployment will reflect either changes in the participation rate or changes in employment. Changes in the former occur when individuals move between the labour force and the non-labour force, with an increase in participation reflecting a net movement into the labour force. Changes in employment can be more complicated, occurring when workers move from employment to unemployment, and vice versa; when workers previously employed leave the labour force; and when those previously outside the labour force take up a job. Clearly, changes in participation can involve either changes in employment or changes in unemployment, while changes in employment will give rise to changes in unemployment or changes in participation.

The flow between employment and unemployment will depend upon the relationship between a number of subsidiary flows, voluntary quits, involuntary terminations and lay-offs (including temporary lay-offs), recalls and new hires. The flow between labour force and non-labour force will be related to factors affecting participation. Such factors might involve decisions affecting education, marriage, child bearing, child-minding and retirement, as well as changes in the remuneration of, and the opportunities for, employment.

Employment will be at a constant level when the flow of new hirings plus recalls (both from amongst the unemployed and from outside of the labour force) are just equal to the flow of retirements, quits and terminations, including lay-offs. Unemployment will be unchanging when the flow of hirings and recalls is just equal to the flow of quits and terminations, including lay-offs, plus the net difference between labour force entries into unemployment and labour force exits from unemployment.

If changes in working age population are not ruled out, as they cannot be when year-to-year, or decade-to-decade, changes are being considered, then changes in both the size and age distribution of the population will affect the flows into and out of the labour force.

Figure 1.1 is a schematic representation of the main flows that take place between the labour force and the non-labour force.

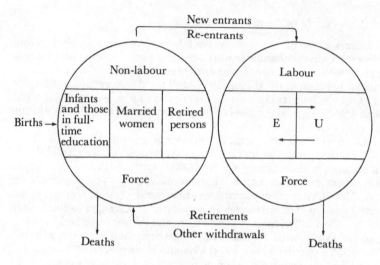

Figure 1.1

The unemployment rate at t, u_t, is defined as the number actually unemployed expressed as a percentage of the labour force, i.e.:

$$u_t = \frac{U_t}{L_t} . 100 = \frac{U_t}{U_t + E_t} . 100$$

which can be rewritten to give:

$$u_t = \frac{U_t}{r_t P_t} . 100$$

Given equations (2) and (3) it would seem that unemployment is unambiguously measured as a residual when employment is subtracted from the labour force. However, if there is ambiguity and uncertainty surrounding the definition of the labour force—and hence its measurement—there will also be ambiguity and uncertainty surrounding the measurement of unemployment. Such ambiguity does in fact exist and arises from the uncertainty that surrounds labour force participation. Although an individual is clearly a participant in the labour market, and hence a member of the labour force, provided that he works for pay[1] and not voluntarily,[2] when an individual is not currently employed his labour market status will depend upon the criteria adopted to distinguish between being unemployed and being outside of the labour force. Different criteria, stemming from different approaches to the measurement of unemployment, are adopted in the UK and the US. These different approaches, and the criticisms that are made of each, are discussed below.

A SNAPSHOT VIEW

While the relative magnitude of the stocks (employment, unemployment and non-labour force population) will determine the level and the rate of unemployment, it is the relationships between the rates of flow between these stocks that determine changes in the level of unemployment. As already noted, the stock of unemployment will vary according to the flows into, and out of work. Since these flows can change from day to day, week to week, and so on, both the size of the unemployment stock and its composition will undergo constant change. This being so, the stock on any one day, or in any particular week, will represent a snapshot view of what may be a changing unemployment situation. Although only relatively small changes in the stock occur from month to month, the flows that are responsible for these changes are much greater. Even where the size of the stock remains constant because the flows into it are just offset by outflows from it, the individuals in the stock will be changing. Thus changes in the characteristics of the unemployed, as well as changes in the distribution of the unemployment stock between different labour market groups, are both consistent with a stock of constant size.

Given that those in the unemployment stock are only identified on a particular day or week in the month, then clearly those who flow into and out of the stock between these dates will never figure in the official count.

MEASUREMENT IN THE UK: THE REGISTRATION APPROACH

In the UK, the Department of Employment (DE) keeps a register of unemployed persons and publishes the 'official' unemployment figures each month. Until, and including, October 1982 the official count consisted of those who, on the day of the count,[3] had registered themselves at the local offices of the Employment Services Agency, or the Youth Employment Service, as being both unemployed and 'capable and available' for work. Registration for work was regarded as being the first test of availability. To prove further his availability for work an individual on the register was expected to accept suitable job offers that were made to him. In this context suitability was judged by reference to the individual's usual employment and also according to whether the wages and conditions associated with the job were at generally acceptable levels.[4]

The British system of collecting unemployment statistics is a by-product of an administrative process since under the National Insurance Acts an individual had, until October 1982, to register in order to qualify for unemployment and supplementary benefit. However, not everyone is covered by the Acts and, since the incentive to register is much weaker for those not covered, the official unemployment count will not include all those who are genuinely available for and desirous of paid work. Furthermore, until October 1982, administrative and legal changes which affected registration clearly affected the official unemployment count.

Although registration was a necessary first step for inclusion in the official unemployment figures until October 1982, it was not in itself a sufficient step. The following categories of unemployed were excluded from the official count: those experiencing a period of sickness lasting more than three days; some categories of the severely disabled; those who were only registered for part-time work and who were not claiming benefit; and women in receipt of a National Insurance maternity allowance. In addition, the temporarily stopped had been excluded from the official count since November 1972, and adult students since March 1976. Apart from the severely disabled these categories will continue to be excluded under the new system.

While qualification for benefit was a strong incentive to register until October 1982, registration was not confined to those in receipt of benefit. For example, in February 1981 only 48 per cent of the unemployed were in receipt of unemployment benefit; almost 20 per cent received neither unemployment nor supplementary benefit.[5] On the other hand, the incentive to register was clearly reduced for several groups, including married females, who, prior to 1977, could opt out of the full National Insurance scheme, sacrificing their entitlement to benefit in return for greatly reduced contributions. However, since that date the withdrawal of this option for new female entrants will have tended to reduce the disincentive effect for married females as a group. The incentive to register was also weaker for young new entrants into the labour force prior to the raising of the minimum school leaving age in 1973 to sixteen years since their lack of contributions disqualified them from unemployment benefit, and their age disqualified them from drawing supplementary benefit. Likewise, the incentive was weaker for those beyond retirement age who, though drawing their pension, were still looking for work. Finally, the incentive to register was—and still is—weaker for those who quit their job voluntarily or were dismissed for misconduct, since in both cases there is a loss of entitlement to benefit during the first few weeks of unemployment.

After the count of October 1982 registration ceased to be a condition of entitlement to unemployment benefit, except for young people under eighteen years of age. This switch to voluntary registration was made on the grounds that it 'will improve the efficiency of the unemployment and benefit services'.[6] Thus, from November 1982 onwards, the official count has no longer been based on registrations for employment because of the expected decline in these; instead it has been transferred to the Unemployment Benefit Offices and is now based upon the computerised records of claimants for benefit. As a result of this changeover a discontinuity in the unemployment series has arisen, since under the new arrangements non-claimants of benefit are excluded from the count while the severely disabled are included.

Before the changeover, claimants accounted for about 96 per cent of registrations in most months, with the exception of June, July and August, when school leavers—who cannot become claimants until the following September—traditionally swell the number of non-claimants.[7] It was therefore expected, prior to the changeover, that the exclusion of non-claimants other than school leavers would reduce the count by about 100,000 per month. On the other hand, the inclusion of the severely disabled was expected to raise it by about 20,000. In addition, the changeover from a clerical to a computerised count will be more accurate because it will identify more quickly those who move onto and off the register on the day of the count. While this is expected to reduce the count, the DE was uncertain about the likely magnitude of this effect prior to the introduction of the new system.

With the exception of the under eighteen age group, the abolition of the registration requirement for all other groups in late 1982 will have reduced the incentive for these groups to register. It is therefore difficult to see how the change in the basis of the count—from compulsory registration to benefit claimants—can lead to an improvement in the efficiency of the employment service.

In the UK there therefore exists a pool of unregistered unemployed that represents an important part of aggregate labour supply because it consists of workers who are both capable and available for work. We discuss further the unregistered unemployed below. Assuming that the incentive to register amongst non-claimants has not been eroded completely since the introduction of the new system, there will also exist a third category of unemployed—those registered but not included in the official count.

Although there is a continuous series of unemployment statistics based on the 'capable of and available for work' definition going back to 1922,[8] the statistics for the inter-war period are not comparable with those for 1948–82. There are two reasons for this. First, while the inter-war figures relate only to the insured unemployed, the more recent figures include some non-insured workers. Secondly, and more importantly, the National Insurance Acts did not cover the whole of the primary work force during the inter-war period as they have done since July 1948. Clearly the official unemployment rate will be biased if there is a differential incidence of unemployment experienced by the insured and non-insured segments of the workforce, as was the case during the inter-war period.

While the official unemployment figures were affected by a large number of administrative and legal changes during the inter-war years,[9] the changes since 1948 have been relatively few, but taken together they mean that the official unemployment rate in late 1982 was over 1 per cent lower than it would have been had the changes not occurred. The raising of the minimum school leaving age from fifteen to sixteen in 1973, which raised the minimum age for inclusion in the labour force, reduced marginally the size of the labour force thereby causing the unemployment rate to rise. Although the effect on the rate has only been marginal (i.e. about 0.05 per cent), it will have been reinforced by the tendency for more young people to remain in full-time education beyond the minimum school leaving age.

There is some variation in the number of temporarily stopped from year to year, but their exclusion from the official count from November 1972 onwards reduced the rate, on average, by about 0.2 per cent over the period. Given the tendency for adult students to register during vacations only, their exclusion from the count in April 1976 had a more marked impact on the rate in certain months than in others. For example, in 1976 the absolute number registered exceeded 100,000 in January, April, July, August and September, and was as high as 179,000 in April. However, the average number on the register throughout the year was about 66,000 and their exclusion from the official count meant that the annual average rate for 1976 was depressed by 0.3 percentage points.

The most important discontinuity in the post-1948 series has been wrought by the changes introduced in October 1982, and which affected the count for the first time in November of that year. In that month the DE estimated the difference between the old and the new counts to be 220,000 (i.e. 0.9 per cent of the labour force).

Finally, in the computation of the unemployment rate the denominator that is used is the number of employees (both employed and unemployed) rather than the working population, or civilian working population. In other words, both employers and the self-employed are excluded from the definition of labour force. If they were included then the rate for 1979 would have been 5.3 per cent rather than 5.7 per cent, while the recorded rate for 1982—which exceeded 13 per cent—would have been about 1 per cent lower. Since there is a considerable time-lag before the mid-year estimate of employees in employment becomes available, the latest available mid-year estimate is used in the calculation of the unemployment rate. For this reason the rate is subject to minor revisions some considerable time after it has first appeared.

THE US APPROACH: MEASUREMENT BY SURVEY[10]

Although statistics relating to insured unemployment are also available in the US, collected by state employment security agencies as a by-product of the unemployment insurance programme, the data are inadequate for the purpose of computing a summary measure of unemployment for the economy as a whole. This is because as late as 1977 only about three-quarters of the civilian labour force was covered by unemployment insurance. Although this fraction has increased since 1978 due to an extension in coverage that brought agricultural workers and local government employees within its scope, the fact that the data are based on claims for insurance means that all those who have exhausted their benefits, or are ineligible because of inadequate contributions, or as a result of disqualification, will not be included. Thus, in contrast to the UK registration approach the Bureau of Labor Statistics (BLS) of the US Department of Labor publishes monthly unemployment (and employment) statistics that are based on the Census Bureau's Current Population Survey (CPS). This is a monthly sample survey of all households in the nation, the sample consisting of about 47,000 households in 923 counties and independent cities across the country. Industry and agriculture, urban and rural areas and other geographic divisions are represented in the same proportion as they occur in the population as a whole. Each month a quarter of the households within the sample are replaced, thereby ensuring that no family is interviewed for more than four consecutive months. However, after eight months each household is brought back into the sample for a further four months before being dropped completely. Such a procedure results in a continuity of data which facilitates short-run comparisons.

The minimum age for inclusion in the survey is sixteen years, and those covered by it are classified as employed, unemployed or not in the labour force according to their activity during the reference (i.e. survey) week. Those who worked for pay or profit at any time during the survey week are classified as employed; thus, part-timers, full-timers and temporary workers are all included. In addition, those who had a job but were absent from work during the survey week because of industrial disputes, bad weather, illness or any other personal reason, are also counted as employed.

Persons classified as unemployed are those who, though available for work, did not work for pay or profit at any time during the survey week but did take active steps in looking for work in the four-week period prior to the survey. In this context, looking for work might involve any of the following: registering for work at a public or private employment office; meeting with prospective employers; checking with friends and relatives; placing or answering advertisements; writing letters of application; being on a union or professional register.

Workers on temporary lay-off—and thus expecting to be recalled by their employer—and those waiting to start a new job within thirty days are exempted from the need to undertake job search even though they are still included among the unemployed. All other persons without a job who fail to satisfy the search criteria are classified as being 'not in the labour force'.

Although unemployment statistics based on CPS data go back to 1940, labour market concepts and definitions have been refined during the intervening period. In the early years neither the test of current

availability nor the four-week job search criterion were applied, and
the lower age limit for inclusion in the official statistics was fourteen
years. Furthermore, those on temporary lay-off or waiting to take up a
new job were regarded as being employed, while those absent from
their job during the survey week as a result of strikes, bad weather,
etc.—but looking for other jobs—were classified as unemployed. It was
not until 1957 that workers laid off and those waiting to take up a new
job were counted as part of the unemployed. The other changes,
namely the raising of the lower age limit to sixteen years, the
introduction of the availability test, the four-week job search criterion
and the transfer of people absent from work because of strikes,
bad weather etc. from the unemployed to the employed category,
took place in 1967. As a result of all these changes unemployment
in 1967 was estimated to be 0.1 per cent lower than under the old
definition.[11]

Up to December 1982 the CPS estimates of labour force have been
based upon the civilian non-institutional population; they have
therefore included the self-employed, but excluded members of the
armed forces. From January 1983 onwards the armed forces have been
included.

Since 1967 CPS has identified discouraged workers as a separate and
distinct group within the 'not in the labour force' category. These are
workers, sixteen years of age and over, who at the time of interview
want a job but are not actively seeking work because they believe they
would be unsuccessful. In other words, it is discouragement over job
prospects that prevents them from searching. Excluded from the
discouraged worker category are those whose main activity during the
survey week is attending school, and those whose lack of job search is
attributable to illness, disability or family responsibilities.

BLS publishes information on discouraged workers quarterly, and
in 1977, out of 59 million persons not in the labour force, only 1 million
were placed in this category, even though 6 million claimed that they
wanted a regular job.[12] Clearly, where genuine cases of discouragement occur, labour resources are being under-utilised and any attempt
to measure the extent of the supply of labour available to the economy
should take account of it.

Given the sample survey approach to the measurement of unemployment in the US, the resulting estimates will be subject to
sampling error. While the sample is sufficiently large to ensure only a
small error in the national estimates of unemployment, the same
cannot be said for estimates of geographical sub-divisions within the
country. Indeed, CPS unemployment estimates for states and localities
are subject to much greater sampling errors than the national estimate.
The problem of sampling error does not arise under the registration
method adopted in the UK and, therefore, there is no reason to
suppose that, given the definitions used, the unemployment estimates
for geographic sub-divisions of the country will be any less reliable

than the national estimate. Indeed, the latter is simply an aggregation of local estimates.

To overcome the problem of sampling error in its estimates of state and local unemployment rates the BLS combines data from CPS, the unemployment insurance programme and the population census. The welding together of these data sources is known as the Handbook Method and makes use of national relationships between unemployment insurance claims and total unemployment. This reliance upon national relationships, coupled with an element of guesswork in the estimation of state and local employment, means that the final outcome is an overestimate of unemployment rates in some states and an underestimate in others.

COMPARISON OF UK AND US RATES

Given the different systems for measuring unemployment in the two countries, there is a need to adjust the statistics to a common conceptual framework before meaningful comparisons can be made. The BLS initiated work in the early 1960s on the international comparison of unemployment rates and has since refined its methods which involve the adjustment of data from other countries to US definitions. Adopting this approach Sorrentino,[13] and more recently Moy,[14] have updated the comparisons and the results for Great Britain and the US are shown in Table 1.1.

Although a substantial upward revision was required to bring the British rate into line with the US rate in the 1960s, by the late 1970s the extent of the revision was negligible, and for 1980-1 no revision was necessary. As Sorrentino has pointed out, this can be explained by three factors, all of which have probably caused an increase in registrations in the UK. First, as economic conditions deteriorate and the level of unemployment increases, the number of registrations will probably increase as those thrown out of work will tend to rely less on their own methods of job search. Secondly, this has probably been reinforced by an increased incentive to register resulting from the introduction of higher unemployment benefits in 1966. Finally, British social security legislation was changed in 1975 in such a way that made it impossible for women marrying after April 1977 to opt out of the National Insurance scheme. As a consequence of this change, recently married females will therefore have a greater incentive to register.

CRITICISMS OF THE UK APPROACH

UK unemployment statistics have come under attack from two different groups—those who argue that the official figures exaggerate the extent of 'real' unemployment, and those who argue that the opposite is true.

Table 1.1: *Unemployment in Great Britain and US Compared*

Year	(1) GB unadjusted rate	(2) GB adjusted rate	(3) US rate	(4) Absolute unadjusted difference (3–1)	(5) Absolute adjusted difference (3–2)
1959	2.2	2.9	5.5	3.3	2.6
1960	1.6	2.2	5.5	3.9	3.3
1961	1.5	2.0	6.7	5.2	4.7
1962	2.0	2.8	6.5	4.5	3.7
1963	2.5	3.4	5.7	3.2	2.3
1964	1.6	2.5	5.2	3.6	2.7
1965	1.4	2.2	4.5	3.1	2.3
1966	1.5	2.3	3.8	2.3	1.5
1967	2.4	3.4	3.8	1.4	0.4
1968	2.4	3.3	3.6	1.2	0.3
1969	2.4	3.0	3.5	1.1	0.5
1970	2.6	3.1	4.9	2.3	1.8
1971	3.6	3.7	5.9	2.3	2.2
1972	3.7	4.1	5.6	1.9	1.5
1973	2.6	2.9	4.9	2.3	2.0
1974	2.6	3.1	5.6	3.0	2.5
1975	4.1	4.6	8.5	4.4	4.1
1976	5.6	6.0	7.7	2.1	1.7
1977	6.0	6.4	7.1	1.1	0.7
1978	6.0	6.3	6.1	0.1	−0.2
1979	5.6	5.7	5.8	0.2	−0.1
1980	7.3	7.3	7.1	−0.2	−0.2
1981	11.3	11.3	7.6	−3.7	−3.7

Sources: C. Sorrentino, 'Unemployment in international perspective', in B. Showler and A. Sinfield (eds), *The Workless State* (Oxford: Martin Robertson, 1981). Joyanne Moy, 'Unemployment and labor force trends in ten industrial nations: an update', *Monthly Labor Review*, November 1982.

John Wood,[15] of the Institute of Economic Affairs, was one of the earliest critics of the official figures, arguing that they include categories that should not be included. In this he has been supported by the influential journalist Sam Brittan[16] and the Centre for Policy Studies.[17] The main categories that these critics have sought to remove are: the temporarily stopped, school leavers, adult students, the short-term unemployed, fraudulent claimants, occupational pensioners, and so-called unemployables. Hughes[18] has already discussed the rationale of this approach and it is not intended to reproduce a lengthy rebuttal of the individual proposals here. However, it is important to stress that all of these critics have been concerned only with the demand-deficient component of unemployment because they believe that concentration on the total measure does, in times of rising unemployment, mislead governments into expanding aggregate demand too much and too quickly, with adverse consequences for the price level. The main criticism of this approach is not simply that it implies—and sometimes makes explicit—that non-demand-deficient types of unemployment are unimportant, but that the excluded categories, when aggregated, do not represent a realistic estimate of non-demand-deficient unemployment.

For example, it is not only illogical to include school leavers as part of the employed labour force if they are successful in obtaining a job, but exclude them from the unemployment figures if they are unsuccessful, it is also wrong to suppose that the number of school leavers on the register can be divorced from the overall state of demand in the economy. Similarly, with the short-term unemployed it is incorrect to equate, quite arbitrarily, the number of persons who have been unemployed for, say, up to eight weeks on the day of the count, with frictional unemployment (i.e. job changing). As the demand for labour falls, and terminations and lay-offs increase, it seems highly likely that initially the proportion of short-term uncompleted spells of unemployment will also increase. Likewise, there is no readily identifiable group that can be termed unemployable. While carrying out intermittent surveys into the characteristics of the unemployed, local DE officials have in the past identified certain individuals as having poor prospects of employment, or as being unenthusiastic for work. However, in categorising the unemployed in this way, local officials have not only been guided by the abilities and motivation of the individuals concerned, but also by the general employment prospects in the locality, and this latter cannot be divorced from the general level of demand. In other words, the number of people placed in this category is itself likely to be cyclically sensitive. Although fraudulent claimants—that is, those who register themselves as unemployed while undertaking paid work unknown to the authorities —should be excluded from the unemployment figures, the number of identifiable cases is small and presumably when they do come to light the individuals concerned are excluded. On the other hand, to exclude occupational pensioners on the grounds that they are in receipt of a private pension implies that they are neither in need of paid work, nor available for it. There is very little evidence to support either of these views.

In 1972, following Wood's indictment of the official statistics, an inter-departmental working party was set up to enquire into the nature of the unemployment statistics and to consider whether the unemployment register contained groups of people who should not be on it because they did not constitute part of the genuine reserve of labour. It concluded that all groups, except the temporarily stopped, should continue to be included in the official count. In addition to reaffirming that the various groups ought to continue to be included, the working party pointed to the insuperable difficulties of identifying these groups, with the exception of the temporarily stopped and adult students. At the time these were already shown separately within the official count, while still being part of it. After the publication of the working party report the temporarily stopped were excluded.

Wood continued to refine his arguments, and in revised versions of his work (1975 and 1982) he suggests the adoption of a 'strategic indicator' as a more reliable guide to policy-makers than the official unemployment rate. If adopted, the strategic indicator would include only male workers aged 25–54 years who have been out of work for six months or more. Thus, all female workers, all male workers below the age of 25 and above the age of 54, together with all males of prime working age who have been out of work for less than six months, would be excluded from the official count. If Wood's strategic indicator had been used to measure unemployment in Great Britain in July 1981, the official count would have been reduced from around 2.75 million to less than 500,000.

Quite apart from the question of whether or not Wood's strategic indicator is a better measure of the *level* of unemployment than the official count, is the question of how it compares with the official measure in recording changes in the level of unemployment. This is something which Wood has not considered. Obviously, the difference in the two measures must reflect differences in the unemployment experience of those groups who are excluded from the strategic indicator and that group that is included (i.e. males, 25–54 years of age, unemployed for more than six months). If the excluded groups tend to suffer disproportionately as unemployment increases, this would cause Wood's measure to lag the official measure. However, this tendency would be offset if long-term male unemployment (i.e. lasting more than six months) increases more quickly than short-term male unemployment.

The opposite view of the official unemployment figures is taken by the Trades Union Congress (TUC). In January 1982, when registered unemployment reached 3 million, the TUC[19] claimed that the real level of unemployment was in excess of 4 million, consisting of 672,000 unregistered unemployed, 350,000 who were benefiting from the government's special employment measures, and 42,000 full-time job equivalents resulting from short-time working in the economy. For including the 350,000 covered by the government's special employment measures, the TUC might fairly be accused of wanting its cake and eating it.[20] Although these jobs depend upon government subsidies of one form or another, the individuals occupying them are being paid for their services and their output contributes to national output and well-being. Therefore, in principle, these jobs are no different from other jobs in other sectors of the economy that are dependent on government subsidy. However, the TUC is on much safer ground when it includes the unregistered unemployed, and it is to this that we now turn.

THE UNREGISTERED UNEMPLOYED

The fact that over fairly short periods of time changes in employment are not mirrored by changes in unemployment suggests the existence of a labour reserve outside the labour force. The unregistered unemployed contribute to this reserve, and Garside[21] has identified several categories of marginal workers who might not register when they become unemployed. These include: married women who are not eligible for unemployment benefit because they have opted not to pay the full National Insurance contribution; occupational pensioners and others who are not eligible to claim benefit, or who have exhausted their entitlement to benefit; those above retirement age who, though they draw a state pension, would like to work to supplement that pension; widows, young entrants to the labour force and the self-employed; those who are unemployed but between jobs (professional and skilled white-collar workers in particular may fall into this category).

In addition, there is evidence of a hidden female labour reserve consisting of married women who, it is reckoned, would enter the job market if only the appropriate employment opportunities presented themselves. In other words, although they might not be looking for work at a particular point, they constitute a labour reserve which could be activated at some time in the future.

Information on the unregistered unemployed can be obtained from three main sources: the decennial Census of Population; the General Household Survey (GHS), which covers 12,000–15,000 households and has been undertaken each year since 1971; and the EEC Labour Force Survey, conducted biannually since 1973 and covering 80,000 households. Each of these adopts different definitions and criteria from the DE for the measurement of unemployment and, therefore, certain adjustments have to be made before estimates of unregistered unemployment can be obtained from them.

In the GHS, unemployment consists of those who in the week prior to interview were looking for work, or would have been looking for work if they had not been temporarily sick, or were waiting to take up a job that they had already obtained. Before comparing the official DE figures with those of the GHS to obtain an estimate of unregistered unemployment, DE data will need to be adjusted downwards to take account of the fact that some of those unemployed on the day of the count will have been employed on other days in the week and would not therefore be counted in a GHS survey. Also, an adjustment will need to be made to take account of occupational pensioners who are included in the DE figures but not in those of the GHS. Similarly, the GHS data will need to be adjusted downwards because it includes those looking for part-time work and adult students. When all of the necessary adjustments have been made the difference between the two series gives an estimate of unregistered unemployment.

According to the GHS, unregistered unemployment has accounted for a declining proportion of total unemployment (i.e. registered plus unregistered) since 1974. Between that year and 1980 the proportion of unregistered male unemployment declined from 15 to 11 per cent; for females the corresponding decline was from 77 to 43 per cent. While indicating the trend, these figures do not take account of the adjustments mentioned above. For example, after making the necessary adjustments, the DE calculated that for 1974 the proportions for males and females were 13 and 67 per cent, respectively.[22]

It is sometimes suggested that the unregistered unemployed are discouraged workers. However, they do not correspond to discouraged workers in the US sense. This is because when those who are unemployed because of temporary sickness are removed from the GHS sample, the GHS estimate of unregistered unemployment will include: (a) those looking for work in the reference week; and (b) those waiting to start a job that they have already obtained. Clearly, category (a)—which accounts for the largest part of GHS unregistered unemployment—would be included in the US definition of unemployment. The same is true for category (b), provided that those included in it intend to take up their new job within thirty days. Thus, the GHS estimate of unregistered unemployment picks up those who would be included in the US survey approach to measuring unemployment. It does not include those who, under US definitions, are regarded as discouraged workers. Indeed, one of the contributory factors to the decline in the proportion of unregistered unemployment among females might be discouragement among those not entitled to unemployment benefit. Other factors might be that the decline in demand for female labour that has occurred during the second half of the 1970s has affected covered workers proportionately more than uncovered workers, and the effect of legislation that has tended to increase the relative size of the covered female labour force.

CRITICISMS OF THE US APPROACH

In the US, criticisms of the BLS unemployment figures, and disagreement over their interpretation (e.g. do they still mean what they used to mean?) have led periodically to the establishment of committees to reassess the statistics and review the underlying definitions and concepts in the light of changing labour market needs. An inter-agency committee of experts was set up in 1955 and the changes that were introduced in 1957 resulted largely from its recommendations. In 1961 a Presidential committee to appraise employment and unemployment statistics,[23] known as the Gordon Committee, was established to review labour force concepts, definitions and the sources of labour market information. In its report it made over 200 recommendations, all designed to improve the quality and scope of existing labour market data and thereby provide a better guide to policy-makers. Although the majority of these recommendations were never adopted, others, which were designed to sharpen labour force definitions (e.g. those relating to availability, job search, minimum age for inclusion in labour force and the reclassification of strikers and absentees from unemployed to employed) were implemented in 1967.

Since the deliberations of the Gordon Committee, the changing structure of the labour force, coupled with the development of interventionist policies within the labour market to combat poverty, discrimination and unemployment, have once again prompted questions about the changing nature of the statistics and highlighted the need for more reliable labour market data. In particular, the allocation of federal funds to employment and training programmes on the basis of state and local unemployment data has raised questions about the adequacy of that data. Therefore in 1976, Congress established the National Commission on Employment and Unemployment Statistics to reassess the system of labour force statistics and make recommendations for improving it. The Commission presented its report[24] in September 1979.

The Commission reaffirmed the distinction between paid and unpaid work as a sound basis for labour force concepts and definitions. Nevertheless, it did make certain recommendations that involve changes for both definitions and methods of data collection. Given the ending of the draft the Commission argued that members of the armed forces ought to be included in the statistics on national employment and labour force. This recommendation, which has implications for the computation of the national unemployment rate, was implemented in January 1983. The Commission did not make the same recommendation for state and local labour force statistics. While implementation of the Commission's recommendation concerning the armed forces implies a lack of definitional consistency as between national and state–local labour force statistics,[25] the Commission nevertheless felt justified in proposing this course given that with a voluntary army individuals are free to choose between employment in the armed services and civilian employment. However, while there is free choice at the macro level, at the local level there are no flows between the local labour market and the military job slots that are available locally. The effect of including the armed forces in the labour force is to reduce the unemployment rate by about 0.2 per cent.

The Commission further recommended that those involved in special employment and training programmes ought to be classified according to whether they are in receipt of money wages, participating in on-the-job training, or exclusively in classroom training. It recommended that those in receipt of wages or involved in on-the-job training ought to be classified as employed, while participants in programmes that provide only classroom teaching be classified as not in the labour force, unless they are also working part-time or searching for work. At the moment, only those who volunteer information on their participation in special employment and training programmes are classified along these lines, the remainder being classified purely on the basis of whether or not they are also employed or searching for work.

In order to improve the reliability of annual statistics for states, Standard Metropolitan Survey Areas and major central cities, the Commission recommended that the CPS sample ought to be expanded by 42,000 households, and that survey resources be concentrated in major population centres. This recommendation was seen as vital given the importance that is attached to state and local unemployment statistics in the allocation of federal aid.

The Commission recommended no change in job search criteria for defining unemployment, or in the age and hours criteria for determining labour force status. However, while recommending that discouraged workers ought to continue to be excluded from the unemployment statistics, it did suggest different criteria for identifying such workers.

DISCOURAGED WORKERS

Table 1.2 shows estimates of discouraged workers for selected years. It shows that changes in the number of discouraged workers exhibit a similar cyclical pattern to that of the official unemployment rate. However, whereas the official unemployment measure increased by 79 per cent between 1979 and 1982, the discouraged worker series increased by 109 per cent.

Table 1.2: *Discouraged Workers, 1971–82 (000s)*

	1971	1973	1975	1979	1980	1981	1982
Total discouraged	774	679	1082	750	971	1103	1568
Females as % of total	69	67	67	63	64	64	63
Official unemployment rate	5.9	4.9	8.5	5.8	7.1	7.6	9.7

Sources: Employment and Training Report of the President, 1981. Employment and Earnings, January 1983.

Females account for about two-thirds of all discouraged workers, and during 1982 three-quarters of all discouraged workers cited labour market factors as the reason for not seeking a job. The remainder cited personal factors (e.g. too young, too old, lacking necessary education or training, etc.).

Any attempt to estimate the number of discouraged workers must necessarily involve distinguishing between different strengths of labour force attachment for those not in the labour force. Since CPS data show that the labour force attachment of discouraged workers is not markedly different from that of others not in the labour force, the Commission argued that there is a need to introduce a more stringent test of attachment. It argued that the test of attachment that is currently employed is both arbitrary and subjective and, therefore, gives rise to unreliable estimates of the number of discouraged workers. It is arbitrary because when reasons other than discouragement are cited for not searching, these are taken to imply unavailability; it is subjective because it is impossible to give a realistic answer to the question 'Are you looking for work now?' without any reference to pay and conditions of work.

In order to introduce a more stringent test of labour force attachment, the Commission advocated that key features of the Canadian Labour Force Survey be integrated into the CPS approach. In essence, this involves incorporating criteria concerning recency of job search and current availability into the test. The Commission advocated a six-month cut-off for recent job search and suggested that current availability could be determined by asking the individual directly whether or not there is any reason why he cannot take a job in the survey week. This would mean that an individual would be classified as a discouraged worker if he is without a job in the survey week but wants one even though he has not searched during the last four weeks, provided that there has been some search during the last six months. In addition, there must be nothing to prevent him taking a job in the survey week if offered one. According to the Commission, tightening up the criteria for estimating discouraged workers along the lines of the Canadian LFS might result in a lower estimate of discouraged workers than that obtained using the current CPS approach.

A NEW MEASURE

If it is to be a useful and reliable macroeconomic indicator, the unemployment rate—or rather changes in it—should reflect changes in the overall level of economic activity. This it does quite well, although usually changes in the rate lag behind changes in GNP—particularly during a period of economic recovery. However, it has been suggested that if the unemployment rate is to reflect the true economic significance of unemployment, as measured in terms of lost output, then some refinements are called for.

Whenever unemployment exists output will always be less than its potential and, provided that the relationship between unemployment and output is linear and stable through time, changes in unemployment will always reflect changes in output. Thus the unemployment rates at different points in time will reflect the relative performance or under-performance of the economy in terms of lost output. But if the relationship between unemployment and output is non-linear, perhaps because of changes in the composition of unemployment, comparison of unemployment rates might not be so good a measure of relative performance. For example, although unemployment might increase by, say, x per cent, output might fall by more (or less) than this. A situation in which output falls more quickly than unemployment is likely to arise in a cyclical downturn, as more productive workers are increasingly laid off as unemployment increases. To compare unemployment rates might, therefore, understate the cyclical change that is taking place. Secular changes in the composition of unemployment might also affect the relationship between output and unemployment and it is conceivable that the output losses associated with a given rate of unemployment could fall. Therefore, in order to take account of changes in the composition of the unemployed, and the labour force too, it has been suggested by both Perry[26] and Peston[27] that a weighted unemployment rate ought to be calculated. The numerator of this rate would be computed by aggregating the absolute levels of unemployment of the various sub-groups within the labour force (e.g. occupations, skills, age and sex groups), weighted by their respective contributions to output, where the weights are proxied by relative wage rates. The denominator is obtained by aggregating the weighted contributions of each of these sub-groups to the labour force. It is argued that such a weighted unemployment rate is a better indicator of macroeconomic performance since it reflects more accurately the economic significance of unemployment in terms of lost output. By not treating all of the unemployed equally it also introduces a qualitative dimension into the measure of available labour supply.

AN ALTERNATIVE MEASURE

In the US it has been suggested by some economists that the employment–population ratio is a better indicator of economic activity than is the conventional unemployment rate. In fact, since 1977 the *Employment and Training Report of the President* has included the employment–population ratio in its annual series of labour market statistics, giving it official status as an important measure of labour market strength. Similar status has not been accorded to it in the UK official statistics.

However, despite the problems involved in measuring both unemployment and the labour force, we believe the employment–population ratio is inferior to the unemployment rate as a measure of unused labour supply, and that reliance on it may give incorrect signals regarding labour market strength.[28] In particular, when the labour force is expanding, use of the employment–population ratio rather than unemployment rate understates weakness in the labour market.

If both the employment-population ratio and the unemployment rate are rising, there is clearly some ambiguity as to whether the economy is performing well in providing jobs for those who want them. It can be shown that this situation—that is, employment-population ratio and unemployment rate both rising—can only occur if employment is growing faster than the population of working age, but slower than the overall growth in the labour force. In turn this must imply an increase in labour force participation which is accompanied by both an increase in employment and unemployment. Only when the participation rate remains constant can the employment-population ratio be seen as a real alternative to the conventional unemployment rate. If the participation rate is changing, then the employment-population ratio will capture only the employment effect of this change; the unemployment effect will go unrecorded. On the other hand, the conventional unemployment rate captures both the employment and unemployment effects of higher participation.

We believe that the strength of the labour market should be measured by the ability of the available labour supply to find jobs.[29] If higher participation is accompanied by both higher employment and higher unemployment, the economy is not strong enough to employ the labour that is available, and the labour market is weak. We find it ironic that while new theories of unemployment emphasise the role of labour supply rather than labour demand as a source of unemployment (see Chapter 3), when it comes to measuring labour market strength there is growing policy support for a standard that ignores the unemployment effects of an increase in the major labour force supply variable, the participation rate.

MORE THAN ONE MEASURE

It has been suggested that 'no single way of measuring unemployment can satisfy all analytical or ideological interests'.[30] For this reason, in 1976 the BLS began to publish six other labour market indicators in addition to the official unemployment rate. A specimen of these different measures is reproduced in Table 1.3. The first six measures are based upon activity status at the time of the count while the seventh, U_7, includes discouraged workers, a category that cannot be estimated with absolute objectivity.

U_5 represents the official unemployment rate and each of the other measures is obtained by adding or subtracting identifiable groups from this measure. As Shiskin[31] has pointed out, each of these measures 'were chosen because they are representative of differing bodies of opinion about the meaning and measurement of unemployment; because they are meaningful and useful measures in their own right;

Table 1.3: *Alternative Measures of Unemployment: US, first quarter 1979*

Measure	%
U_1 Persons unemployed 15 weeks or longer as a percentage of civilian labour force	1.2
U_2 Job-losers as a percentage of civilian labour force	2.4
U_3 Unemployed persons 25 years and over as a percentage of civilian labour force 25 years and over	3.9
U_4 Unemployed full-time jobseekers as a percentage of full-time labour force	5.2
U_5 Official unemployment rate—persons 16 years and over as a percentage of civilian labour force 16 years and over	5.7
U_6 Full-time job-seekers plus half part-time job-seekers plus half total on part-time for economic reasons as a percentage of civilian labour force less half part-time labour force	7.2
U_7 Numerator of U_6 plus discouraged workers[a] as a percentage of denominator of U_6 plus discouraged workers	7.9

Note:[a] Those who say they want a job but are not looking because they think no work is available for them.

Source: US Department of Labor, Bureau of Labor Statistics, The Employment Situation (News Release), Table A–7, 1 June 1979.

and because they can generally be ranked along the scale from low to high.' Although each measure will reflect a particular set of value judgements concerning what should and should not be included in the measure of unemployment, their publication by BLS does not imply that that body either approves or disapproves of the value judgements that are implicit in any of the measures. They are published simply to enable analysts to choose for themselves what they consider to be the appropriate measure of unemployment for the job in hand.

Although the DE separates out certain categories within the unemployment total, thereby enabling analysts to compute their own preferred measure of unemployment, there is a lot to be said for following the BLS lead and publishing a range of measures around the official rate. The official rate would always be the one that is quoted in press releases etc., but the very fact that the other measures are there for individual analysts to choose from might at least serve to narrow future debate about what groups should and should not be included in the official measure.

SUMMARY AND CONCLUSIONS

Although we have concentrated here on the measurement of aggregate unemployment and its rate in the two countries, both countries produce a massive amount of detailed statistical information on other aspects of unemployment, including duration. Furthermore, these aggregates are broken down to cover many different identifiable groups. In the US alone about 700 different series, each relating to some aspect of employment or unemployment, are published regularly.[32] Despite this wealth of statistical detail, disagreements over what constitutes the correct measure of total unemployment and over the interpretation of the published official statistics still occur. This is because there is no single 'correct' measure of unemployment. Not only are there possible differences in the method of measurement, as seen by a comparison of the actual methods adopted in the UK and the US, but there are many different purposes for which unemployment data are wanted, and no single measure can serve all of these purposes. The purpose for which the unemployment measure is needed will largely determine what is included in the measure and, therefore, which groups should be excluded.

The debate over unemployment statistics in the UK must be seen against the background of the wider debate between Keynesian economists on the one hand, and monetarists or market economists on the other. What the debate reveals is that there is almost no limit to which certain individuals will go in order to minimise their estimates of Keynesian unemployment, particularly when total unemployment is on the increase. Our criticism of them is not that they attempt to disaggregate total unemployment into its component parts, isolating that part that would be susceptible to expansionary demand management policies, but that some of them carry out this exercise in a totally arbitrary and indiscriminate fashion. Demand management is not the only policy that serves the interests of the unemployed, but even if policy-makers were only concerned with that unemployment that is susceptible to demand management, they would still need to estimate realistically the other components of unemployment in order to introduce the right policy mix. What this implies is not that these other categories can be ignored, but that more information is required in order that they can be estimated more accurately. Furthermore, since the official UK measure of unemployment only captures those with a strong labour market attachment, it would be useful if, from time to time, *official* estimates of the hidden labour reserve were made.

On the other hand, in the US, the debate seems to have been more technical, concentrating upon such issues as sample size and the statistical significance of variations in the unemployment rate across regions and localities, the adjustments in the rate that are necessary in order to take account of demographic changes, and discussion of the methods of estimating the reserves of labour that lie outside the labour force. No doubt the debate will continue in the UK and US and, from time to time, changes in the underlying concepts, definitions and the methods of measurement will be introduced. So long as these changes reflect the changing need of analysts and policy makers, and do not result from political pressure from any quarter, then all will be well. Of course, the problem will be to keep these separate influences separate.

NOTES AND REFERENCES

1. The self-employed are not included in the labour force in the UK, but are included in the US.
2. Voluntary workers are not usually regarded as being part of the labour force. In practice the distinction between paid and voluntary workers is not always clear cut, especially where family firms draw upon family labour.
3. In October 1975 the day of the count was changed from Monday to Thursday. This obviated the need for adjustments in the count to take account of amendments notified on the four days following the count.
4. W. R. Garside, *The Measurement of Unemployment: Methods and Sources in Great Britain 1850-1979* (Oxford: Basil Blackwell, 1980), p.65 fn 4.
5. However, even those who have exhausted their entitlement to benefit would still have an incentive to register, namely to continue to receive National Insurance credits and thereby build up future benefit entitlement, including retirement pension benefits.
6. Department of Employment, *Employment Gazette*, September 1982.
7. Ibid.
8. A. R. Thatcher, 'Statistics of unemployment in the United Kingdom', in G. D. N. Worswick (ed.), *The Concept and Measurement of Involuntary Unemployment* (London: Allen & Unwin, 1976).
9. Garside, *op.cit.*, pp.49–53, Table 8.
10. This section draws heavily on the article by the Bureau of Labor Statistics, US Department of Labor, entitled 'How the government measures unemployment', reprinted in *Readings in Labor Force Statistics*, Appendix Vol.III to *Counting the Labor Force*.
11. *Counting the Labor Force*, National Commission on Employment and Unemployment Statistics (Washington, 1979), p.26.
12. T. A. Finegan, 'The measurement, behaviour, and classification of discouraged workers', in *Concepts and Data Needs*, Appendix Vol.I to *Counting the Labor Force*.
13. Constance Sorrentino, 'Unemployment in international perspective', in Brian Showler and Adrian Sinfield (eds), *The Workless State* (Oxford: Martin Robertson, 1981).
14. Joyanne May, 'Unemployment and labor force trends in ten industrial nations: an update', *Monthly Labor Review*, November 1982.
15. John B. Wood, *How Much Unemployment?* (IEA, 1972). See also Robert Miller and John Wood, *What Price Unemployment?: An Alternative Approach* (IEA, 1982).
16. Sam Brittan, *Second Thoughts on Full-Employment Policy* (London: Centre for Policy Studies, 1975).

17. The Centre was founded by Sir Keith Joseph and Margaret Thatcher in 1974. It is independent of the Conservative Research Department and in the mid-1970s it began to issue its own press releases on the unemployment situation.
18. James J. Hughes, 'How should we measure unemployment?', *British Journal of Industrial Relations*, Vol.XIII, No.3, 1975; and 'The measurement of unemployment: an exercise in political economy', *Industrial Relations Journal*, Winter 1976/77.
19. *Programme for Recovery*, TUC Economic Review, 1982.
20. The TUC's inclusion of this group certainly runs counter to the recommendation of the National Commission on Employment and Unemployment Statistics in the US. See pp.17–18 below.
21. Garside, *op.cit.*
22. DHSS, *General Household Survey*, 1980.
23. President's Committee to Appraise Employment and Unemployment Statistics, *Measuring Employment and Unemployment* (Washington: Government Printing Office, 1962).
24. *Counting the Labor Force, op.cit.*
25. The recommendation to adopt different definitions of labour force at national and local levels for the purpose of calculating unemployment rates runs counter to the recommendation of the inter-departmental working party in the UK. (See Cmnd 5157.) This committee decided not to expand the definition of labour force to include employers, self-employed and HM forces, because this information would be unavailable for local areas. Thus, to use estimates of working population at the national level and not at the local level in the calculation of unemployment rates would have implied the adoption of different definitions, which is undesirable in itself.
26. George L. Perry, 'Changing labor markets and inflation, *Brookings Papers on Economic Activity*, No.3, 1970.
27. Maurice Peston, 'Unemployment: why we need a new measurement', *Lloyds Bank Review*, April 1972.
28. James J. Hughes and Richard Perlman, 'On the comparison between current and past rates of unemployment', *Journal of Post-Keynesian Economics*, Vol.5, No.1, Fall 1982.
29. This argument is contrary to that of Carol Leon, 'The employment-population ratio: its value in labor force analysis', *Monthly Labor Review*, 124 (February 1981), pp.36–43, who puts great value on the employment-population ratio because it measures the success of the economy in providing jobs. We believe it is more important to measure the success of the economy in providing jobs *relative to the number wanting them*.
30. Julius Shiskin, 'Employment and unemployment: the doughnut and the hole', *Monthly Labor Review*, February 1976.
31. Ibid.
32. 'How the government measures unemployment', *op.cit.*

2. Classification of Unemployment Types

INTRODUCTION

There are many different ways of classifying unemployment, and no single classification can be regarded as definitive or correct. According to one commentator it has been estimated that, as a result of all of these different classifications, no fewer than seventy different types of unemployment have been referred to in the literature on the subject.[1] There are basically two reasons for this multiplicity of overlapping labels. First, different analytical approaches to the unemployment problem might give rise to the adoption of different classifications. For example, a preoccupation with the *causes* of unemployment might lead to the adoption of one particular classification, while an emphasis on the *cures* for unemployment might favour another. Secondly, the availability of certain types of statistical information on unemployment might give rise to other classifications. While 'analytical' classifications will pervade the theoretical literature on the subject, the 'statistical' classifications will tend to dominate the empirical literature. More often than not, categories of unemployment arising out of an analytical classification will have no direct statistical counterpart. For this reason, the testing of theories relating to analytical types will often prove difficult.

In this chapter, we begin by discussing the classification of unemployment that identifies four main types: frictional, seasonal, structural and cyclical. This classification is familiar to most students of economics and we refer to this as the traditional classification. Next, we discuss growth gap and technological unemployment and see how these relate to the traditional classification. This is followed by a brief discussion of the classification based upon the adequacy of aggregate demand which gives rise to demand deficient and non-demand-deficient unemployment. Next, we discuss the voluntary–involuntary distinction and, finally, the classification based on duration which gives rise to short- and long-term unemployment.

THE TRADITIONAL CLASSIFICATION

Frictional Unemployment

Both frictional unemployment and structural unemployment arise because the labour market is not perfect in matching the vast number of individual suppliers of labour services with the large number of employers who demand those services. In a dynamic economy, with changes occurring on both sides of the labour market, some job-changing is inevitable. This is because some firms will be contracting their traditional lines of business—perhaps to the point of ceasing to trade altogether—while others will be expanding. At the same time, many firms will be diversifying their activities and, taken together, all of this will mean that the demand for labour will be undergoing continuous change, both with regard to type of skills and location, and perhaps also with respect to the number and pattern of hours. On the supply side, some workers will withdraw from the labour market; others might return to it, or enter it for the first time, while the job preferences of those who remain might be undergoing change.

The net result of all these changes on the supply side will be that at any point in time some workers will have quit their jobs, others will have been laid off, while others will have just entered or re-entered the labour market. On the demand side, there will be some vacancies for old, established jobs together with some new job openings. In short, unemployment and job vacancies will co-exist, given that the labour market does not adjust instantaneously to these changes. It is the unemployment arising from a lack of instantaneous adjustment of supply to demand, caused by imperfections in knowledge and mobility, that is called frictional unemployment. It is sometimes referred to as search unemployment and is always regarded as being of short duration because it is assumed that jobs exist for those who are frictionally unemployed. If these jobs are suited to the skills of the frictionally unemployed, are within the local labour markets in which they are searching, and are at standard rates of pay, all that is required to bring worker and job together is a period of search. Search unemployment is treated analytically in the next chapter.

It follows from this that the level of frictional unemployment in any period will depend upon the number of workers changing their jobs for whatever reason, the number of new entrants into the labour force, and the average duration of job search for both groups. Since each of these three factors can vary with the level of aggregate demand, frictional unemployment will be a function of the level of aggregate demand. Voluntary quits and the rate of entry and re-entry into the labour force will tend to vary directly with the number of job openings, and thus with the level of aggregate demand. On the other hand, the average duration of job search could rise or fall as aggregate demand rises according to whether workers—and employers too—become more or less fussy in accepting job offers. Finally, involuntary terminations and lay-offs will probably decline as aggregate demand rises. It is, therefore, impossible to predict, *a priori*, whether frictional unemployment will increase or decrease as aggregate demand expands. For this reason it seems sensible to think in terms of the full-employment level of frictional unemployment. Alternatively, frictional unemployment is sometimes regarded as the irreducible minimum level of unemployment.

Seasonal Unemployment

Seasonal unemployment, which is often lumped together with frictional unemployment, arises from identifiable seasonal fluctuations in the demand for, and supply of, labour. The former, which gives rise to seasonal changes in production and employment is often associated with changes in climate, as for example in the construction and tourist industries. On the supply side of the labour market an influx of school leavers and adult students during the summer months often leads directly to an increase in unemployment. In order to eliminate seasonal fluctuations from the month-to-month changes in unemployment, the official statistics are usually presented on a seasonally adjusted basis.

Demographic factors apart, the extent to which an economy suffers from seasonal unemployment will therefore depend upon the variation in climatic conditions from one season to another; the extent to which seasonal activities mesh together and offset each other; and the ease with which workers can move from one seasonal job to another. Clearly, although seasonal unemployment might not be a major problem from the point of view of the national economy, it might still pose a problem for isolated communities which are heavily dependent upon seasonal trades.

Structural Unemployment

Structural unemployment also arises from the problem of adjusting labour supply to labour demand in a dynamic economy. However, whereas for frictional unemployment the mismatch is simply a problem of timing, in the case of structural unemployment it is more fundamental, arising from the fact that workers are not perfect substitutes for each other. It also has occupational, industrial and geographical dimensions. As its name implies, structural unemployment arises out of structural changes in the pattern of labour demand caused by changes in consumer tastes, production techniques, location of industry, etc., or changes in the characteristics of labour supply. As a result of these changes particular skills might be less widely demanded, some might even become obsolete. Although the demand for other skills might be expanding, including that for new skills, those individuals possessing redundant skills will remain unemployed unless their skills can be adapted to meet the new requirements, or they can acquire new skills, or they can be relocated to those areas where the old skills are still in demand.

As with frictional unemployment, structural unemployment exists alongside an unsatisfied demand for labour—i.e. job vacancies. The distinction between the two types of unemployment is somewhat blurred and structural unemployment has been described as a 'severe case',[2] or even a 'particular species',[3] of frictional unemployment. However, whereas frictional unemployment is short-term unemployment arising from labour and business turnover, structural unemployment is more long-term and, therefore, is usually regarded as being more serious. Notwithstanding this, in the empirical literature there is sometimes no attempt to distinguish between the two types of unemployment. Even in the theoretical literature the two are sometimes lumped together and called frictional, or search unemployment.

A special sort of structural unemployment might arise where one type of worker is complementary to another type of worker who is in short supply. For example, where unskilled and skilled workers complement each other and there are vacancies for skilled workers, the employment of unskilled workers might be lower than it would otherwise be. In this sense unskilled workers might be said to be structurally unemployed. Scott[4] goes even further and suggests that workers can be structurally unemployed due to an inadequacy of labour-using investment. Since labour-saving investment tends to reduce employment, it needs to be balanced by a sufficiently large amount of labour-using investment if employment overall is not to fall, and structural unemployment emerge. He argues that when comparing unemployment at business cycle peaks, any changes in unemployment that cannot be attributed to frictional changes must result from structural factors. This presupposes, of course, that demand is expanded to the same point in each cycle, or alternatively, that full employment coincides with the peak of each boom.

Workers who are discriminated against and not employed because of their age, sex, race, etc., even though they have the experience and training that are necessary to hold down the jobs for which they apply, might also be regarded as being structurally unemployed, providing that jobs that they could fill remain vacant.

Also included within the structural category are the so-called 'unemployables'. These are individuals who, because of personality defects, physical and mental disabilities, or lack of motivation for work, experience difficulty in finding a job and keeping it, especially if some sort of training is involved. In short, they are unsuitable for permanent employment. However, employability is a slippery concept and someone who is declared unsuitable for employment when the labour market is slack, with several workers chasing every job vacancy that appears, may well be regarded as employable when the market tightens and competition among employers is much stronger. It is, therefore, extremely difficult to identify just what group constitutes the unemployables. Membership is likely to be a shifting one, with the size of the group varying inversely with the pressure of aggregate demand.

As Lipsey[5] and Bergman and Kaun[6] have pointed out, it is important to distinguish between the 'structure of unemployment' and 'structural unemployment'. The former simply describes the 'array' of unemployment rates across different labour market groups (i.e. age, sex, occupation, etc.), while structural unemployment implies imbalances and mismatches. If the unemployment rates for all groups vary in the same proportion as the overall rate, the structure of unemployment would remain constant as aggregate demand changes. However, because the rates for some groups are more sensitive to changes in aggregate demand than the rates of other groups, the structure of unemployment will vary with changes in aggregate demand. This variation in the structure of unemployment, measured by changes in the dispersion of group rates about the overall rate, tells us nothing about whether structural unemployment itself has increased or decreased independently of the level of aggregate demand. However, since a larger dispersion in group rates, other things being equal, implies greater sectoral imbalances in the labour market, a worsening in the structure of unemployment at full employment, or at a given pressure of aggregate demand, is indicative of an increase in structural unemployment.

In practice—as we shall see later—structural unemployment is likely to be cyclically sensitive. It will tend to increase as aggregate demand increases up to the point of full employment. Thereafter it will tend to 'melt'[7] under the pressure of further increases in demand. Once again the full-employment level of structural unemployment becomes the focus of attention.

Cyclical Unemployment

Cyclical unemployment, sometimes referred to as Keynesian unemployment, occurs during the recession phase of the business cycle when investment and consumption expenditures begin to fall off and the economy is unable to generate the same number of jobs as existed at the previous cyclical peak. Although different sectors of the economy are affected to differing degrees, with capital goods industries more seriously affected than consumer goods industries, and durable consumer goods industries more seriously affected than non-durable consumer goods industries, the underlying cause of cyclical unemployment is the inadequacy of short-run aggregate demand. This view, that large-scale unemployment can be caused by a deficiency of overall demand, has only come to be accepted over the last fifty years as a result of the seminal work by Keynes[8]—and in recent years the Keynesian thesis has suffered a partial eclipse.[9]

Prior to Keynes, the 'so-called'[10] classical theory of employment and unemployment dominated economic thinking. According to classical theory, full employment was the natural order of things. That is to say, there was an automatic tendency to full employment resulting from the fact that supply generates its own demand. Any departure from full employment was regarded as a purely temporary dislocation, caused only by the failure of prices, wages and interest rates to adjust sufficiently to changed economic circumstances. Assuming that prices and interest rates adjust fairly quickly to market forces, the tendency for unemployment in excess of frictional to arise would be caused by the inflexibility of wages, and could therefore be regarded as voluntary. Indeed, it was the flexibility of prices, wages, etc. which, together with the tendency of supply to create its own demand, ensured full employment.

Clearly, classical theory was at odds with the experience of both the UK and the US during the inter-war period when large-scale unemployment prevailed.[11] Keynes set out to reconcile economic theory with the evidence that was plain for all to see. He stressed the importance of aggregate demand in determining the level of employment and unemployment, and refuted the notion of an automatic tendency to full employment. He argued that the economy would only settle at full employment by the merest of chances, if the total of all demands in the economy were sufficient to absorb its capacity to produce (i.e. aggregate supply). Within a closed economy Keynes stressed the need for investment to fill the gap between income and consumption, since investment and consumption together determine the level of aggregate demand. He argued that, whereas consumption is fairly stable in the short run, investment is not, and that it is this volatility of investment that causes fluctuations in the level of employment and unemployment. Given that businessmen invest in the expectation that they will make profits, Keynes argued that it is changes in businessmen's expectations that cause changes in investment. Therefore, given that decisions to save and decisions to invest are taken by different groups, there is no guarantee that investment will be sufficient to ensure full employment. If the economy starts from a position of full employment a change in investment intentions will move it away from this position because the equality between savings and investment—a necessary condition for equilibrium—can only be achieved by an adjustment in output and employment. The change in businessmen's expectations will therefore push the economy beyond full employment and into inflation, or give rise to a deficiency in aggregate demand and involuntary unemployment.

GROWTH GAP AND TECHNOLOGICAL UNEMPLOYMENT

Whereas cyclical unemployment stems from a deficiency of short-run aggregate demand, when the capacity of the economy is not changing as a result of economic growth, growth gap unemployment only emerges in the longer term. Although it has not been referred to much in the UK literature, it has in the US, particularly during the debate that centred on the higher levels of unemployment during the period

1958-63.[12] Growth gap unemployment can exist at cyclical peaks as a result of the gap between full employment output and actual output. It arises because output does not grow in line with capacity. Thus, when technological change, or growth in the labour force, allows output to grow faster than what it actually does, growth gap unemployment will emerge. It differs from that particular species of structural unemployment referred to by Scott in that it is caused by a long-run deficiency in aggregate demand, whereas Scott's structural unemployment is caused by an inadequate stock of labour-using capital. However, since its causes only emerge in the long run rather than short run, it is conceptually different from cyclical unemployment. For the sake of completion it should therefore be added to the traditional classification.

Technological unemployment is sometimes referred to as a separate and distinct category. However, the concept adds very little to our understanding of unemployment in that technological unemployment can easily be slotted into the other types of unemployment that have already been discussed. The technologically unemployed are those who lose their jobs as technological advance results in the substitution of capital for labour—a process that has gone on almost since the beginning of time. The individuals who are displaced as a result of such change might be redeployed within the firms for which they work; alternatively, they might become unemployed. If jobs that they are qualified to fill exist they will find alternative employment after a short period of time, and their unemployment is best described as frictional. If the technological change is such that the skills of those displaced are rendered redundant, even though the demand for labour generally is buoyant, then those displaced are structurally unemployed. If the economy is expanding only slowly, so that the overall growth in jobs is insufficient to keep pace with the number of workers displaced, technological change gives rise to unemployment that is similar to cyclical unemployment in that it stems from a deficiency of aggregate demand, but different in that it involves economic growth. In other words, the technological change gives rise to what has been described above as growth gap unemployment.

A NOTE OF CAUTION

Although conceptually it is possible to distinguish between the various types of unemployment discussed above, it is not possible to assign individuals to these categories. That is, it is not possible to say individual A is frictionally unemployed, while B is structurally unemployed and C cyclically unemployed. There are two reasons for this. The first is that particular job vacancies are not reserved for individual unemployed workers. The second is that the various categories of unemployment are not always as distinct and separate as has been suggested. The boundary between frictional and structural will be blurred; if there is an overall adequacy of demand seasonal will merge into frictional, but might be regarded as part of cyclical if aggregate demand is not adequate. Furthermore, during the contractionary phase of the business cycle it might not always be possible to distinguish between cyclical unemployment and that arising from a longer-run deficiency in aggregate demand. Similarly, at business cycle peaks it might prove difficult to distinguish between growth gap unemployment and what Scott describes as structural unemployment.

However, notwithstanding these problems it might be possible, and indeed it is desirable, to obtain estimates of the extent to which the various categories of unemployment contribute to the total. This will not only require precise definitions of the various categories of unemployment, but also definitions which are operational. Such precision is not necessary if all that one is looking for is 'evidence of increases or decreases' in the components.[13] But in testing for increases or decreases in the components one is still constrained by the data that are available.

In order to disaggregate unemployment into its component parts, data on vacancies as well as unemployment are necessary. And these data need to be at reasonably disaggregated levels for occupations and localities, and possibly industries too. It is, of course, desirable to have reasonable estimates of the disaggregated components of unemployment in order that the correct remedial policies, or rather the correct mix of such policies, can be pursued.

AGGREGATE DEMAND AS CRITERION

Given the problem of overlap between the various categories of unemployment in the traditional classification, it is not surprising that a simpler classification is sometimes adopted. The frictional, seasonal and structural categories are lumped together to give non-demand-deficient unemployment, that is unemployment that is dependent upon non-demand factors for its elimination. On the other hand, ignoring temporal considerations, the cyclical and growth gap varieties can be subsumed under the heading of demand-deficient unemployment, unemployment that can be remedied through expansionary demand policies.

Although there is a loss in analytical detail when such a simplified classification is adopted, it might nevertheless be necessary from an operational point of view.

THE VOLUNTARY-INVOLUNTARY DISTINCTION

The distinction between voluntary and involuntary unemployment lies at the heart of the Keynesian theory of employment and unemployment. Although the classical economists believed that all unemployment in excess of frictional was voluntary—that is, caused by the unwillingness of workers to accept employment at lower real wages—Keynes argued that involuntary unemployment could exist if 'in the event of a small rise in the price of wage goods relatively to the money wage, both the aggregate supply of labour willing to work for the current money wage and aggregate demand for it at that wage would be greater than the existing volume of employment.'[14] This definition implies that involuntary unemployment exists when there is an excess supply of labour at a given money wage, and that an expansion in aggregate demand and a reduction in the real supply price of labour are both required in order to eliminate it. (The theoretical controversies arising from this definition are treated more fully in the next chapter.)

More recently Lord Kahn has stressed that Keynes' definition of involuntary unemployment was unnecessarily complicated and that it is not necessary to include a decline in real wages as a condition for its reduction. Kahn says that it is sufficient to define involuntary unemployment as occurring when 'at the current money wage and with the current price level, the number of men desiring to work exceeds the number of men for whose labour there is a demand.'[15] Thus, all that is required to eliminate this type of unemployment is an increase in the demand for labour.

Although Keynes accepted that voluntary unemployment could exist, he stressed that when involuntary unemployment is also present money wage cuts will not ameliorate the unemployment situation. In other words, when the two types of unemployment co-exist, the reluctance of the voluntary unemployed to accept real wage cuts is not a hindrance to the solution of the unemployment problem. This reluctance only becomes important when aggregate demand rises. As Perlman[16] has argued elsewhere, when aggregate demand is deficient even the voluntarily unemployed might be considered to be involuntarily unemployed since they could not price themselves into a job by accepting a wage cut, even if they wanted to.

However, the ideas of the classical economists continue to have some currency. For example, Samuel Brittan believes that 'In one sense all unemployment could be regarded as voluntary because there is a wage level at which almost any individual could price himself into a job.'[17] Brittan still retains a foot—or perhaps just a toe—in the Keynesian camp when he goes on to state that 'Even if we regard all unemployment as voluntary, some is clearly more voluntary than others.'[18] Similarly, Lucas argues that 'there is an involuntary element in all unemployment in the sense that no one chooses bad luck over good; there is also a voluntary element in all unemployment in the sense that however miserable one's current work options, one can always choose to accept them.'[19]

The belief that all unemployment is voluntary is, in essence, an acceptance of the view that there is a 'natural rate of unemployment' towards which the economy tends to move. The term natural rate was introduced by Friedman;[20] it is consistent with a non-accelerating rate of inflation and is determined by those real factors that underlie the structure of the labour market and the composition of the labour force. Since both of these factors can change, so too can the natural rate. For example, if the labour market becomes less efficient, or more imperfect, then the natural rate will increase. It will also increase if the composition of the labour force changes in favour of women, teenagers and part-time workers, since these groups engage in more frequent job changes and move into and out of the labour force more frequently than do other groups.[21] (Discussion of the natural rate is taken up in the next two chapters.)

Given a commonsense interpretation of terminology, it is not difficult to agree with the first part of Lucas's statement, quoted above, namely that in practice both voluntary and involuntary elements might often be present. However, the second part seems to ignore the fact that when unemployment is high, many unemployed individuals have no real choice. They have no job offers that they can accept; their only choice is enforced idleness.

Some might argue that so long as a single job vacancy exists all of those who turn it down are voluntarily unemployed. However, as Rees[22] has pointed out, such reasoning suffers from an aggregation fallacy. For example, if one job vacancy remains unfilled because 100 unemployed workers have turned it down on the grounds that the wages and conditions that attach to it are unacceptably low, it is fallacious to regard all of the 100 as voluntarily unemployed. Although it might be legitimate to regard one of these as voluntarily unemployed, the remaining 99 would not be voluntarily unemployed if this individual had accepted the job—unless of course there were another 99 vacancies that they refused to fill for similar reasons.

Despite the precise theoretical distinction between voluntary and involuntary unemployment, attempts to apply the terminology to different unemployment situations lead to difficulties and misunderstanding. This is particularly true of voluntary unemployment which is often equated with frictional unemployment on the grounds that the frictionally unemployed are assumed to be those who have already refused job offers in order to continue to search for better ones. This is wrong in that not all of the frictionally unemployed will have quit their jobs voluntarily. Some—perhaps many—will have been thrown out of work involuntarily as a result of lay-offs or redundancies; others might have just joined the labour force and be searching for their first job. Even though they might engage in search activity, not all of these will have turned down job offers. But even if a redundant worker does not accept the first job that is offered to him, is it correct to regard him as being voluntarily unemployed when he was thrown out of work in the first place? If not, then at what point in time, or after how many job refusals, is it reasonable to regard him as being voluntarily unemployed?

Voluntary unemployment is also assumed to cover all of those who quit their jobs voluntarily, or are dismissed for industrial misconduct. Once again, using the term in this way is wrong because it confuses voluntary job-leaving with voluntary unemployment. As Hughes[23] has commented elsewhere 'an individual might voluntarily quit one job in the expectation that he will be able to obtain another within a certain time period—say four weeks. During his four weeks of job search he might best be described as voluntarily unemployed. But what if he takes twelve weeks to find a new job rather than the expected four? Is he voluntarily or involuntarily unemployed from the beginning of the fifth week to the end of the twelfth week?' In other words, if the reality of the job market differs from his earlier expectations, does the individual's unemployment status change during his period of job search?

It is obvious from these examples that modern use of the voluntary–involuntary terminology is sometimes wrong, and therefore misleading. This arises from the failure to draw the distinction between voluntary and involuntary job-leaving on the one hand, and unemployment on the other. Also, from a measurement point of view, the voluntary–involuntary classification does not seem to be very useful. The same is not true of the next broad classification that is discussed below.

CLASSIFICATION BY DURATION

The availability of statistics, both in the UK and US, on the duration of unemployment makes it possible to classify unemployment as either short- or long-term, although clearly this involves the adoption of some arbitrary dividing line, e.g. 15, 26 or 52 weeks, as the point where short-term unemployment ends and long-term unemployment begins. Since duration figures refer to uncompleted spells of unemployment, whatever arbitrary dividing line is chosen the short-term measure will be biased upwards, and the long-term measure downwards, as estimates of completed spells. This is because part of what is observed to be short-term unemployment will be the beginning of long-term unemployment. However, analyses of short- and long-term unemployment based upon duration figures can be useful, particularly if supplemented by other labour market indicators.

Since frictional unemployment is short-term, it is tempting to argue that changes in short-term unemployment—as measured from data on uncompleted spells—reflect changes in the frictional component of total unemployment. However, there are at least two reasons for rejecting this line of reasoning. First, as noted above, an increase in short-term unemployment might simply reflect the beginning of an increase in longer-term unemployment. Second, uncompleted duration figures tell us nothing about completed spells of unemployment. For example, individuals who suffer from repeated spells of short-term unemployment—i.e. periods of unemployment alternating with periods of employment—cannot be regarded as just being frictionally unemployed.

Both structural and demand-deficient unemployment will involve longer-term unemployment. An increase in long-term unemployment could therefore imply an increase in either, or both, of these types of unemployment. Although it is impossible to separate out these two types from the long-term measure, it might be possible to control for the effect of a change in aggregate unemployment on long-term unemployment and thereby determine whether long-term unemployment has increased independently of aggregate demand. If it has, this would be indicative of an increase in structural unemployment.

However, if long-term unemployment increases because of a deficiency of aggregate demand, and if it persists for a number of years, then a pool of very long-term unemployed is likely to emerge. It might be somewhat academic to quibble about whether the individuals in it are unemployed as a result of demand-deficiency or structural factors. Although the reason for their prolonged unemployment might be said to be a deficiency in aggregate demand, to all intents and purposes they might be regarded as being structurally unemployed. This is because they will probably have suffered some erosion of their skills, while their motivation for work will have been blunted, so that when demand picks up again they will probably experience extreme difficulties in finding employment. Even if their skills and motivation remain intact employers might well perceive that an erosion has occurred and the end result will be just the same—difficulty in finding work when the economy picks up again. Thus, very long-term unemployment might be equated with structural unemployment.

Different Measure of Duration
The magnitude of the unemployment stock will be a function of the number of people flowing into the stock and the average time that each spends in unemployment (i.e. the average duration of a completed spell of unemployment). Although the average duration of completed spells of unemployment will be affected by changes in the rates of inflow and outflow, both of which will be influenced by changes in the aggregate demand for labour, the average duration of unemployment can also vary independently of the pressure of labour demand. However, assuming the average duration of completed spells to be constant and unrelated to inflows, an increase in the rate of inflow

would cause the stock of unemployment to rise. After a period of time—equal to the average duration of unemployment itself—there would be a corresponding increase in the rate of outflow from the stock and unemployment would stabilise at a new higher rate of flow. Until this point is reached, however, the average duration of uncompleted spells would be lower than what it was before the increase in the rate of inflow occurred. On the other hand, if the rate of outflow from the stock remains constant, an increase in the rate of inflow will be reflected in an increase in the average duration of completed spells, although initially the average duration of uncompleted spells would fall before eventually rising. If the rate of inflow remains unchanged while there is an autonomous increase in the average duration of completed spells, the rate of outflow from the stock will decrease—at least for a time—while the stock of unemployment will increase.

Changes in outflow might reflect earlier changes in inflow or autonomous changes in the average duration of completed spells itself. Where they reflect the former, an increase in the rate of outflow will result in a fall in the duration of completed spells, thus offsetting the increase caused by the higher inflow. However, the effect of a change in the rate of outflow on the duration of uncompleted spells is not so clear cut. For example, if it is concentrated among relative newcomers to the stock (i.e. those who have been unemployed less than the average), an increase in the rate of outflow will cause the average duration of uncompleted spells of those who remain to rise. A reduction in the rate of outflow concentrated among this group would cause average duration to fall. Where the changes in outflow are concentrated largely among those who have experienced an above average duration of unemployment, the effect on the duration of uncompleted spells will be opposite to those outlined above.

Although we have referred to the average duration of completed spells of unemployment, there are in fact two such measures. First, there is the terminations weighted average duration, (D_2), which calculates the average duration of all unemployment spells that terminate within a given period of time. This provides an estimate of the length of time that a newly unemployed person can expect to remain unemployed. The second is the experience weighted average duration (D_3), which measures the average length of unemployment spell experienced by those who are unemployed at a particular point in time. Main,[24] has discussed these two measures, and how they relate to the average duration of uncompleted spells (D_1), by reference to Figure 2.1.

This figure shows the unemployment experience of a population that consists of six people. Persons 1, 2, 5 and 6 are all unemployed at t_0, which represents the day or week of the count. Persons 3 and 4, although not unemployed at t_0, both experience two spells of unemployment within the time period $t_{-1}t_1$. If the completed spell lengths of the individuals are denoted by S_1, S_2 etc., and the

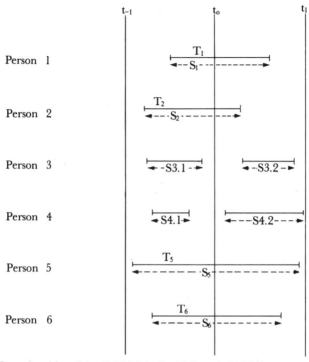

Source: Reproduced from Brian G. M. Main, *Scottish Journal of Political Economy*, Vol.28, No.2., June 1981.

Figure 2.1: *Spells of Unemployment*

uncompleted spell lengths by T_1, T_2 etc., the average duration of the uncompleted spells, D_1, is given by:

$$D_1 = \frac{T_1 + T_2 + T_5 + T_6}{4}$$

D_1 is an upwardly biased measure of duration since long spells of unemployment are over-represented while short spells that occur between counts (e.g. $S_{3.1}$ and $S_{3.2}$) are excluded altogether. Indeed, the probability of being observed and, therefore, included in the measure of D_1 is proportional to the length of the completed unemployment spell. As Main has observed, if D_1 were not an upwardly biased measure of duration then, in a steady state, doubling D_1 would 'provide a sensible estimate . . . of average spell length as each individual would on average be observed half way through his total spell of unemployment.'

The terminations weighted average duration, D_2, is given by:

$$D_2 = \frac{S_1 + S_2 + S_{3.1} + S_{3.2} + S_{4.1} + S_{4.2} + S_5 + S_6}{8}$$

Although this measure has no statistical biases, its welfare implications can be 'quite misleading', particularly if short spells constitute a high proportion of total spells but a high proportion of total unemployment days are accounted for by long spells. For example, ten people might be unemployed for 300 days each, while 90 people are unemployed for only 1 day each. This means that there are 100 spells of unemployment involving a total of 3090 days of unemployment, giving an average duration of spell length of 30.9 days. This can be quite misleading given that 97 per cent of total days of unemployment are accounted for by spells lasting 300 days.

Ackerlof and Main[25] claim that the difference between duration measures of uncompleted spells, D_1, and that for completed spells, D_2, is 'exactly analagous' to the difference between average age of the population and average lifespan. The relationships are analagous, but not exactly so. The average duration (span) of existing spells (lives) is less than the average length of completed spells (lives) because the duration of each spell (life) in progress is less than its completed length. However, since the frequency of short completed spells of unemployment is greater than the frequency of short lives, the estimates of average duration of completed and uncompleted spells of unemployment will be much closer than the corresponding estimates of average age of population and average lifespan.

The experience weighted average duration, D_3, is given by:

$$D_3 = \frac{S_1 + S_2 + S_5 + S_6}{4}$$

This measures the average duration of the unemployment spell in which the observation day of unemployment is spent. As Main points out, in the steady state this is not only true of the observation day, but of all days. That is, D_3 measures the average duration in which a typical day of unemployment is spent. D_3 gives more weight than D_2 to longer spells of unemployment in which comparatively more unemployment is spent. In a steady state $D_3 = 2\ D_1$. Of course, if a steady state does not apply, then estimates of D_3 obtained by doubling D_1 will be biased. If unemployment is rising as a result of an increase in the rate of inflow, the stock of unemployment will consist of a relatively high number of people with low uncompleted spells of unemployment even though they might go on and complete lengthy spells. Therefore D_1 will be biased downwards compared to the steady state estimate and, accordingly, doubling D_1 will lead to an underestimate of D_3. When unemployment is non-steady and declining, estimates of D_3

derived from observations of D_1 will be upwardly biased. (Empirical estimates of D_3 are discussed in Chapter 7.)

DISAGGREGATION OF UNEMPLOYMENT INTO FRICTIONAL, STRUCTURAL AND DEMAND-DEFICIENT COMPONENTS

Adopting a threefold classification of unemployment, frictional (U_f), structural (U_s) and demand-deficient (U_{dd}), we can write down the macro relationships if it is assumed that a reduction in any one of the three components will lead to a reduction in aggregate unemployment (U_T). If we assume initially that U_T is greater than aggregate job vacancies (V_T), then we have:

$$U_T = U_f + U_s + U_{dd} \tag{1}$$

With job vacancies, we can distinguish between those vacancies which are of the right type to absorb the unemployed (V_R), and those which are of the wrong type (V_W). Total job vacancies, V_T, which is the stock of unfilled job openings that firms wish to fill, is given by:

$$V_T = V_R + V_W \tag{2}$$

Since a worker is assumed to be frictionally unemployed if he possesses the right attributes (qualifications, skill, experience, etc.) to fill a vacancy, and structurally unemployed if he possesses the wrong attributes, then:

$$U_s = V_W = V_T - V_R \tag{3}$$

and

$$U_f = V_R = V_T - V_W \tag{4}$$

Given the assumption that $U_T > V_T$, all of the vacancies that exist will be either frictional or structural. That is:

$$V_T = U_s + U_f \tag{5}$$

Substituting (5) into (1) gives

$$U_{dd} = U_T - V_T \tag{6}$$

If instead of $U_T > V_T$, the macro labour market condition is $V_T > U_T$, then $U_{dd} = O$ and (1) is rewritten as:

$$U_T = U_s + U_f \tag{7}$$

Similarly, given that $V_T > U_T$, some of the vacancies that exist will be the result of excess demand and therefore (3), (4) and (5) will not hold; however, (3) and (4) will become:

$$U_s = V_W = U_T - V_R \tag{8}$$

and

$$U_f = V_R = U_T - V_W \tag{9}$$

Given accurate macro data on unemployment and vacancies, the amount of demand-deficient unemployment can therefore be estimated from (6). However, it is not possible to obtain measures of structural and frictional unemployment from these macro relationships unless total vacancies can be broken down into those which are of the right type and the wrong type to absorb the unemployed. This would require much more detailed information at the micro (i.e. occupational) level. Assuming that these data exist, Perlman[26] has suggested a way of disentangling structural and frictional unemployment. According to him the key to the measurement of structural unemployment lies in what he labels the Structurally Overemployed Counterparts (SOC), that is, occupations in which there is an excess of vacancies over unemployment.

If it is assumed that all workers attached to a particular occupation (say the ith) are able to fill a vacancy in that occupation, then all vacancies for that occupation will be frictional, provided that $U_i > V_i$. The excess of unemployment over vacancies (i.e. $U_i - V_i$) in this labour surplus occupation will contribute either to structural unemployment (U_s), or demand-deficient unemployment (U_{dd}). If the full amount of the excess is to contribute to U_s it must be matched by an excess of vacancies over unemployment in SOC occupations. What this means is that $\Sigma (V_i - U_i)$ for all SOC must be greater than $\Sigma (U_i - V_i)$ for labour surplus (i.e. non-SOC) occupations, which implies that the macro condition of $V_T > U_T$ must hold. When $\Sigma (V_i - U_i)$ for all SOC is less than $\Sigma (U_i - V_i)$ for all non-SOC—i.e. when $U_T > V_T$—the full excess of vacancies over unemployment does not count since for structural unemployment to exist there must exist vacancies for the structurally unemployed to fill. Thus when $U_T > V_T$, U_s is given by $\Sigma (V_i - U_i)$ for all SOC.

Therefore, when the macro state of the labour market is known, structural unemployment can be calculated by aggregating the surplus of vacancies over unemployment in all SOC (when $U_T > V_T$), or surpluses of unemployment over vacancies in all non-SOC (when $V_T > U_T$). Frictional unemployment can then be calculated easily from (5) and (7). Table 2.1 summarises how the three components of

Table 2.1: *Structural, Frictional and Demand-Deficient Unemployment Under Different Macro Conditions*

	$U_T > V_T$	$V_T > U_T$
$U_{dd} = U_T - V_T$	O	
$U_s = \Sigma \ (V_i - U_i)$ for all SOC		$\Sigma \ (U_i - V_i)$ for all non-SOC
$U_f = V_T - \Sigma \ (V_i - U_i)$ for all SOC		$U_T - \Sigma \ (U_i - V_i)$ for all non-SOC

unemployment can be estimated under the different macro conditions. Four important points need to be born in mind in connection with the above analysis.[27]

(i) Starting from a point in which there is some slack in the economic system, i.e. when $U_T > V_T$, a general expansion in labour demand will lead to both an absolute and a relative increase in U_s; this increase will be greater the more concentrated the increase in labour demand is in SOC occupations. There is also likely to be an increase in structural imbalance, as measured by differential unemployment rates across occupations.

Once $U_T = V_T$, a further general increase in the demand for labour will lead to a fall in absolute U_s so long as some of the new demand falls in non-SOC occupations. The greater the concentration in non-SOC, the greater will be the decline in U_s and the more likely is structural imbalance to decline. Whether or not the decline in absolute U_s will cause it to rise or fall relative to total unemployment depends upon how the increase in labour demand is distributed between SOC and non-SOC occupations, and on whether the demand is satisfied or not. Increases in demand that affect non-SOC occupations will cause U_s to fall relatively, while increases that affect SOC and are satisfied will cause U_s to rise relative to U_T. Increases that fall in SOC but are not satisfied will leave U_s relatively unchanged.

Thus, up to what might be termed the Beveridge[28] full-employment point (i.e. where $U_T = V_T$), U_s will rise as aggregate demand rises; once the point of balance is passed, U_s will begin to melt away in absolute terms, although relative to total unemployment it might still increase. If as a result of demand expansion all labour surplus (non-SOC) occupations disappear, structural unemployment will also disappear.

(ii) The predictions concerning U_f are less sharp and cannot be made on the basis of knowledge concerning the overall state of the labour market. Both the magnitude and the direction of change in U_f that accompany an expansion in aggregate demand will depend on how the new demand is distributed among occupations, and whether it is satisfied or not. For U_f to decline the new demand must be distributed in such a way that the reduction in unemployment in SOC occupations is greater than the increase in vacancies in non-SOC.

(iii) The estimates of U_s and U_f that result from this approach will clearly depend on the extent to which occupations are disaggregated.

If the occupational classification is not sufficiently disaggregated, this will mean that occupations which are essentially different, requiring different skills, training and labour market experience, will be grouped together giving rise to estimates of U_f that are too large, and estimates of U_s that are too low. This is because the underlying assumption that an individual who is attached to an occupation will be able to fill any vacancy in that occupation will not hold. With insufficiently disaggregated occupations the mobility that actually exists between occupations will be exaggerated. On the other hand, if the occupational disaggregation is made too fine, this will understate the extent of active mobility between occupations with the consequence that U_s estimates will be too high, and U_f estimates too low.

(iv) Similar problems arise in connection with geographical mobility. Up to now there has been no mention of this because we have implicitly been assuming a single, national market for labour. This is clearly unrealistic since workers attached to an occupation in one part of the country will usually not be able to offer themselves for a vacancy in the same occupation in another part of the country. Given geographical immobility, the method of analysing occupational unemployment and vacancy data to estimate U_s and U_f will lead to an underestimate of the former, and an overestimate of the latter. Ideally, the analysis needs to be carried out for individual localities and the results aggregated to obtain estimates for the economy as a whole. However, in practice, defining the boundaries of a local labour market is not easy. For the purpose under discussion they need to be defined in such a way as to ensure that all workers within a local labour market are sufficiently mobile to take up any job, at any point, within that market. But if the boundaries are drawn in order to ensure absolute mobility within, this would probably give rise to mobility across boundaries and an overestimate of U_s would result. In practice, possibly the best that can be aimed for is to achieve a level of geographic disaggregation in which any immobility within the local labour market area is matched by mobility across its boundaries.

THE UV CURVE

Given the sensitivity of the U_s and U_f measures to changes in demand, it is necessary, when testing to see if either component has increased, to compare estimates at points in time when the pressure of aggregate demand is the same. A variant of this approach is to define full employment and then test to see whether the full-employment estimates change. If full employment is defined to occur at the point of balance between aggregate unemployment and aggregate vacancies,[29] then non-demand-deficient unemployment can be estimated.

The simplest approach, suggested by Solow,[30] is to graph unemployment and vacancy data through time. When plotted these two series exhibit an inverse parallellism and estimates of non-demand deficient unemployment are obtained from the points of intersection of the two series. The two series are illustrated in Figure 2.2; non-demand-deficient unemployment is shown to decline between t_1 and t_2, rise between t_2 and t_5 and thereafter decline again.

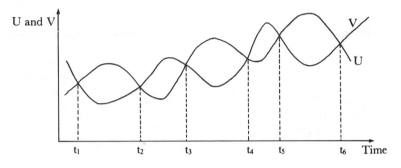

Figure 2.2

The problem with this approach is that the U and V series might not cross very often. Thus if the economy is run for a long period at either a very high or very low level of unemployment, it is impossible to determine whether there has been a change in the amount of non-demand-deficient unemployment. An alternative approach is to plot UV curves for different time periods by regressing V on U. Such a curve, UV_1, is shown in Figure 2.3.[31]

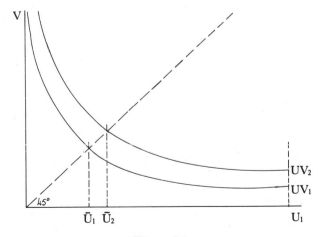

Figure 2.3

Starting from a point of high unemployment, U_1, an expansion in aggregate demand will cause unemployment to fall quickly at first, with only a small rise in vacancies. However, as demand continues to expand an increasing part of it will go unsatisfied, until eventually most of the incremental increase in demand results in vacancies, with very little reduction in unemployment. The point at which the curve cuts the 45° line indicates the amount of non-demand-deficient unemployment, $\bar{U}_1$, associated with UV_1.

If the structure of the economy and the efficiency of job search remain unchanged, there will be a stable UV curve for the economy. However, if either or both of these change, the UV curve will shift—inwards if the efficiency of job search or the structure of the economy improves, and vice versa. Thus, in Figure 2.3, the outward shift from UV_1 to UV_2 indicates a reduction in the efficiency of the labour market, and a consequent increase in the level of non-demand deficient unemployment to U_2. For any given level of unemployment, there is always a higher level of vacancies associated with UV_2 than with UV_1. Similarly, for a given level of vacancies, UV_2 is always associated with a higher level of unemployment. If UV curves are estimated for different periods of time, changes in the non-demand-deficient component of unemployment can be measured.

THE IMPORTANCE OF VACANCY STATISTICS

It is obvious from the foregoing discussion that vacancy statistics, on an occupational and regional basis—and preferably for industries too—are a prerequisite for the disaggregation of unemployment into its component parts. Vacancy data are needed in order to know what resources should be directed towards structural and frictional cures, and what emphasis should be placed on demand expansion. Thus, if unemployment is to be reduced in a non-inflationary way, vacancy data are vital. However, given that today's vacancies might not be good indicators of tomorrow's vacancies, they will not be a perfect guide to training and retraining policies. In addition to information on the stocks of vacancies remaining unfilled at discrete time intervals, it would also be useful to have information on vacancy flows.[32] Jobs for which the rate of vacancy flow (i.e. the flow of new vacancies relative to the stock of old ones) is high might be jobs with a high turnover and a short vacancy duration. It is not these jobs, but those which have vacancies of longer duration which should be the object of training and retraining policy.

The UK is better placed than the US as far as the availability of vacancy data are concerned. The DE publishes monthly, or quarterly, unemployment and vacancy data on an industrial, regional and occupational basis. The vacancy data relate to jobs notified to employment offices and remaining unfilled on the day of the vacancy count. However, notification has not been compulsory since 1956, and only about one-third of all vacancies are notified.[33]

In the US, national vacancy data on an occupational and industrial basis were collected during the second world war, but the practice was discontinued thereafter, with the exception of the period of the Korean War. During the 1950s, Arthur Burns, later Chairman of the Council of Economic Advisers, strongly supported the collection of national job vacancy data, but to no avail. In 1965 he argued that the unavailability of vacancy data was 'the most serious gap in [the US's] entire scheme of economic intelligence',[34] and that its collection was a necessary adjunct to the Employment Act, 1946. But apart from limited programmes of data collection in the mid-1960s, nothing happened on a national scale until after the 1968 amendment to the Manpower Development and Training Act, which mandated a programme of regular collection. To be included in the count 'a position had to be unoccupied on the last day of the month, immediately available, and the object of an active search for a new worker from outside the firm.'[35] However, the programme was short-lived, beginning in 1969 and ending in 1973.

In the US, organised labour has not favoured the collection of job vacancy data, fearing that such data could be used to minimise the seriousness of unemployment and justify inaction over stimulating aggregate demand, by giving rise to arguments that 'the jobs are there: people just don't want to work.'[36] While recognising the conceptual appeal of vacancy statistics, the National Commission on Employment and Unemployment Statistics—like the Gordon Committee before it—did not recommend the introduction of a programme of collection. The Commission felt that the cost of obtaining data at a level of disaggregation that would be useful would be exorbitant.

COMBATING FRICTIONAL AND STRUCTURAL UNEMPLOYMENT

Both frictional and structural unemployment co-exist with job vacancies. In the case of the former, this is because unemployed workers have limited information about the jobs that are available, while employers have limited information about the workers who are available to fill these jobs. The acquisition of information involves both time and resources. The time element can be expressed as the cost of a unit of time spent in job search. For the employed worker, the loss of income while searching is a time cost and probably the most important of the worker's search costs. For the employer, output and profit forgone as a result of having a job unfilled is the corresponding time cost.

For the unemployed worker facing a job offer, the cost of turning down that offer in order to continue to search for a better one will be higher in a slack labour market than in a tight one. This is because the probability of receiving a similar, or better, offer will be lower in a slack market than in a tight one. Thus, an unemployed worker will engage in less 'voluntary' search the slacker is the labour market environment. For the employer the time costs of search are likely to be higher when demand is buoyant and order-books full and, therefore, at such times he will engage in less voluntary search. Since buoyant demand and full order-books will tend to coincide with tight labour markets, employers and workers will differ in their search strategies at any point in time.

Anything that raises the unit time cost of job search for either worker or employer will reduce the time spent in job search and thereby reduce frictional unemployment, although the matching of workers and jobs might be inferior, giving rise to greater job dissatisfaction and/or lower productivity. A reduction in unit time costs will have the opposite effects. For unemployed workers one of the variables that will determine the unit time costs of job search is the level of unemployment benefit. Thus, an increase in the level of benefit would reduce the unit time cost, giving rise to a longer period of search and higher frictional unemployment, although this might be accompanied by a better matching of available workers and jobs.

The costs of job search might be expressed differently. Instead of unit time cost we can think in terms of the total cost per search. For the worker this would be the total cost per job searched; for the employer the total cost per worker searched or 'vetted'. Clearly the cost per search will be influenced by the unit time cost of search. If the cost per search is reduced for the individual worker or employer, the tendency will be to engage in more searches. If there is no change in the number of searches per unit of time, frictional unemployment will increase as the unit time cost of search and, therefore, the cost per search decline. However, if the number of searches per unit of time increases it is then not certain whether frictional unemployment will increase or decrease as the cost per search declines.

Similarly, the existence of a public employment service will affect search, and thus the resulting level of frictional unemployment, in two ways. First, it will reduce the cost per search to individuals using it, thereby tending to increase frictional unemployment. Second, it will tend to increase the efficiency of job search by increasing the number of searches per unit of time. This will reduce the time necessary to match worker and vacancy and will thus tend to reduce frictional unemployment. It is therefore impossible to predict whether frictional unemployment will increase or decrease as a result of the introduction, or extension in coverage, of a subsidised public employment service. However, it will lead to a better matching of workers and jobs. Furthermore, once the job service is in existence, any improvements which increase its efficiency (i.e. reduce the time involved per search) will lead to a reduction in frictional unemployment. But if improvements in efficiency are associated with an extension in coverage, the effect on frictional unemployment once again becomes uncertain. Returning to unemployment benefit, if this is reduced relative to average earnings it will lead to a reduction in frictional unemployment, provided that it does not impair the efficiency of worker job search. Such an impairment is less likely to occur if the reduction in benefit is accompanied by the provision of search grants for those who are unemployed and actively engaged in search, and by an improvement in the efficiency of the public employment service.

Structural unemployment persists because of an occupational, industrial or regional mismatch between unemployed workers and job vacancies. Where the problem is essentially one of regional mismatch, a policy of relocation is necessary if unemployment is to be reduced. This can either involve taking workers to the work, or work to the workers, or some combination of the two. Attempts to relocate workers to those areas where their skills are in demand might take several forms: financial incentives to help with relocation costs; guaranteed jobs for a minimum period to ensure that the benefits of relocation continue for a minimum period of time; assistance with housing. This latter might be necessary where the potential migrants live in municipal housing, perhaps at subsidised rents, or when they are moving from an area of housing surplus to an area of shortage. Attempts to relocate work away from areas of labour scarcity towards areas of labour surplus might well require both stick and carrot. That is to say, prohibiting the location or expansion of firms in one area might need to be backed up by the provision of incentives to locate, or relocate, in others.

Where the mismatch is an occupational one, a policy of manpower training and retraining will be called for. Unskilled workers, and workers possessing redundant skills, will need to be trained or retrained and equipped with those skills for which there is likely to be a future demand. It is therefore necessary to have some way of forecasting what occupations and skills will be needed in the future. Clearly, vacancy data are inadequate for this purpose and need to be supplemented by manpower forecasts on an occupational and skill basis. Only if retraining is directed towards skill shortage occupations will it contribute towards a reduction in aggregate unemployment. If it equips the unemployed with skills which are already oversupplied, retraining will simply lead to a reshuffling of unemployment as trainees displace other non-trainees who are qualified to fill posts without undergoing retraining.

To encourage structurally unemployed workers to undergo retraining it will be necessary to offer incentives in the form of maintenance grants during the period of retraining. In order to act as an incentive, these grants need to be fixed at a level that is higher than what the trainee would receive in unemployment benefits and welfare payments.

While it makes sense to concentrate as much retraining as is possible during cyclical troughs—because it minimises costs—retraining is no substitute for aggregate demand policies. Indeed, the two policies are complementary in that the economy needs to be operated at a fairly high level of demand to ensure that there are vacancies for the retrained workers to fill. If the economy is operated at a low level of demand over a prolonged period of time, then the benefits from retraining will be low, or non-existent, because trainees will either return to unemployment or cause displacement once their retraining is over.[37]

Although the discussion so far has centred on retraining for skilled occupations, in reality there will need to be a range of programmes, starting with job orientation and job motivation at one end of the spectrum, and ending up with training for high level skills at the other.

Industrial mismatch might require manpower retraining or regional relocation, or both. But whatever the cause of the mismatch, resources will need to be devoted to counselling in the first instance to ensure that the unemployed are channelled into those programmes which best suit their needs.

SUMMARY

The traditional classification of unemployment into frictional, structural, seasonal and cyclical components provides a useful framework within which to discuss the causes and cures of unemployment, but it is by no means exhaustive; many other categories are referred to in the literature. Since these different categories often overlap, care must be taken when aggregating categories in order to ensure that double counting does not occur. Disaggregation of unemployment into its frictional and demand-deficient components requires data on job vacancies as well as unemployment, disaggregated by occupations and regions. Although it might be possible to measure particular categories, or test for changes over time, it is not possible to allocate unemployed individuals to these various categories because individual jobs (and vacancies) are not earmarked for individual workers.

Frictional unemployment is not synonymous with search unemployment, but anything that reduces job search will, *ceteris paribus*, reduce frictional unemployment. The reduction of structural unemployment requires the transfer of workers from labour surplus occupations and regions to those occupations and regions in short supply (i.e. SOC). Since the number of SOC is likely to increase with the pressure of aggregate demand, as too is the number of vacancies within each SOC, structural cures will contribute more towards a reduction in unemployment when aggregate demand is high than when it is low. Put differently, structural cures are not a substitute for demand-management policy, but are complementary to it.

NOTES AND REFERENCES

1. Robert H. Ferguson, *Unemployment: Its Scope, and Effect on Poverty* (Ithaca, New York: New York State School of Industrial and Labor Relations, Cornell University, 2nd edn), p.75.
2. Richard G. Lipsey, *An Introduction to Positive Economics* (London: Weidenfeld & Nicolson, 3rd edn, 1971), p.693.
3. F. S. Brooman, *Macro-Economics* (London: Allen & Unwin, 4th edn, 1970), p.89.
4. Maurice Scott with Robert A. Laslett, *Can We Get Back to Full Employment?* (London: Macmillan, 1978), pp.11–12.
5. Richard G. Lipsey, 'Structural and deficient-demand unemployment reconsidered', in *Employment Policy and the Labor Market*, ed. Arthur M. Ross (Berkeley: University of California Press, 1965).
6. Barbara R. Bergmann and David E. Kaun, *Structural Unemployment in the United States* (US Department of Commerce, Economic Development Administration, 1966), pp.7–8.
7. Samuelson likens the hard core of structural unemployment to a core of ice that can be melted under the pressure of aggregate demand. See Paul A. Samuelson, *Economics* (New York: McGraw-Hill, 1970, 8th edn), p.802.
8. J. M. Keynes, *The General Theory of Employment, Interest and Money* (London: Macmillan, 1936).
9. This has been as a result of the revival of classical monetary economics in the economics literature, and its adoption by both UK and US governments under Mrs Thatcher and President Reagan.
10. 'So-called' because Keynes labelled it as the classical theory when it should have been labelled neo-classical.
11. Large-scale unemployment was a characteristic feature of both the 1920s and the 1930s in the UK. In the US it emerged only after 1929.
12. For such a definition of structural unemployment see E. Gilpatrick, *Structural Unemployment and Aggregate Demand* (Baltimore: Johns Hopkins Press, 1966).
13. Barbara R. Berman, 'Alternative measures of structural unemployment', in *Employment Policy and the Labor Market, op.cit.*.
14. Keynes, *op.cit.*, p.15.
15. R. Kahn, 'Unemployment as seen by Keynesians', in G. D. N. Worswick (ed.), *The Concept and Measurement of Involuntary Unemployment* (London: Allen & Unwin, 1975), p.21.
16. Richard Perlman, *Labor Theory* (New York: Wiley, 1969), pp.146–9.
17. Samuel Brittan, *Second Thoughts on Full-Employment Policy* (Barry Rose, 1975), p.35.
18. Ibid, p.36.
19. R. E. Lucas 'Unemployment policy', in *Studies in Business Cycle Theory* (Oxford: Basil Blackwell, 1981), p.242.
20. Milton Friedman, 'The role of monetary policy', *American Economic Review*, Vol.58, March 1968, pp.1–17.
21. Milton Friedman, 'Inflation and unemployment', *Journal of Political Economy*, Vol.85, No.3, 1977, pp.451–472.
22. Albert Rees, *The Economics of Work and Pay* (New York: Harper & Row, 1979, 2nd edn), p.105.

23. James J. Hughes, 'How should we measure unemployment?' *British Journal of Industrial Relations*, Vol.13, No.3, pp.317–33.
24. Brian G. M. Main, 'The length of employment and unemployment in Great Britain', *Scottish Journal of Political Economy*, Vol.28, No.2, June 1981, pp.146–64.
25. George A. Akerlof and Brian G. M. Main, 'Unemployment spells and unemployment experience', *American Economic Review*, 70, December 1980, pp.885–93.
26. Perlman, *op.cit.*, pp.167–96.
27. These points are all discussed more fully in James J. Hughes, 'The use of vacancy statistics in classifying and measuring structural and frictional unemployment in Great Britain 1958–72', in *Bulletin of Economic Research*, Vol.26, No.1, May 1974, pp.12–33.
28. W. H. Beveridge, *Full Employment in a Free Society* (London: Allen & Unwin, 1944).
29. This is a reasonable definition of full employment assuming that unemployment is measured in such a way as to reflect adequately unused labour supply, and vacancies to reflect unsatisfied demand for labour. However, use of this definition of full employment should not be taken to imply anything about inflation.
30. Robert M. Solow, *The Nature and Source of Unemployment in the United States* (Wicksell Lecture, Stockholm, 1964).
31. For the derivation of this curve, see A. J. Brown, 'UV analysis', in Worswick (ed.), *op.cit.* In fitting these curves for industries and regions, Thirlwall found that linear regression gave the best fit. See A. P. Thirlwall, 'Types of unemployment: with special reference to non-demand-deficient unemployment in Great Britain', *Scottish Journal of Political Economy*, Vol.16, No.1, February 1969, pp.20–49.
32. The need for vacancy flow statistics is mentioned by Harry Frumerman in 'Job vacancy statistics', in *Concepts and Data Needs*, Appendix Vol.1 to *Counting the Labor Force*, National Commision on Employment and Unemployment Statistics.
33. See *Employment Gazette*, Vol.90, No.6, June 1982, Table 3.2, p.342n.
34. Frumerman, *op.cit.*
35. *Counting the Labor Force*, National Commission on Employment and Unemployment Statistics (Washington, 1979), p.119.
36. Frumerman, *op.cit.*
37. For more discussion on these points, see James J. Hughes, 'Training for what?', *Industrial Relations Journal*, Autumn 1978, pp.27–33.

3. Macroeconomic Issues: The Evolving Debate

Emotion runs high even in the most academic analyses of the causes and cures of unemployment. Keynes in the *General Theory*[1] was never soft on the classicists, and the microeconomic school sometimes stoops to rhetoric as a substitute for logic. In the very first paragraph of *Microeconomic Foundations*,[2] Phelps disparages the core of Keynesian economics by his description of the 'road from the fall of aggregate demand to the fall of output and employment airily reached by Keynes'. On the Keynesian side, one has only to note the sub-title of Hines'[3] critique of the microeconomic approach to employment and inflation theory, 'Bad Old Wine in Elegant New Bottles', to realise that both sides spice their analyses with strong language.

The vital importance of the issue can explain the emotion in the arguments. In discussing the overall level of unemployment we are concerned with the very nature of unemployment; whether it arises out of the deliberate choice of workers not to accept lower real wages or different lower paying jobs (i.e. voluntary), or whether it is the result of broader economic forces which are beyond the ability of firms and workers to control (i.e. involuntary). We are also concerned with the appropriate policy measures for reducing unemployment.

In this chapter we study the three theories of unemployment—the classical, Keynesian and new microeconomic—and the policy implications that derive from them. An attempt is then made to reconcile the Keynesian and microeconomic approaches. A final section deals with the difficulty of measuring unemployment that is tractable to remedial measures, an issue which neither Keynesian nor microeconomic theory can handle adequately.

THE CLASSICAL THEORY OF UNEMPLOYMENT

The classical theory of unemployment, closely linked with the writing of Pigou, and in particular his *Economics of Welfare* and *Theory of Unemployment*, is sometimes referred to as the neo-classical theory in that it rests explicitly on the older, classical, macroeconomic dictum of Say's law, namely that supply creates its own demand. It also rests implicitly on the basic microeconomic formulation of Walras' general equilibrium model, in which price adjustments restore and maintain system-wide market-clearing equilibrium. Given the rigidity of its assumptions, the return to full employment from a condition of unemployment is easily attained.

In fact, a basic weakness of the theory is that it is not clear how a disequilibrium state of unemployment, above the frictional level, arises in the first place. The Walrasian system does not allow for market imperfections in the form of unions, minimum wage laws, etc., and Say's law does not allow for excess supply in markets. However, even with the effect of such imperfections on excess supply, an exogenous shock to the system will still trigger an adjustment mechanism which, though it takes longer, will automatically give rise to market equilibrium.

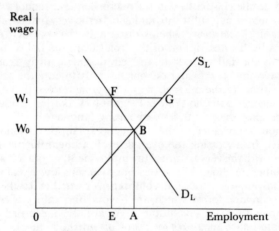

Figure 3.1. *Classical Unemployment*

In Figure 3.1 we present the traditional graphical description of the classical adjustment process. With employment and real wages on the X and Y axes, respectively, labour demand and supply curves fit their traditional patterns. The demand curve, based as it is on real wages, is the aggregate marginal productivity schedule of labour, assuming that factors other than labour are fixed and that diminishing returns are present. The labour supply curve is upward sloping, with each point on it depicting the equilibrium trade-off between the value of a marginal hour of leisure and the market wage for the work force as a whole.

Full-employment equilibrium is established at the intersection of supply and demand, with employment at OA and real wage OW_0. Now suppose that, for whatever reason, a disequilibrating real wage becomes too high at OW_1. Firms will bring their marginal labour cost back into line with marginal revenue through the mechanism of rising marginal productivity which can be achieved by reducing their work force to OE. Meanwhile, on the supply side, there is disequilibrium as excess supply FG arises.

In this classical sense, disequilibrium and excess supply mean that the marginal disutility of work is not equal to, but is less than, the wage. It is this disequilibrium which itself sets in motion equilibrating forces. Workers accept a reduction in their real wages, inducing the re-employment of labour, and at the same time reducing labour's marginal productivity as firms move down along their demand curves until equilibrium is restored at B, where once again workers are on their supply curves.

This adjustment takes time—how long depending on how fast workers react to their predicament (i.e. disequilibrium) by adjusting their wages to put themselves back on their supply curve. There is nothing in Walrasian analysis to tell just how long this 'groping' towards equilibrium takes, but it occurs rapidly enough so that there is no room in the analysis for a 'great depression', or any other long period of high unemployment.

Not only does the disequilibrium last a relatively short time, or alternatively the restoration of full employment occur quickly, but also—and what is more important for policy—it occurs automatically within the operation of the system itself. There is no need for any special efforts or government programmes to reduce unemployment. If things are left alone, unemployment will take care of itself.

The theory would even admit to some small amount of long-run unemployment, if workers refuse to lower their real wages because of institutional factors such as union wage policy or minimum wage legislation. In the extreme if, say, unionisation creates a supply schedule of $W_1 FGS_L$ in Figure 3.1, then the excess supply of labour, FG, could not be reduced. Although this unemployment would be of national concern, it would be attributable to worker (or union) recalcitrance and not to weakness of the economic system. While this form of voluntary or frictional unemployment could be of substantial magnitude, it would be inconceivable to think of mass unemployment being created by market imperfections. The barriers would crumble under the force of workers striving to achieve supply equilibrium.

This is a very convenient theory, but regrettably it does not always mesh with the facts. Ten years of depression in the US, and even longer in the UK, would have been sufficient to put to rest a theory that sees only brief periods of self-correcting high unemployment, or chronic low-level unemployment, arising only from market imperfections, had not the Keynesian analysis refuted it on theoretical grounds.

THE KEYNESIAN THESIS SIMPLY STATED

So much has been written about Keynes' contribution to macro-economics and to the theory of employment and unemployment, with almost every page of the *General Theory* cited to show what Keynes said, what he meant, and what he did not mean, that sometimes the argument reads as if it were conducted by Biblical scholars rather than by economists.

For example, consider the discussion over the major Keynesian contribution to the theory of (un)employment. Leijonhufvud[4] claims that the 'revolutionary element' in the *General Theory* is the reordering of the Marshallian (and Walrasian) ranking of adjustment velocity, with quantity responses to a shortage of total demand being more rapid and complete than price adjustments, with the result that markets do not clear and the actual quantities of labour and goods bought and sold differ from those represented by demand and supply schedules. But Grossman[5] points out that nowhere in Keynes' own analysis does this argument appear, and that it is just Leijonhufvud's interpretation that Keynes had this emphasis on non-clearing markets in mind along the line developed by Clower.[6] In his turn Clower argues that Keynes must have had this sequence in mind, or else most of the theory would be 'theoretical nonsense'.

While it is true that the translation of excess supply in the product market to the excess supply in the labour market (Patinkin's[7] analysis) does not appear explicitly in the *General Theory*, and Keynes' treatment of the consumption function might not spell out the connection between the supply schedule of labour and the effective demand for labour based on the consumption function (Clower's argument), these disequilibrating processes are implicit in Keynes when he, in effect, denies the macroeconomic application of the Walrasian model as well as Say's law. In any case, they are only processes by which Keynes arrives at his truly path-breaking conclusion with its strong policy implications.

In what respect did Keynes break with the classicists? It is not that the latter saw the real wage as determining the level of employment, while Keynes reversed the order with the level of employment determining the real wage. In fact, as we shall develop below, the Keynesian theory is not weakened if the real wage is independent of the level of employment. Moreover, Keynes himself implied this independence when he noted that a fallacy of composition would result in translating the declining marginal productivity based labour demand curve for the firm to the economy as a whole under different levels of employment related to different levels of aggregate demand (p. 259). Stated as simply as possible, the unique feature of the Keynesian thesis is that the economic system is capable of experiencing a long period of unemployment without generating forces within itself to restore full employment.

Although this statement is not a particularly strong one, and purposely so, it has far-reaching policy implications, mainly that special efforts must be exerted to reduce unemployment. There is no mention of underemployment equilibrium because too much time and mental effort has been spent on arguing whether the Keynesian analysis leads to less than full employment equilibrium or disequilibrium.[8] Patinkin expresses the issue forcefully, arguing that since the money wage rate would tend to fall with an excess supply of labour, equilibrium could not be reached at less than full employment (since equilibrium implies that nothing tends to change in the system). According to Patinkin[9] this theorem (the concept of underemployment equilibrium)

tells us nothing about the nature of the forces which generate unemployment. It tells us nothing about the relationship between the height of the real wage rate and the existence of unemployment. It tells us nothing about the proper practices to follow to combat unemployment. And—most importantly of all—it tells us nothing about the central question which divides classical and Keynesian economics, the efficiency of an automatically functioning market system with flexible money wages in eliminating involuntary unemployment.

Solow[10] puts the equilibrium-disequilibrium argument into perspective when he states, 'From the standpoint of policy prescription it hardly matters whether the economy is at rest in a "bad equilibrium" [Keynesian involuntary unemployment] or merely takes a long time to get back to a good equilibrium [classical *and* Keynesian full employment].'

Thus, while the debate over whether Keynes described a possible condition of less-than-full employment equilibrium or disequilibrium may not be settled, the outcome of that debate is unimportant as far as the essential Keynesian message is concerned, namely that the economic system itself does not generate forces to re-establish full employment and that underemployment can persist for a long period in the absence of demand stimulation.

Given the often unproductive debate over equilibrium–disequilibrium in Keynesian theory, we outline below the unmodified version of Keynes' theory of involuntary unemployment—i.e. as it appears in Keynes' writings. We then discuss recent modifications to the theory.

KEYNES' THEORY OF INVOLUNTARY UNEMPLOYMENT

Keynes made only a partial, albeit all-important, break with the classical theory. While he denied the easy restoration to full employment from a disequilibrating movement towards (high) unemployment, he did accept the classical (marginal product) labour demand curve. The operation of the Keynesian labour market, when there is a departure from full-employment aggregate demand, is presented graphically in Figure 3.2. In this analysis we follow early Keynes in that a fall in aggregate demand and employment leads to a rise in the real wage.

Starting from a full-employment equilibrium with employment, OA, and real wage, OW_0, assume a reduction in aggregate demand resulting from a decline in planned investment compared with

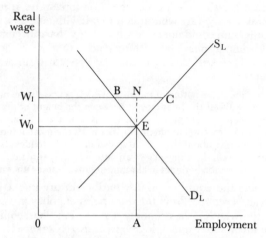

Figure 3.2:   *Keynesian Involuntary Unemployment*

planned savings or, what is less likely, a weakening of consumption demand. The initial decrease in aggregate demand makes its way through the operation of the multiplier to a stable lower level of demand and output, at which planned savings and investment are equal. At this reduced level of aggregate demand, less labour is required and the demand for labour moves up the demand curve to real wage OW_1, where excess labour supply, or unemployment, of BC arises. The real wage rises as employment falls in accordance with Keynes' view, as stated in the *General Theory*.

What is significant is that any unemployment which arises is 'involuntary' in that it is not within the workers' power to reduce it.[11] They will not be able to reduce their unemployment by trying to lower their real wages because any reduction in money wages they might accept would, in the absence of an increase in demand, result in an equivalent reduction in prices. Full employment will be restored at OA only through an increase in aggregate demand as workers *accept* the decline in the real wage required to re-employ them at the previous lower point on the labour demand curve.

Keynes argued initially that workers will not allow a reduction in real wages by taking money wage cuts because of labour market imperfections caused by unions, etc., or because of 'mere human obstinacy' (p. 6). The classicists were also agreed that such behaviour would prevent full employment, with the resulting unemployment considered by both themselves and Keynes as frictional–voluntary unemployment.

But Keynes points to a means by which workers would allow a cut in real wages when he argued that the same workers who will refuse a cut in money wages will not resist a cut in their real wages through a price increase that exceeds a money wage rise. Keynes attributed this asymmetrical behaviour to workers' strong interest in maintaining their *relative* wage level, which is, of course, undisturbed by a price rise which reduces all real wages by the same percentage, but is lowered for any particular group which accepts a money wage cut.

Whatever the reason for workers' acceptance of a real wage cut—and there is nothing of 'money illusion' in Keynes' own argument for their acceptance—this dependence on a decline in real wages for the restoration of full employment does not make Keynes a classicist. For, to repeat and re-emphasise, the classicists viewed the decline in the real wage as being initiated by workers, while Keynes regarded it as something they have to accept since the increase in aggregate demand, the only source for eliminating involuntary unemployment, requires them to accept this decline if they want to see the demand stimulation translated into higher employment.

These relationships can be understood more clearly by reference to Keynes' definition of involuntary unemployment:

Men are involuntarily unemployed if, in the event of a small rise in prices of wages-goods relatively to the money-wage, both the aggregate supply of labour willing to work for the current money-wage and the aggregate demand for it at that wage would be greater than the existing volume of employment. (p. 15)

Thus, in accordance with this definition, from Figure 3.2 we see that if workers allow a relative price increase (during a period of rising aggregate demand)—behaviour which Keynes called 'fortunate', in that it prevents labour recalcitrance from being a bottleneck to recovery—the involuntary unemployment will be eliminated as the aggregate demand determined real wage slides down the demand curve from B to E.

Note that there is no reference to money illusion in this definition either. Keynes did not argue that workers have to increase their labour supply at a lower real wage; the greater volume of employment, at E rather than C, occurs at a lower level of supply, and results if workers just maintain their supply schedules.[12] Not only is money illusion unnecessary, but similarly the alternative relative wage argument after worker acceptance of real wage cuts through inflation is not needed to explain the rise in employment during recovery.[13]

Even if workers tried to lower their real wages by taking money wage cuts when aggregate demand is below its full-employment level, they would be unable to do so since prices would fall in proportion to wage cuts. Keynes chided the classicists for thinking that an independent cut in money wages (i.e. unrelated to aggregate demand stimulation) would not reduce prices more or less proportionately, since they saw the price level as being determined by prime costs and money wages are by far the chief component of these costs (p. 12).

Workers may try to gain employment by lowering their money-wage rate, but this practice would be fruitless because, with no change in demand, prices would fall *pari passu*. Perhaps the resulting deflation would stimulate aggregate demand somewhat through increased consumption resulting from the increase in the real value of cash balances (i.e. through the Pigou effect), but the movement towards full employment through this process would be slow and tortuous. Similarly, the stimulating effects of an expansionary monetary policy would be weak and incomplete. As Friedman[14] expresses it, 'Monetary policy is twice damned'; first because to Keynesians the existence of the 'liquidity trap' means that an increase in the money supply exerts little downward pressure on interest rates, and secondly because in bad times investment is interest-inelastic.

If workers are involuntarily unemployed, so that wage policy will not help re-employ them, and monetary policy will not work, the policy prescription for recovery is clear; an expansionary fiscal policy must be adopted to raise aggregate demand, which will lead to the re-employment of workers as they 'fortunately' allow their real wages to fall as prices rise.

Keynes was so sure of the strength of his theory that he welcomed a statistical inquiry into the cyclical pattern of money-wage–real-wage changes, and predicted in accordance with his theory that the relationship would be inverse. In particular he believed that real wages would rise during the downturn. Such studies were made but, contrary to Keynes' expectations, they revealed a tendency for money wages and real wages to move together.[15] Undaunted, Keynes[16] welcomed these findings, pointing out that they freed him from the inconvenient conclusion of his theory, namely that real wages would fall during recovery, a conclusion that he himself would not have reached had he followed through his fallacy of composition argument against the application of the firm's labour demand curve to the economy as a whole under changing levels of aggregate demand (p. 259). Then he would not have accepted the classical downward sloping labour demand curve, based on marginal productivity theory, as applicable to the economy at large. What remained unaffected by these findings was Keynes contention that employment could only be increased through a rise in aggregate demand for output regardless of the movement of real wages in the process. But it remained for Patinkin to advance the Keynesian argument by analysing the effect on aggregate labour demand of a change in product demand.

MODIFYING KEYNES: PATINKIN'S ANALYSIS

Patinkin[17] criticises the underlying assumption of the classical–Keynesian input (labour) demand curve, namely that it is not subject to quantity constraints operating from the output market, and points to the adjustment that is necessary in the Keynesian theory. If there is a decline in the aggregate demand for goods, Patinkin suggests that this will be translated into the labour market by a movement of employment and wages off both the demand and the supply schedules. This is shown in Figure 3.3. Following Keynes, there is an initial drop in employment from ON_0 to ON_1. According to Keynes, real wages would rise from N_0B to N_1E as output declines and the economy moves upwards along its labour demand curve in response to the decline in aggregate (product) demand. But Patinkin points out that such a movement implies firms can sell all they can produce. In reality, no more than the output produced by ON_1 labour can be sold, thus there is no upward push on real wages above $N_1C(=N_0B)$ from the demand side. In effect, Patinkin argues it is as if firms have experienced a leftwards shift of their demand curves, although he does not develop

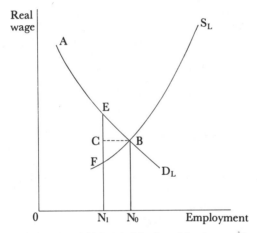

Figure 3.3: *Patinkin's Modification of Involuntary Unemployment*

this point.[18] Instead, he points out that individual firms are output-constrained, even if they do not realise it. No more than the output equivalent of ON_1 employment of labour can be sold, so that the marginal product of labour is indeterminate at this level of output. In effect, the labour demand curve becomes $AECFN_1$.

As Patinkin explains in an agonising footnote,[19] if real wages are at N_1C individual firms might try to increase output since their own real wage seems to lie below labour's marginal product, but if they do so they will find they have unsold, unwanted inventory. They will therefore cut back production and for such firms C does not represent a static situation. Since at any time there are some firms expanding and others contracting, 'as long as commodity demand conditions remain unchanged, never is the aggregate succeeding in moving to the right of C.'

In fact, there is no reason for the real wage to settle at $N_1 C$ since alternating upward and downward processes will move it along the vertical path bounded by EF. The real wage will remain indeterminate and unstable over this path, in purist Keynesian disequilibrium, with instability and mobility, but without the economy moving towards a higher level of employment.[20]

If the real wage rises to its upper (*General Theory*) level at $N_1 E$, there is no pressure towards excess production in the product market, but there is a clear disequilibrium in the labour market, with excess labour supply putting downward pressure on real wages. On the other hand, at the lower limit of real wages, $N_1 F$, there is equilibrium in the labour market. In fact, as Patinkin points out, there is, 'by definition', full employment, even if there has been no increase in employment, since the quantity of labour supplied declines to the level of labour demand.[21]

Thus at any time, if aggregate demand remains unchanged, the level of real wages is indeterminate but bounded by the limits EF. Patinkin's contribution to Keynesian theory is that it has formally freed the real wage from the static, marginal productivity labour demand curve. As noted above, Keynes argued that evidence of actual independence of the real wage from the level of unemployment strengthened his theory in that it was thereby made less contrived. Thus Patinkin[22] was able to claim that 'we are more Keynesian than Keynes'.

But, in one important respect, Patinkin's argument breaks with Keynesian theory, and in fact the break is unjustified by his own analysis. It is one thing to say that the real wage is indeterminate at reduced output and labour demand, but it is quite another, and unKeynesian at that, to say that it can move freely over a wide range. There is nothing in Patinkin's analysis to warrant denial of Keynes' contention that at a given level of aggregate demand the real wage can only move over a limited range, if at all, irrespective of supply–demand pressures in the labour market and monetary factors trying to push it up or down.

Thus, for example, the possibility that full employment is reached by the classical–microeconomic device of lower real wages, at F in Patinkin's analysis, albeit at lower employment, may not be a realistic one. As will be argued below, it is the sluggishness of real wage adjustment which serves as the basis of our attempt to reconcile Keynesian and microeconomic analysis.

THE MICROECONOMIC THEORY OF UNEMPLOYMENT

As its name implies, this theory makes a complete break with Keynesian analysis. According to this theory unemployment is caused by microeconomic disruptions and is cured only if the appropriate microeconomic adjustments take place. As such its theoretical underpinning lies in the Walrasian system of general equilibrium equations, with modifications. These modifications refer to the labour market imperfections which prevent full application of the adjustments to market-clearing equilibrium with excess demand and supply eliminated in all markets. The microeconomic theory received its clearest expression in Friedman's[23] definition of the 'natural rate' of unemployment:

The 'natural rate of unemployment' . . . is the level that would be ground out by the Walrasian system of general equilibrium equations, provided there is imbedded in them the actual structural characteristics of the labour and commodity markets, including market imperfections, stochastic variability in demand and supply, the cost of gathering information about job vacancies and labour availability, the costs of mobility, and so on.

As Friedman clearly explains, if the unemployment rate is above the natural level there is conventional Walrasian adjustment; this excess labour supply will exert downward pressure on real wages, which in turn will reduce the rate to its natural equilibrium level, comprised of the frictional elements contained in Friedman's definition. Nothing could be further from the Keynesian–Patinkin analysis. Real wages not only move when non-frictional unemployment rises, the direction of change is such as to reduce unemployment to its frictional level. Instead of the Walrasian system being denied,[24] it serves as the basis for adjustment of a temporary disequilibrium.

More than one writer has pointed out the weakness of a theory that, in effect, treats the money wage as just another price in the Walrasian system. With wages accounting for such a dominant share of costs and product prices, as Keynes himself argued,[25] any substantial wage change would have strong repercussive (disequilibrating) effects on other prices in the system. In Weintraub's arch expression, 'To interpret money wages as "simply another price" is to mistake elephants for flies.'[26]

While the microeconomists may postulate much too close a money-wage-real-wage employment nexus, it is unfair to claim that their analysis runs 'full circle'[27] back to the classical starting-point. Although both theories see the adjustment to full employment (frictional unemployment) achieved through falling real wages, the modern theory adds the microeconomic element of job search as a barrier to freely falling real wages. Search represents the utility maximising activity of individual workers who incur the costs of looking for work—including the loss of wages from being unemployed while searching—in order to improve their employment conditions, mainly their wage.[28] Such a search constitutes an investment in information.[29]

Thus, while the classicists see no barriers to workers accepting a lower real wage to restore full employment, except for market imperfections, or perhaps Keynesian 'worker obstinacy', the microeconomists argue that the reluctance of many workers to accept the going wage is the natural consequence of two factors. The first is the paucity of information on the (changed) real wages that will employ them; the second is their utility-maximising search for higher-paying work.

As a result of this search for the 'best' job, unemployment may persist for a long time before workers realise that they can only get a job at a lower real wage than they had been seeking. While this argument makes the difference between the classicists and the microeconomists only one of duration of unemployment, this is not an insignificant difference given that we are discussing cyclical unemployment. Keynes, in minimising the possible stimulation of aggregate demand from cash balance and liquidity-interest rate effects of money wage declines, would have agreed that a difference based on adjustment time is one of kind and not simply of degree.

But search theory itself has been subject to criticism, which though forceful does not undermine it entirely. It is argued that the greater portion of job search is conducted by the employed rather than the unemployed. Of course, to the extent this is so, the unemployment rate is unaffected by job search utility maximisation, but as long as some workers trade employment for search opportunities, the theory holds. Also, the fact that unemployment might be concentrated in the secondary labour market, that is, among workers who when they quit jobs do so not for better-paying ones but because they are dissatisfied with the dead-end nature of their previous employment, does not seriously damage the theory. Regardless of the reason for their current unemployment, these are the workers who are most likely to hold out for a high wage to compensate for the distaste of their employment opportunities. Furthermore, recent studies suggest that it is not realistic to regard high unemployment as being caused by groups of secondary market workers moving in and out of bad jobs. Secondary market workers also suffer disproportionately from long-term unemployment indicating that they bear the brunt of demand-deficient unemployment when this reaches serious proportions.[30]

Another criticism of the microeconomic school is that it suggests that those who suffer most from unemployment invest most in search because it is assumed that longer and more frequent spells of unemployment are associated with heavier investments in utility-maximising search. This implies that those in bad jobs, or subject to high unemployment because of low skills or outright labour market discrimination (e.g. minorities and women), make rational decisions to invest more in search. But this suggestion implies that all search is efficient, leading to a utility-maximising equilibrium between unemployment and search gains. In effect this extreme view is reflected in the position adopted by Lucas and Rapping[31] that all unemployment (in excess of frictional) represents an equilibrium (natural) level since it is caused by utility–maximising job searchers. However, once we allow for inefficient, non-maximising job search, then it can be argued that many, especially low-wage workers who hold out for higher paying jobs, are really engaging in rather long-term inefficient search. (The subject of inefficient job search is taken up in Chapter 6.)

Fullest support for the microeconomic view is given by Lucas.[32] According to his analysis, deviation from the natural rate of un-employment—say a movement above the rate—may occur when workers are unaware that the market wage has fallen even though they are aware of receiving lower wage offers themselves. As utility-maximisers they reduce their effective supply to the market, investing in longer job search or opting for the leisure associated with unemployment until their information about the market becomes clearer.

In the process of these mistakes, a cycle is generated about the natural rate. In fact, the title of Lucas's collection—*Studies in Business Cycle Theory*—reflects the progress of his analysis towards pre-Keynesian views of fluctuations. Cycles are recurrent systematic movement in output and employment. To Lucas they are generated by supply-side influences, particularly workers' responses to their perception of current and future available wage opportunities when making their work–search–leisure choices. At the beginning of his book (page 3) Lucas writes: 'the way households vary hours of work in response to changes in perceived current and future wages and prices is at the center of everything that follows in this volume.'

There is no role for aggregate demand fluctuation in Lucas's supply-response generated cycles. But even more antithetical to the Keynesian view than the emphasis on supply factors as a cause of economic fluctuations, is Lucas's acceptance of the pre-Keynesian view of recurrent and systematic cycles themselves, a position supported by his quantitative findings. With actual unemployment revolving about its natural rate, as a matter of course, there is no need for outside forces to correct a level of unemployment above that rate.

Critics of the microeconomic approach evoke the Great Depression as proof against the validity of the microeconomic–natural rate hypothesis. Lucas readily admits that his explanation of fluctuations about the natural rate cannot apply to the extremely high unemployment rates that persisted during the Great Depression. He writes: 'The Great Depression, however, remains a formidable barrier to a completely unbending application of the view that business cycles are all alike' (p. 273). Then, more directly, he writes: 'If the Depression continues, in some respects, to defy explanation by existing economic analysis (as I believe it does), then perhaps it is gradually succumbing to the Law of Large Numbers' (p. 284). That is, if the Great Depression cannot be explained by the natural-rate hypothesis, the pattern of cyclical behaviour both before and since would suggest that that experience was an aberration. Certainly, Keynesian prescriptions would be inappropriate to these other cycles and the risks involved in applying them are greater the more the endogenous pattern of cyclical movements is ignored.

For example, in the late 1950s and early 1960s in the US both the Council of Economic Advisers and the Administration thought Keynesian policies (i.e. large tax cuts) were needed to reduce the unemployment rate below 5 per cent—the then generally accepted upper limit for the frictional–structural base. The 1964 tax cut succeeded in lowering the rate below this level, but was followed, with a two-year lag, by persistent inflation. In natural rate terms, it would be argued that the authorities had not realised that the natural rate had risen, and that they were in effect applying fiscal policy to drive the actual unemployment rate below its natural level, with consequent inflationary effects.

The purpose of these counter-arguments in support of the micro-economic theory is not to claim that this theory can explain long periods of high unemployment. Indeed it cannot do so. Rather, the purpose is to defend it as having some validity for explaining relatively low, but above normal, levels of unemployment. This is something to which we shall return in the next section, in which Keynesian and microeconomic theory are reconciled.

But what are the policy implications of microeconomic theory? To Friedman *et alia*, monetary expansion is an inefficient means of reducing unemployment below its natural rate. To Keynes, as was discussed above, monetary expansion would be at least partially[33] ineffective, whereas to Friedman it is even counterproductive. Higher prices resulting from an expansion of the money supply would result in only a temporary decrease in real wages and fall in unemployment until workers bid up their money wages to restore real wages to their former level. Eventually, even the short-run Phillips curve would not arise as inflation becomes fully anticipated, and there would no longer be any short-run gains in employment, although there would be harmful inflationary side-effects of uncertainty and balance of payments problems. (These issues in the relationship between inflation and unemployment receive fuller treatment in the following chapter).

The natural rate changes over time because of changes in the underlying impediments to full employment detailed in Friedman's definition. The only feasible policy measures for a long-run reduction in the natural rate of unemployment would be in the reduction of labour market imperfections and better information on job avail-ability to reduce frictional and structural unemployment. This might seem like nothing more than the classical prescription, but for the classicists the steps would suffice to eliminate non-frictional unemploy-ment and reduce the frictional level. For the microeconomists, though, there would still remain the need for information on attainable real wages, not just the more readily available information on job openings at current wages.

RECONCILING KEYNES AND THE MICROECONOMISTS

To make such diametrically opposed theories as the Keynesian and microeconomic compatible, it is necessary to establish that they apply to unemployment under different economic conditions. If Keynesian theory is applicable to the conditions of its birth, i.e. periods of heavy unemployment, microeconomic theory is only applicable to milder, albeit more numerous, recessions. For example, concerning the applicability of Keynesian theory to periods of heavy and persistent unemployment Weintraub[34] has written: 'Currently [1975] with 9 per cent unemployment, assorted Keynesians breathe new life; the sect is always intellectually comfortable with [high] unemployment.' As for the microeconomic view, many, including Lucas himself, have pointed out the weakness of a theory that would try to explain a long period of very heavy unemployment as resulting from fruitless search for non-existent better paying jobs. Again, according to Weintraub, unemployment statistics for 1975 reflected more depression conditions than 'a sloppy failure in job search'.[35]

But even its proponents imply that the microeconomic theory applies to relatively good times when workers can search for better jobs, secure in the knowledge that they can always have slightly worse ones. Alchian,[36] who presents a detailed exposition of search theory based on voluntary quitting, explains lay-offs on the ground that firms know that workers would quit rather than agree to the wage cuts necessary for their profitable retention: 'And so lay-offs are announced without fruitless wage negotiation.' However, in 1982–3—years of high unemployment—several large unions in the US, led by the Auto Workers and Teamsters, have settled new contracts, or reopened existing ones, agreeing to wage concessions which will, even under fairly low rates of inflation, guarantee that their members will have lower real wages over the next few years. Similarly, although it was not a common occurrence, it was not entirely unknown for individual groups of workers to accept wage cuts rather than lay-off during those years.

Accepting that only Keynesian unemployment applies to periods of high unemployment, and assuming that within a Keynesian framework, as modified by Patinkin, microeconomic theories apply to periods of moderate—but higher than frictional—levels of unemployment, we can explain the persistence of long periods of unemployment under both economic conditions. Let us consider heavy unemployment first, by reference to Figure 3.3, which describes Patinkin's modification of Keynesian theory. Recall that Patinkin considers that the real wage, when it is not itself an independent force raising unemployment in that it is not set higher than the 'right' market clearing level, moves indeterminately between C and F. But, in addition, he argues that point F would be an unstable one in that firms would tend to lower prices and thus raise the real wage. However, although this adjustment makes it unnecessary for the theory to have to explain what Patinkin[37] calls '"by definition" a full-employment situation', it somewhat contradicts his own earlier argument that other points along ECF are not off the employer's labour demand curve. This curve, in effect, becomes $AECFN_1$ when aggregate demands falls, so that firms never experience upward pressure on real wages anywhere along the vertical range of the new demand curve. Real wages will depend upon how prices respond to excess capacity, but, what is important in this context, they will not be raised by employers' labour demand. Then, according to Patinkin's own analysis, F could not only be attained but, what is more important, maintained.

We also noted above that although Barro and Grossman see the possibility of point F being attained, they do not argue that it will be an unstable real wage. Rather, they argue that it is not a position of full employment but one of 'voluntary unemployment', with the unemployed consisting of those holding out for a higher real wage than $N_1 F$. But if the supply curve has any meaning, these workers are unwilling to settle for $N_1 F$, and as such should not be counted in official unemployment statistics.

Both of these arguments to explain away the full-employment situations of real wages $N_1 F$ are unnecessary if Keynesian limitations on the range over which the real wage can decline are acknowledged. The simple conclusion that then follows is that the real wage can fall a little below $N_1 C$, but not nearly so far as NF, so that substantial long period Keynesian unemployment can be maintained.

Let us now introduce the microeconomic approach under conditions of moderate unemployment. Figure 3.4 is a blown-up version of Figure 3.3, with one important difference; the decline in aggregate demand is assumed to be only moderate, so that, in theory at least, the real wage could fall as far as $N_1 F$. However, the distance between N_0 and N_1 would be much less if Figure 3.4 were on the same scale as Figure 3.3.

With the decline in aggregate demand, there is a decline in output and employment from ON_0 to ON_1, and the appearance of unemployment measured by $N_1 N_0$, or CB. Now many workers will accept a lower real wage as downward pressure on the real wage arises, say to $N_1 G$, but short-run labour supply is not described by H on the supply curve, but by I which lies inside the supply curve. I represents the number of workers who would take available jobs immediately at the lower real wage. J includes the number, IH, who would be willing to work at the lower real wage *if they had to*, but they are still seeking employment at the previous higher wage $N_0 B$.[38] J also includes those, HJ, *who will not work at the lower real wage, but are still seeking jobs at the old real wage.*

In time, when they become aware of the fact that they cannot find jobs at this wage, some, IH, will accept the lower wage $N_1 G$ and look for jobs at that wage; others, HJ, will drop out of the labour force in accordance with the behaviour described by the actual supply

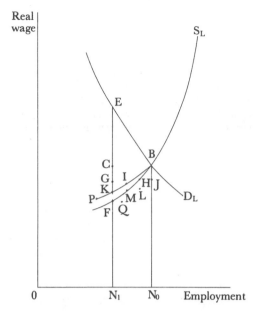

Figure 3.4: *Keynesian–Microeconomic Theories of Moderate Unemployment*

curve.[39] Although there is an adjustment time required, this variant of the microeconomic theory, which allows for differential search time, is consistent with a willingness to accept lower real wages.[40]

Now, suppose the real wage is driven down to K. In accordance with the above argument, the labour supply measured by KL represents those workers who are searching for a higher-paying job (at wage $N_1 G$), but what is important, in the short run they are not available for employment to employers. In time, many (KM) will accept the lower wage, and some (ML) will drop out of the labour force as the supply of labour moves to its longer-run position on the supply curve, at M.

But what is most important, wages cannot fall below $N_1 K$ in the short run because employers want this amount of labour to meet reduced production associated with the decline in aggregate demand. They would prevent wages from falling further in the short run, even with unemployment, because at lower real wages labour would become a production bottleneck as available supply falls to only P.

BIKP is a form of short-run supply curve. It is the supply available at given wage rates which will be augmented in time by others, currently holding out for a higher real wages, who will eventually accept jobs at these wages if offered. Of course, at wage $N_1 K$, over time the available labour supply would push out to M as more workers accepted the lower real wage and others dropped out of the labour force. Then, the real wage would be in a position to fall towards F. But whether this would in practice occur is doubtful since we are discussing cyclical behaviour and the time period of adjustment would probably be too long to represent a realistic path towards full employment. Anyway, the argument that search unemployment will eventually lead to full employment, if only one waits long enough, is similar to the argument that in time cash balance effects might lead to full employment, even if money wage declines *in themselves* cannot do so.

Note that we are implying that F represents a full-employment situation. There is a difference between F and K even though both points seem to describe a position of zero excess labour supply at the going real wage. But at K, there is an unemployed supply, KM, that would work at the prevailing real wage if it discovered through search that it could not find better-paying jobs. On the other hand, at F, there is a supply seeking better-paying jobs, FQ, which correspond to Barro and Grossman's 'voluntary unemployment', but they are unwilling to work at $N_1 F$ and will drop out of the workforce when they accept the fact that they cannot find better-paying jobs. They are not truly part of search unemployment, nor are they a component of the 'natural rate'.

AN UNRESOLVED ISSUE: MEASURING KEYNESIAN INVOLUNTARY UNEMPLOYMENT AND THE 'NATURAL RATE'

While the concepts of Keynesian involuntary unemployment and the microeconomic 'natural rate' are themselves elusive enough, the practical issue of their measurement is even more difficult to solve. Consider first Keynesian involuntary unemployment. Edwards[41] notes that while Keynes went into great detail defining the concept, he never explained how it can be measured. And, of course, measure it we must if we are to test the effectiveness of policies designed to reduce it.

Referring to Figure 3.2, which depicts the unmodified Keynesian presentation, what is the level of involuntary unemployment at real wage OW_1? If we interpret Keynes accurately, then in order to answer this question the Bureau of Labor Statistics (BLS) in the US, and the Department of Employment (DE) in the UK, should ask the unemployed worker the involved theoretical question, 'Would you be willing to work at a lower real wage, if necessary, should it be offered as a consequence of increased production?' The question then arises, 'What level of the real wage will eliminate involuntary unemployment? We know that from Figure 3.2 this is AE, but can the BLS or the DE be expected to know this wage?

In actual fact the question that is asked to determine whether those without jobs should be included in the unemployment count is: 'Will you take a job at the current wage?' This would suggest that involuntary unemployment is measured by BC, the volume of excess labour supply at the current real wage OW_1. Given the upward sloping supply schedule, this clearly overstates the number, BN, that would be willing to work at the lower real wage, OW_0. This shows how difficult it is to translate the concept of involuntary unemployment into practical measurement.

While Patinkin's modification, introduced to explain the pro-cyclical nature of movements in the real wage, may make the concept of involuntary unemployment more consistent with reality, it makes its measurement no easier. Referring to Figure 3.3, at first view Patinkin's modification seems to make the measurement of involuntary unemployment much simpler. Here the movement away from the initial equilibrium—i.e. from B to C—is not accompanied by a rise in the real wage, as in the basic Keynesian model, and at C involuntary unemployment is clearly CB and the unemployment test implicit in the question put by the BLS or DE: 'Would you accept a job at the going wage?' applies.[42] However, since workers can reduce their real wages somewhat by doing this, even if they cannot increase their employment, unemployment would thereby be reduced as a result of shrinkage in the labour supply.

Thus, it might be more appropriate to ask workers if they would be willing to lower their wage to find a job, with an affirmative answer indicating the presence of involuntary unemployment. But then, if real wage $N_1 F$ were reached, there would be no involuntary unemployment, or any unemployment for that matter. However, as Barro and Grossman point out, this condition would be a sub-optimal policy goal in that output and employment could be raised, without unemploy-ment, at a higher real wage, $N_0 B$, if only aggregate demand were strengthened. Obviously the BLS and DE cannot round up people at real wage $N_1 F$ who are not unemployed and ask them if they would work at a higher real wage, should a higher-paying job become available as a result of an expansion in output.

The same problem of sub-optimality arises at any real wage between C and F, although, of course, to a lesser degree than at F. Thus, we can conclude that only if the real wage is coincidentally at C does the labour market test not only measure existing involuntary unemploy-ment, but also coincide with the optimal policy for its reduction.

As for measuring the natural rate of unemployment, Friedman[43] himself admits: 'Unfortunately we have no method to estimate accurately and readily the natural rate . . . and the natural rate will itself change from time to time.' Measurement of the natural rate is closely tied to the important policy issue of an attainable, non-inflationary unemployment rate. Consequently, while we have touched on its measurement problems in this chapter, these will be discussed more fully in the next, which concentrates on the inflation-unemployment relationship.

SUMMARY

All three basic theories of unemployment—the classical, Keynesian and microeconomic—see unemployment associated with too high a real wage for the restoration of full employment. The fundamental difference between the unmodified Keynesian theory and the other two is that the former regards the high real wage as only a manifestation of unemployment, the other two see it as the cause. The fundamental difference between the classical and microeconomic theories is that the former sees no barrier to the fall in real wages, which will occur as a matter of course unless impeded by institutional market imperfections, while the latter sees the path to lower real wages blocked, not only by labour market impediments, but also by the optimising decision of workers who include unemployment as a rational investment cost of search.

The classical theory is based on Say's law and Walras' general equilibrium model, both of which Keynes rejected. This rejection led him to a theory that explains the persistence of heavy unemployment for long periods of time. Patinkin's modification of the Keynesian analysis frees it from its unrealistic assumption of contra-cyclical movements in real wages, but leaves the basic Keynesian view of involuntary unemployment, resulting from inadequate aggregate demand, intact. While doing this, however, he overstates the degree of real wage flexibility.

The microeconomic approach also applies the Walrasian system, but differs from the classical interpretation in that it allows for complete information and consequent job search as an element retarding adjustment to unemployment. The microeconomic theory can be made compatible with the Keynes–Patinkin system for explaining the persistence of moderate unemployment, with search time slowing the process of falling real wages and reduced unemployment. But putting it in that system makes any reduction in unemployment the result of reduced labour supply, at unchanged employment, rather than an increase in employment. For example, referring to Figure 3.4, at the real wage denoted by K, the BLS or DE may decide to call this a full-employment situation in that there is no more labour currently available at this wage above the number actually working. However, there is a large number, KL, that is actively seeking work at a higher wage. Not all of these should be counted as part of search unemployment; KM should be counted in that in time they will come to accept a lower real wage than they are currently holding out for.[44] As if these measurement problems are not difficult enough, there is the added problem of sub-optimality at any measured unemployment at real wage levels below C. This path to sub-optimally reduced unemployment is one that an unreconstructed microeconomist might not want to follow.

Remedial policies differ for the three theories. Put briefly, the classicist requires only better labour market services on job availability and a reduction in institutional market impediments. To these, the microeconomist adds the need for better information on attainable wage rates. The Keynesian requires aggregate demand stimulation, not through monetary policy, which all three theories reject as ineffective or counterproductive, but through expansionary fiscal policy.

Both Keynesian involuntary unemployment and the microeconomic natural rate defy easy measurement. Policy measures are obviously hampered by this weakness.

NOTES AND REFERENCES

1. J. M. Keynes, *The General Theory of Employment, Interest and Money* (New York: Harcourt Brace, 1936), herein referred to as *The General Theory*. Citations from this work will be noted in the text rather than in footnotes.
2. Edmund S. Phelps, 'Introduction: the new microeconomics in employment and inflation theory', in Edward S. Phelps (ed.), *Microeconomic Foundations of Employment and Inflation Theory* (New York: Norton, 1969). p.1.
3. In G. D. N. Worswick (ed.), *The Concept and Measurement of Involuntary Unemployment* (Boulder Col.: Westview, 1976).
4. Axel Leijonhufvud, *On Keynesian Economics and the Economics of Keynes* (New York: Oxford University Press, 1972), pp.55-6.
5. Herschel Grossman, 'Was Keynes a "Keynesian"? a review article (of Leijonhufvud)', *Journal of Economic Literature*, X, March 1972, pp.26-30.
6. Robert Clower, 'The Keynesian counter-revolution: a theoretical appraisal', *The Theory of Interest Rates*, ed. F. K. Hahn and F. R. Brechling (London: Macmillan, 1965).
7. Don Patinkin, *Money, Interest, and Prices* (New York: Harper & Row, 1965).
8. E. Malinvaud, *The Theory of Unemployment Reconsidered* (Oxford: Basil Blackwell, 1977), maintains that equilibrium can be established when markets do not clear in a non-Walrasian system.
9. Patinkin, *op. cit*, p.315.
10. Robert Solow, 'Alternative approaches to macroeconomic theory: partial view', *Canadian Journal of Economics*, 1979, p.343.
11. Whether the entire amount of excess supply, BC, at real wage, OW_1, represents unemployment is an issue to be discussed below in the 'Unresolved Issue' section.
12. For this point, see Richard Perlman, *Labor Theory* (New York: Wiley, 1969), p.143; and John T. Addison and W. Stanley Siebert, *The Market for Labor: An Analytical Treatment* (Santa Monica: Goodyear, 1979), p.385. Chapter 11 of this comprehensive reference work treats many of the issues raised in this chapter.
13. This alternative is discussed by James Tobin, 'Inflation and unemployment', *American Economic Review*, Vol.62, March 1972, pp.1-8; and J. A. Trevithick, 'Money wage inflexibility and the Keynesian labour supply

function', *Economic Journal* Vol.85, 1976, pp.327–32. For a critical evaluation of the Tobin–Trevithick position, see John Addison and John Burton 'Keynes analysis of wage and unemployment reconsidered', *Manchester School*, March 1982, pp.1–23.

14. Milton Friedman, 'The role of monetary policy', *American Economic Review*, Vol.58, March 1968, p.2.

15. For a review of these studies, see Ronald G. Bodkin, 'Real wages and cyclical variations in employment', *Canadian Journal of Economics*, August 1969.

16. J. M. Keynes, 'Relative movements of real wages and output', *Economic Journal*, 49, March 1939, p.40.

17. Patinkin *op. cit.*, Chapter 13.

18. The labour demand curve would actually shift to the left if capital or other factors could vary with labour, and/or some firms closed down rather than all having their output limited, as Patinkin's argument implies. With fewer firms, and less use of other factors, the marginal product of labour could remain unchanged at lower output, with C being the marginal product of labour at the lower demand curve. For the earlier literature on demand shift with variable non-labour factors, see Perlman, *op. cit.*, pp.161–5.

19. Patinkin, *op. cit.*, p.323, n.9.

20. Patinkin does argue that extraneous (to Keynes) cash balance effects will raise employment, but this change, if it occurs, is irrelevant to the present discussion.

21. Robert J. Barro and Herschel J. Grossman, 'A general disequilibrium model of income and employment', *American Economic Review*, LXII, March 1972, p.86, argue that at E there is a form of voluntary unemployment rather than full employment. But this argument is based on faulty application of Bureau of Labor Statistics standards for measuring unemployment. This argument will be examined below.

22. Patinkin, *op. cit.*, p.340. Patinkin's modification gained acceptability among Keynesians. As explained by Abba Lerner 'On generalising the general theory', *American Economic Review*, L, March 1966, p.134, with reference to an earlier edition of Patinkin's work, 'What is relevant is not the inability of labor to reduce its real wage, but the inability to bring about an increase in demand which increases employment, whether this would lower the real wage or raise it.'

23. Friedman, *op. cit.*, p.8.

24. As Clower, *op. cit.*, pp.110–11, forcefully expresses it, *'Either Walras' law is incompatible with Keynesian economics, or Keynes had nothing fundamentally new to add to orthodox (classical) economic theory.'* (Italics in original.)

25. See, for example, James Tobin, 'Inflation and unemployment', *American Economic Review*, LXII, March 1972; and Hines, *op. cit.*

26. Sidney Weintraub, 'The missing theory of money wages', *Journal of Post-Keynesian Economics*, 1, Winter 1978–79, p.73.

27. A description used by both Tobin, *op. cit.*, p.2, and Hines, *op. cit.*, p.77.

28. Hahn contrasts job search unemployment with Keynesian demand-deficient unemployment by noting, 'In much of the recent literature on the labour market it is mostly assumed that workers search for the best wage and not for a job at the going wage.' F. H. Hahn, 'Unemployment from a theoretical viewpoint', *Economica*, 27, August 1980, p.288.

29. The basic theory of investment in information was developed by George Stigler, 'Information in the labor market', *Journal of Political Economy*, October 1962.
30. Kim Clark and Lawrence Summers, 'Labor market dynamics and unemployment: a reconsideration', *Brookings Paper on Economic Activity*, 1, 1979, find that unemployment is concentrated in relatively small groups of people who are out of work for long periods of time.
31. Robert Lucas and Leonard Rapping, 'Real wages, employment and inflation', in Phelps, *Microeconomic Foundation, op. cit.*
32. Robert E. Lucas, *Studies in Business Cycle Theory* (Cambridge, MA: MIT Press, 1981). This volume consists of a collection of Lucas's papers on micro-theory, with commentary.
33. See note 10 above. In the *General Theory*, p.173, Keynes wrote: 'If . . . we are tempted to assert that money is the drink which stimulates the system to activity we must remind ourselves that there may be several slips between cup and lip.'
34. Sidney Weintraub, *Keynes, Keynesians, and Monetarists* (University of Pennsylvania Press, 1978), p.39. In a similar vein, Richard Kahn, 'Some aspects of the development of Keynes' thought', *Journal of Economic Literature*, XVI, June 1978, p.553 writes, 'His [Keynes'] failure to consider adequately how wages would, or might, behave under conditions of fairly full employment is attributable to the high level of unemployment with which he was faced and to his belief that, apart from war, unemployment would never fall to a really low level.'
35. Ibid. p.56.
36. Armen A. Alchian, 'Information costs, pricing, and resource unemployment', in *Microeconomic Foundations, op. cit.*, p.39.
37. Patinkin, *op. cit.*, p.327.
38. Hahn, *op. cit.*, p.287, makes the significant point that the willingness to trade a lower real wage for increased probability of unemployment must not be taken to mean a willingness to accept the wage. The latter clearly depends on the calculation of the agent of what the actual trade-off is. Hahn repeats the point on p.293.
39. Kaldor's claim that 'the notion of a "natural rate" of unemployment falls to the ground if real wages are positively correlated with employment' only holds if there is no search unemployment. Nicholas Kaldor, 'An introduction to "A Note on the General Theory"', *Journal of Post-Keynesian Economics*, Spring 1979, p.4.
40. For the tendency for workers to lower their wage aspiration the longer their search, see Charles C. Holt, 'Job search, Phillips wage relations, and union influence: theory and evidence', in *Microeconomic Foundations, op. cit.*
41. Edgar O. Edwards, 'Classical and Keynesian employment theories: a reconsideration', *Quarterly Journal of Economics*, 73, August 1950, p.423.
42. Thus, with probably the Patinkin modification in mind, Kahn is able to claim that the involuted Keynesian definition of involuntary unemployment could be replaced by the DE (and BLS) test, in that 'there is involuntary unemployment to the extent, at the current money-wage and with the current price-level, the number of men desiring work exceeds the number of men for whose labour there is demand'. Richard Kahn, 'Unemployment as seen by the Keynesian', in Worswick (ed.), *The Concept and Measurement of Involuntary Unemployment, op. cit.*, p.21.

43. Friedman, *op. cit*, p.10. Criticism of attempts to measure the natural rate is noted in Chapter 4.
44. Of course, at F, excess labour at FQ should not be counted because they will drop out of the labour force once they realise they can get no higher wage than F.

4. Unemployment and Inflation

While Chapter 3 on macroeconomic issues focused on the question of whether unemployment can be caused by demand-deficiency, or is primarily a supply-side phenomenon, the current chapter expands on the controversy in its discussion of whether unemployment and inflation are functionally related. The issue is an important one because it deals with the serious policy questions that arise when the economy approaches full employment.

Two basic themes form the structure of the analysis:
(i) does the movement towards full employment lead inexorably to inflation?
(ii) is (inflationary) monetary policy effective in reducing unemployment?

A yes answer to the first question and a no answer to the second lead to very dismal policy conclusions. If a reduction in unemployment results in inflation, then policy-makers are faced with what Phelps calls the 'cruel dilemma' in selecting a mix of inflation and unemployment, both of which are undesirable. The no answer to the second question means that what was once considered a valuable tool for controlling unemployment, monetary policy, is ineffective for that purpose. But in this chapter we conclude that there is cause for optimism in pursuing a policy of reduced unemployment by judicious combination of aggregate demand and monetary measures.

These two themes are examined in this chapter, the first in relation to the early Phillips–Lipsey analysis, the second by reference to the natural rate-microeconomic approach which stresses the short run nature of the Phillips curve. After presenting the two main threads of the inflation–unemployment relationship, we argue that they do not describe a true controversy, but in fact discuss two different aspects of the unemployment–inflation relationship. In a policy section we develop the argument that the two are not incompatible. It is not that they can be reconciled; rather, we argue, that they can both be descriptive of reality since they are not treading the same path in the unemployment–inflation field. Both can therefore contribute to full-employment policy.

THE PHILLIPS CURVE: PHILLIPS–LIPSEY ANALYSIS

Ever since the initial Phillips study,[1] policy-makers have been aware of a possible trade-off between inflation and unemployment reduction.

(Although Phillips related *wage* changes to unemployment, the translation into price changes is an easy one considering the close relationship that exists between wages and prices via the productivity link.)

Phillips explained the inverse relationship between wage changes and unemployment by reference to labour market conditions. When unemployment is low, employers bid up wages in competition for scarce labour. Conversely, when the labour market is weak, firms do not have to pay as much to hire available labour, or alternatively, competition among plentiful labour for jobs exerts downward pressure on wages—and consequently prices.

Phillips attributed the non-linearity in the curve, specifically its flattening out at the bottom, to the reluctance of workers 'to offer their services at less than the prevailing rates when the demand for labour is low and unemployment is high so that wage rates fall only very slowly.'[2] Here we see adumbrations of search theory in the micro analysis of the next section. If 'previously' is inserted before 'prevailing rate', and 'causing unemployment to rise above the natural level' is substituted for 'and unemployment is high', we are close to the arguments of Alchian, Holt *et al.*[3]

Phillips' more or less *ad hoc* explanations of the nature and shape of his curve were replaced by Lipsey's[4] more rigorous theoretical argument. Close examination of the curve reveals important unanswered questions in Phillips' explanation. For one thing, steepness at the high levels of demand and flatness at the low levels have policy implications which are far too important for glib explanations. According to Phillips such explanations rely on strong demand-pull forces when the economy is strong, and cost-push forces when it is weak. For another, the basic curve in Figure 4.1 seems to imply that employers experience no learning process as they find plenty of labour available at higher wages.

It is too early in the discussion to bring in 'adaptive expectations', but consider the implication of point A in Figure 4.1. At A, in period 1, there is still substantial unemployment. Let us assume that the actual level is above the frictional-structural level, say at an unemployment rate of 8 per cent, and a wage rate increase of 5 per cent. According to Phillips, wages are bid up because employers think they have to pay a higher wage to attract workers. But once they find that labour is abundant, as it is at that unemployment rate, the question arises why employers do not learn about labour market conditions and offer the same wage, if not a lower one, in the next period (year). According to the curve, if unemployment remains unchanged so will the extent of wage inflation. Surely this peculiarity of the curve, or in employer behaviour, needs explanation.

Secondly, one might ask the question, 'Why are employers bidding up wages at all at point A?' If the unemployment rate is above its frictional-structural level labour is not scarce so why do employers feel

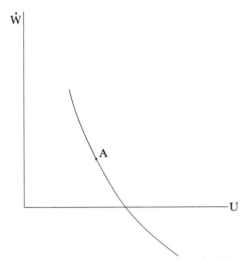

Figure 4.1: *The Basic Phillips Relationship*

the necessity to raise their wage offers, particularly in the absence of inflationary expectations?

Lipsey's analysis of the Phillips relationship answers these questions —non-linearity in the curve, persistence of wage inflation at a given (above frictional-structural) unemployment rate, and the presence of wage inflation in any case when unemployment is above this level. In effect, Lipsey explains all three by his theory of sectoral Phillips curves. Wages, in his analysis, are related linearly to the degree of excess demand in the labour market. When supply exceeds demand, and excess demand is, in effect, negative, wages tend to fall to an extent measured by the surplus of labour. This surplus, in turn, equals the unemployment rate. Hence, the Phillips curve is linear for high levels of unemployment.

But when there is excess demand in the labour market, so that wage pressure is positive, this excess demand is not reflected in the Phillips curve since it tends to rise more than unemployment falls, the difference between the two reflecting unfilled job vacancies. Thus, as aggregate demand has to cut deeper and deeper into the frictional-structural base, there might be little or no reduction in unemployment. Although wage inflation still bears the same relationship to a given degree of excess demand, the degree to which unemployment is reduced by employer efforts to hire workers becomes smaller and the Phillips curve grows steeper for lower level of unemployment, eventually becoming vertical before reaching the Y axis.

But this steepness in the curve occurs before a declining overall unemployment rate reaches its frictional-structural base because, while there is more excess supply in labour markets than there is excess demand (assuming equal-sized markets) when demand-deficient unemployment is present, the upward wage pressure in labour-shortage sectors will outweigh the downward pressure in labour-surplus sectors over a certain range of unemployment. This follows because, as was explained above, the amount of excess labour demand required to reduce unemployment is greater than the excess supply required to increase it by the same amount.[5]

The sectoral approach to the labour market also explains why a given level of unemployment above the frictional–structural base, even if maintained, will generate continuous wage inflation. Although the overall unemployment rate may be above the combined frictional-structural rate, the sectoral rate is below the frictional–structural rate in enough sectors to make the overall wage pressure from labour-deficient sectors outweigh the wage-depressing forces from the labour-surplus sectors. Thus, while there is, on balance, a labour surplus, the continuous inflationary pressure from unemployment at this level is not dependent on the failure of employers to realise that there is a labour surplus; it arises from the force of excess demand—greater than that indicated by the unemployment rate—in labour shortage sectors.

While Lipsey's analysis goes far in explaining the shape and nature of the Phillips curve, it provides little guidance for policy-makers. The Phillips relationship itself indicates that efforts should be made to move the curve to the left, but this is easier said than done. Lipsey's analysis recommends that the labour market be improved to make the frictional[6] base smaller, but natural rate theorists would agree with programmes to this end, and it is an obviously beneficial policy for any efforts to reduce unemployment. Similarly, the reduction of structural imbalances through training for occupations and jobs that hold the promise of a strong future demand does not need Lipsey's analysis for support. What Lipsey does claim, though, is that these imbalances are a source of inflationary pressure long before full employment, defined as the overall frictional–structural level, is reached.

While the Phillips–Lipsey analysis held sway as the dominant explanation of the inflation-unemployment relationship for about a decade, it was subject to criticism and refinement from the beginning. The loose fit of the curve—particularly in the US—and its changing position were attributed by some analysts to the influence of such variables as prior price change, expectations, lags, unemployment rate changes and profits.[7]

Apart from the effect of other variables on the price level, arguments have been raised that the unemployment rate is not a strong factor in wage determination, especially in a union setting,[8] and that the unemployment rate itself is not a good measure of labour market tightness.[9] A further argument holds that since wage-price changes and labour market tightness are not causally related, Phillips curve analysis serves only to provide a convenient vehicle for justifying the suppression of a full-employment policy, when in fact such a policy could be pursued without 'inflationary cost'.[10] Thus, in the late 1960s, the Phillips curve faced a two-pronged attack, from theory and events. The theoretical opposition will be discussed in the next section, but here we mention the inability of the Phillips curve to deal with stagflation.

Inflation in the US increased in the late 1960s, with no appreciable change in the unemployment rate. Defenders of the analysis explained the phenomenon as a rightward shift in the curve. For example, Perry[11]—as noted in Chapter 1—held that a compositional shift in the labour force, and in unemployment, towards workers who contributed less to total output, resulted in a given rate of unemployment being associated with a greater degree of labour market tightness than had been the case in earlier years.

But even this hypothesis broke down under the full force of stagflation in the recession of 1974–5. The Phillips curve was not capable of dealing with a situation of 11 per cent inflation and 9 per cent unemployment. The view still prevails that the curve shifted to the right mainly because of the shock effect on prices of a sudden sharp rise in oil prices, and because US agricultural exports raised food prices. However, a Phillips curve that is so volatile as to jump around frequently and unpredictably leaves little basis for policy-makers to forecast the quantitative effect of expansionary demand policy on the wage or price level. What remains of the Phillips curve is the qualitative conclusion that a reduction in unemployment will lead to more inflation, and an increase in unemployment to less inflation.[12]

THE NATURAL RATE AND THE PHILLIPS CURVE

The Long-Run Phillips Curve

While in the years immediately following its introduction analysts used the Phillips curve to examine the degree to which unemployment reduction raised wages and prices, in the late 1960s Friedman posed the question of whether the functional relationship between unemployment and inflation was reversible, that is, whether inflation could lead to a reduction in unemployment. In the next section we shall examine the confusion resulting from the failure of the two approaches to mesh with regard to the issues they are addressing, but here we simply describe the Friedman–Phelps argument.[13]

According to this view, as discussed in Chapter 3, unemployment tends to gravitate towards its natural rate. Furthermore, any short-run deviation above this rate represents supply-induced unemployment, which will be eliminated once workers lower their wage aspirations and accept lower money *and real* wages.[14] In our discussion of the role of search theory below, we shall examine the question of whether expansionary monetary policy can substitute for this adjustment by workers in reducing unemployment to its natural rate, but here we address the question posed by the natural rate theorists of whether monetary expansion can lower unemployment below the natural rate.

The familiar[15] graphical analysis of the natural rate theory is shown in Figure 4.2. We begin with unemployment at its natural rate, U_N, at the current wage level; that is, with no wage inflation. Now the monetary authorities decide that they want to reduce the unemployment rate below the natural rate through expansionary monetary policy. We might wonder why the authorities would want to do this, but here we do not question the wisdom of the policy, but just describe its effect on unemployment.

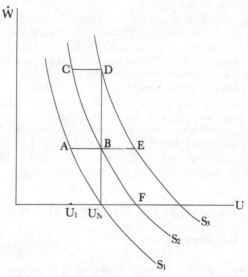

Figure 4.2: *The Long-Run Phillips Curve*

Monetary expansion raises wages up to A on the short-run Phillips curve S_1, while unemployment falls to U_1. The increase in wages leads to an increase in prices. The reduction in unemployment occurs because, although prices have risen, workers have not yet adjusted to the inflation and, in effect, through the influence of money illusion accept a lower real wage, even though the money wage has increased. Thus money illusion plays a central role in the generation of the short-run Phillips curve, even though—as was argued in Chapter 3—it is not necessary for Keynesian theory, but simply acts as a *deus ex machina*, allowing recovery to occur without labour bottlenecks.[16]

Firms are led to expand output and employment in response to this lower real wage which drives a wedge between marginal revenue and marginal cost. But eventually workers realise they have been deluded by the wage increase that in fact lowers their real wage, and demand higher wages.[17] The process of adjustment is not instantaneous, but it is simultaneous between employer and workers. While the latter are 'learning' about the decline in real wages and demanding higher money wages, employers contract their demand for labour as labour costs rise. A new equilibrium is reached at B on a higher, short-run Phillips curve with the previous level of unemployment. Only the price level has changed—not real production costs, nor employers' demand for labour. If wage inflation is maintained at A or B, this implies that workers have adapted to the new level; in fact, they expect it. Thus, there is no further movement along S_2 as long as the same wage inflation rate is maintained.

But policy-makers can generate a new short-run Phillips curve by raising the wage–inflation rate to C along S_2. The same process of adjustment and adaptive expectations arise and a new equilibrium is attained at D on S_3. Thus, what is known as the accelerationist view of the short-run Phillips curve unfolds. Unemployment can only be temporarily reduced from one period to the next by an accelerating wage and price level. Short-run Phillips curves are generated in the process, during which unemployment is reduced; but the long-run Phillips curve is vertical and is described by Points U_NBD in Figure 4.2 at the natural rate of unemployment. This vertical, long-run curve indicates the absence of an unemployment–inflation trade-off. No matter how high the wage–price level is pushed, the unemployment level remains constant in the long run. The trade-off exists only in the short run, and depends upon the steepness of the short-run Phillips curve.[18] If a given reduction in unemployment is to be maintained in the long term, then the price that has to be paid is an accelerating rate of inflation.

There is an optimistic element in Figure 4.2. The relationship is reversible. Thus, while expansionary monetary policy will not reduce unemployment in the long run, neither would a contractionary policy raise it in the long run. Starting from point D, a contractionary monetary policy would lead to U_N via E and F. In other words, successive 'doses' of contractionary policy would give rise to successive increases in short-run unemployment, until eventually there is zero inflation at the natural rate of unemployment.

Returning to the short-run gains in reduced unemployment arising from movement along a short-run Phillips curve, an important policy question arises as to how long the short run is. If adjustment is slow and the same level of inflation persists over several periods before workers anticipate price increases, then, as a practical matter, although the long-run equilibrium will not be associated with a reduction in unemployment, the lengthy short-term gains might make the effect (inflation) worthwhile. In other words, we have a favourable counterpart to the Keynesian argument that a slow movement towards equilibrium may lead to irrelevant results. In the Keynesian case there is continued high unemployment while the unemployment reducing effects of wage reductions work themselves out. In the case under discussion, the unemployment-reducing effect may be significant if it takes a long time for the offsetting equilibrating adjustments to take place.

A literature[19] has developed over the length of the short run, the period of adaptation after which a given inflation rate is fully anticipated and, what is more important, incorporated into current wage demands. While most studies[20] emphasise that full adaptation is hampered by price stickiness, this is not a universal view.[21] Rees[22] considers that barriers to wage flexibility, such as long-term union contracts, prevent quick full-wage responses to initiating price changes, thereby lengthening the adjustment period and allowing a 'longer' short-run trade-off. While agreeing that unions slow down the adjustment in the short run, Ashenfelter *et al.*[23] argue that unions increase the pressure for higher wages later on, with the consequence that inflation is more severe in the longer term. The adaptive hypothesis in this literature have their ultimate refinement in the theory of rational expectations.

Under adaptive expectations, derived from Friedman, agents anticipate price changes based on past inflation and a short run Phillips curve can be generated. But under rational expectations, as described, analysed and tested by Lucas and Sargent,[24] anticipated inflation depends upon far more variables than the past rate of inflation. As a result, future inflation is more fully and quickly anticipated. Thus, the Friedman-type short run Phillips curve becomes much steeper, or even vertical,[25] and short run gains in reduced unemployment arising from a given monetary expansion are very slight, or non-existent.

On the positive side, the costs of a contractionary monetary policy that reduces the rate of inflation are negligible. As Lucas points out: '*any* average inflation rate [is] consistent with *any* level of unemployment' (*Business Cycles*, p.228). While he attributes this conclusion to the long run analysis of Friedman–Phelps, it is also implicit in the shorter run analysis of the rational expectations model.

Nevertheless, if employers—and especially workers—adjust quickly to inflation there will be only very short-run benefits, in the form of reduced unemployment, to be gained by inflationary monetary policy. On the other hand, the costs of a contractionary monetary policy, in terms of higher unemployment, will be negligible.

SEARCH UNEMPLOYMENT AND THE NATURAL RATE HYPOTHESIS

Search theory, developed in Chapter 3, provides the link between the natural rate hypothesis and the long-run Phillips curve along the path of adaptive expectations. Search behaviour provides two services to the theory. First, it strengthens the view that unemployment is basically a labour-supply phenomenon, an argument presented in Chapter 3. Second, and more relevant to the present discussion, it helps explain both the short-run Phillips trade-off and the vertical long-run nature of the curve.

According to search theory, workers tend to accept jobs which offer wages within their acceptance range, which in turn is partially determined by their wage expectations. They are quicker to perceive wage changes than they are price changes, which is understandable since the changes in wage offers that they receive will be relatively few, and will affect them immediately. However, changes in the price level are the composite of changes in many individual prices which only affect workers in the future as they consume those goods which have increased in price. Thus when prices rise as a result of inflationary monetary policy, a time-lag develops during which workers stop searching and accept what may turn out to be a reduction in their real wage. They accept job offers which now appear to be above their acceptance (real) wage level. During this period, employers as well as workers are motivated to reduce unemployment in that real wages are temporarily lower and there are profits to be earned by expanding their work forces.

In this manner, the upward movement along the short-run Phillips curve is generated. But, in time, workers become aware of their mistake, or rather, they adjust to the higher price level. They demand higher money wages to restore their real wages and the extra profits earned by employers evaporate, reducing labour demand to its old level.

But this is not the end of the adjustment because search theory requires a supply side response, otherwise the implication of the theory that jobs are available if workers will take them at the real wage offered is that once they adjust to the price level they would be willing to hold jobs that they would not have accepted before the wage–price increase. In fact, though, as the theory unfolds, they behave rationally and quit the jobs they have mistakenly taken under the belief that the wage increase was a real one. Labour supply stabilises when the previous level of unemployment, which represents search unemployment, is reached. Then the rightward movement of the short-run Phillips curve is generated. The worker will not be fooled a second time; inflation is anticipated, and if the authorities want to generate another short-run reduction in unemployment they will have to raise the inflation rate. Hence the accelerationist model is generated.

The main contribution of search theory to the natural rate hypothesis is that it adds realism to the adjustment process by postulating a world, or at least a labour market, of imperfect knowledge and adaptation to inflation that is rational, but at the same time not immediate.[26] In effect, search theory creates a policy choice. Whereas, under more

rapid adjustment, expansionary monetary policy offers little scope for
reducing unemployment even temporarily, search theory offers the
choice of a short-term reduction in unemployment at the cost of
inflation. These short-term gains will be greater the slower the
adjustment process, or the less rational are expectations.

Search theory can also explain why expansionary monetary policy
cannot serve as a long run substitute for a willingness on the part of
workers to accept a lower real wage to bring unemployment back to
the natural rate if it is above that rate. To avoid the initial condition of
deflation, which would arise if unemployment were above its natural
non-inflationary rate, assume a situation of stagflation in which
unemployment is high (above its natural or frictional–structural rate),
but in which prices are rising. This situation is described by point A in
Figure 4.3 in which N is the natural rate.

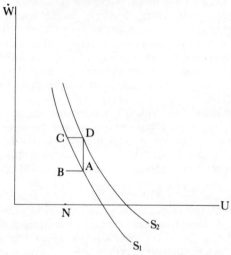

Figure 4.3: *Inflation at the Natural Rate and Search Unemployment*

Under search theory there are jobs available at the prevailing wage,
which is below the acceptance level of those searching for a job. If these
jobs were taken, employment would move to B, which coincides with
N. BA then becomes voluntary unemployment, in accordance with the
natural rate hypothesis. To substitute for this worker reluctance to
accept the going wage, stronger inflationary monetary measures move
the workers along the original short-run Phillips curve, S_1, to C. We
can assume that this is simply a supply phenomenon, with no lag in
wages behind prices. But workers have not yet adjusted to the higher
prices, simply to the higher wages. Once they do adjust they quit jobs
as they realise the acceleration of inflation yields no improvement in
the real wages of their jobs and job offers. They move to D on the

new higher short-run Phillips curve S_2 and will stay there as long as they anticipate that inflation will be at the new, higher rate. The unemployment rate at D is the same as that at A.

The logic of the argument is that real values have not changed and there is no reason for workers to change their negative attitude towards the same real wage at which they refused jobs before. Thus, search theory does not require workers to quit their jobs while unemployment is rising, as is sometimes argued. Just as they preferred not to take available jobs at the going wage when at point A, they would also prefer to hold out at C for an even higher money wage once it becomes apparent to them that the higher money wage at C yields no increase in the real wage.

The natural rate hypothesis does not deny that the actual rate can lie above the natural rate for long periods of time, at least for as long as workers resist employment at the prevailing wage, or are ignorant of this wage. But it does deny that expansionary monetary policy can overcome this resistance or ignorance.

Criticism of search theory is on firmer ground when the argument is raised that jobs might not be available at the prevailing wage. Search and natural rate theorists would counter with the argument that the prevailing wage is too high and that a lower wage would be required to bring a high unemployment rate back to the natural level. Indeed, they would stress the failure to realise that wages have fallen as the cause of workers holding out (searching) for jobs at the old wage.[27] But if this is the natural rate theory's explanation for the persistence of recessions, then as we stated in Chapter 3, the theory becomes indistinguishable from classical theory which stresses that the path to full employment is via lower wages, and as such becomes vulnerable to the Keynesian argument that acceptance of lower money wages itself has little or no effect in reducing unemployment. The only way out is for search theory and the natural rate hypothesis to deny the existence of demand-deficient unemployment.

THE EARLY PHILLIPS CURVE AND NATURAL RATE HYPOTHESIS—THEORIES APART

A great deal of the controversy between Phillips curve supporters and natural rate theorists would be avoided if both sides realised they are discussing different events. The argument is not brought into focus by noting that Phillips was interested in the question of how a change (usually a reduction) in unemployment affects the wage-price level, while natural rate theorists are more concerned with the effect of monetary policy on unemployment. Given that more attention is paid to Phillips' expositors and critics than to his original article, certain misunderstandings have come about. One such misunderstanding is the belief that Phillips' relationship is reversible, with unemployment falling if prices rise. But this is not the case. Time and again in his paper Phillips stressed that wage inflation is the dependent variable and unemployment the independent variable. The reverse is true for the natural rate theory. Phillips would not have been the least surprised to find that inflation in itself did not reduce unemployment; in fact, he expected this to be the case and took it into account in his data analysis.

The central difference between the two arguments lies in the treatment of prices. In the first part of this section we examine the different role of prices in Phillips curve analysis and in the natural rate theory. Then we examine the policy implications of both contributions.

The Role of Prices

Turning first to Phillips, he was well aware of the importance of prices in the trade-off relationship he discovered between wage–price inflation and the unemployment rate. In effect, he considered two types of price increases, one related to the reduction in unemployment, which is endogenous to his system, the other exogenous—mainly arising from sharp increases in import prices. To Phillips, these latter price changes were equivalent to inflationary monetary policy in that, in themselves, they have nothing to do with an increase in aggregate demand, which has its own endogenous inflationary aspect. In fact, in the detailed analysis of the sub-periods that he studied, he explained points significantly to the right of the curve as being the consequence of sharp rises in import prices which push up the general price level.

Thus, in practice, he might be said to have presented his curve net of exogenous forces on the price level which have no impact on unemployment. In other words, there is no unanticipated inflation, no 'fooled' workers suffering from money illusions, and no consequent windfall profits in Phillips' original analysis. According to this interpretation there are not even the short-run gains resulting from a rise in the price level unassociated with the pressure of aggregate demand; there is no short-term movement along the curve, but rather a jump off the curve. A new, higher curve would be generated if the same inflationary force continued. However, in the years covered by Phillips' study, inflationary elements, such as abnormally high import prices, occurred sporadically and therefore such random factors resulted in points off (above) the curve rather than new curves.

But what of the endogenous price changes? These are at the core of the trade-off and represent the negative *consequence* of the quickening of the labour market, and presumably the product market, in response to the strengthening of aggregate demand. Phillips saw the rise in the cost of living that resulted from these pressures as giving rise to one-off wage increases rather than continuing inflation. For example, assume for the sake of simplicity that there is no growth in productivity, that labour market tightening raises wages by 3 per cent, and that the growth in aggregate demand raises other factors prices and the general price level by the same amount, 'Then the introduction of cost of living adjustments in wage rates under a Cost of Living adjustment plan will have no effect [on wages or prices], for employers will merely be giving under the name of cost of living adjustments . . . the wage increases which they have given as a result of their competitive bidding for labour.'[28]

Even though there are no changes in real values, there is no force operating to make inflation higher in the next period to maintain the new lower level of unemployment. This result holds even if there is perfect knowledge, or full anticipation, that increases in labour and other factor prices will not lead to real income changes. Implicitly, workers were willing to take jobs at the previous (and unchanging) real wage had they been available, and take them as the rise in aggregate demand creates openings. Workers accept the fact that a rise in real wages can only result from a gain in productivity, although total labour income, of course, will rise with reduced unemployment. Phillips' unemployment model is clearly one of job shortage and not job search.

Thus, if the now higher level of aggregate demand is maintained, wage inflation remains constant, while if demand falls to its previous level there is movement down the curve to the previous rate of wage inflation. In any case, if there is no exogenous inflationary force, such as a sharp rise in import prices, or a sudden jump in agricultural prices, or expansionary monetary policy, the short-run Phillips curve is also the long-run curve.

Very often textbooks on macroeconomics or labour combine the Phillips and natural rate theories with a garbled result. Their exposition of the vertical long-term curve hypothesis under adaptive expectations may begin with a statement such as: 'Assume an increase in aggregate demand moves the trade-off between unemployment and inflation to a higher point on the Phillips curve . . .', and go on from there to describe the process of reduced job search, temporary profits from marginal revenue being above marginal cost and the whole stimulus to unemployment reduction collapsing with anticipated inflation, the long run result of this assortment of short-term elements being a movement up to the same unemployment level on a higher Phillips curve.

In response to all this one might ask: 'What happened to the increase in aggregate demand?' Surely, the term has more meaning than the feeble ephemeral secondary stimulus from inflation of windfall profits, 'fooled' workers, and money illusion? If the initial upward movement along the curve comes from an increase in demand for goods and factors, then none of the natural rate consequences would ensue since these are associated only with a monetary, and not a real, expansion of demand. Basically, the error in this exposition of the natural rate hypothesis, which begins with an increase in aggregate demand, is that it fails to recognise that the hypothesis does not consider demand expansion as an initiating force.[29]

Thus, to repeat, the main difference between the two schools is the treatment of price changes, and the possibility of demand-deficient involuntary unemployment. Both agree that monetary expansion in itself would not reduce unemployment in the long run. But for the Friedman–Phelps hypothesis there are short-run reductions in unemployment from inflation. The main difference, though, is that while expansionary price changes were exogenous in the original Phillips analysis, in the natural rate analysis they are central to the system, and are the vehicle by which short-term changes in unemployment may—or in the case of rational expectations, may not—come about.

But unemployment as well as prices are treated differently in the two theories. In the Phillips-type model, changes in unemployment are the cause of price changes within the system. To Friedman and Phelps unemployment is the temporary outcome of price changes. Their position is consistent with their view of unemployment as a search-related phenomenon. In such a system, changes in aggregate demand have no role as a determinant of the unemployment level since unemployment above the frictional level, being voluntary, is basically unaffected by the level of aggregate demand. Workers, though, must adjust their wage aspirations downward when demand is weak.

The different role of prices and unemployment can explain the conflicting results of testing or applying the theories. As to the Phillips position, the weakness of the fit in different periods for different countries reflects the presence of extraneous inflationary pressures which result in observations that lie above the curve. Similarly, efforts such as Perry's to explain shifts in the curve have their theoretical logic, but the experience of the late 1960s and 1970s, when the curve seemed to break down completely, really does not destroy the traditional Phillips curve concept. Exogenous price shocks from oil and food prices, together with an expansionary monetary bias and in the presence of significant changes in the level of aggregate demand, did not give any new (higher) Phillips curve a chance to operate. What were observed were a series of points on higher incipient curves that never had the opportunity to develop into complete curves.

In modernisation of the Phillips analysis, Wachter[30] denies that the wage inflation–unemployment trade-off actually broke down in the mid-1970s. The normal tendency for an inverse relationship, with wage inflation receding with rising unemployment, was more than offset by the continual rise in prices which led to continual inflationary expectations on the part of workers, who in turn pushed for still higher wages. Thus, wage inflation was independently generated by continual price increases. But this conclusion is not substantially different from that reached by Phillips—except for the central role given to expectations—that exogenous price increases lead to observations to the right of the curve. In the 1970s though, the extraneous force was inflationary policy rather than rising import prices.

In his Nobel lecture, Friedman[31] speculates that persistent high and unanticipated inflation might generate real forces that give rise to a positive Phillips curve, or a rise in the natural rate of unemployment. The uncertainty that arises during these periods, while prices and wages are rising, might lead to the forestalling of economic commitments by economic agents, including decisions to hire or take jobs.[32] Friedman's arguments, along with Wachter's price expectation effect on wage inflation, are alternatives to the hypothesis that the Phillips curve broke down in the mid-1970s.

During the mid-1970s stagflation developed in both the UK and US. Adherents to the traditional Phillips curve argue that this condition implies the co-existence of continuous inflationary pressure and steady, but low, aggregate demand. According to the natural rate hypothesis, the condition represents continued efforts to stimulate the economy through expansionary monetary policy against a background of correctly anticipated inflation, and a probable rise in the natural rate.

Tests of the natural rate hypothesis involve finding whether initiating price increases, when fully expected, lead to equivalent wage changes which presumably would lead to a vertical Phillips curve. The results are inconclusive. Some analysts find the conditions for the vertical curve confirmed.[33] Others find expected inflation less than actual inflation, with a long-run trade-off possible. But the difference between the two inflationary rates is never large, so that monetary policy is at best a weak and highly inflationary method for achieving a given (small) decrease in unemployment.[34]

Tests of the natural rate hypothesis and, by implication, attempts to measure the rate itself have been criticised. Thirlwall[35] points out that there are elements other than the structure of unemployment that affect the wage–change–price–expectations relationship. For example, the estimate of the natural rate would rise if mark-ups are reduced, as they tend to be in a recession. Furthermore, as Thirlwall demonstrates, the natural rate estimate rises with a decline in productivity, which again occurs during recessions. Thus recent sharp increases in natural rate estimates may reflect declines in productivity growth related to low aggregate demand and may not simply measure the strength of frictional–structural elements, such as the shift in labour force composition towards groups (e.g. women, teenagers and minorities) that have higher frictional–structural rates. But as Thirlwall points out, frictional and structural unemployment, which estimates of the natural rate are supposed to capture, may themselves be influenced by the overall level of unemployment itself, rising when overall unemployment is high. Thus, a measured short run increase in the natural rate might simply reflect bad times and be susceptible to demand management for correction. Therefore, even if the theory underlying the natural rate is flawless, incorrect measures of the natural rate itself might give rise to incorrect policies, or failure to pursue the correct policy. For example, too high an estimate of the natural rate might cause policy-makers to desist from expanding aggregate demand, even though such a policy would reduce unemployment without accelerating inflation.

POLICY IMPLICATIONS

Both theories have their negative side. For the traditional Phillips curve, a reduction in unemployment leads to inflation, and for the monetarist-accelerationist-natural rate approach, a rise in prices will give only temporary unemployment reduction, or at best a slight trade-off at the expense of great inflation. But we should emphasise the positive policy implications both contribute.

Adherents to the traditional Phillips curve must admit the fundamental postulate of the natural rate hypothesis, that unemployment cannot be reduced below the natural rate without causing inflation; in fact the resulting inflation is an important element in the traditional approach. However, while for the traditionalists inflation is a consequence of unemployment, for the natural rate adherents it is the moving force behind (temporary) unemployment reduction. Thus, both schools recognise that to lower unemployment below the natural (frictional-structural) rate is inflationary. Nevertheless, the Friedman-Phelps argument is not attacking a straw man when it points out the inflationary effect of actually trying to lower the rate below the natural level, because this rate might be so high as to be politically and economically disturbing. This condition is described in Figure 4.4 in which the economy is at the natural rate, (N), at point A on Phillips curve S_1.

The economy is thus experiencing a rate of wage inflation measured by NA. While demand stimulation would lower unemployment to N_2, even if the equilibrium were stable at B the inflation rate at B might be intolerable. A better policy would be to try to shift the curve to the left and make it flatter, such as S_2. Then the reduction of unemployment to N_2 would involve much less inflation. The leftward shift could be achieved, admittedly with the risk of dampening the unemployment-reducing effects, by a contractionary monetary policy limiting the growth of money supply rather than by the direct depressant of higher interest rates. The effect of this monetary policy is to shift the curve downwards to S_2, with N_2 being attained with less inflation at C. The curve can also be shifted to the left by reducing frictional and structural elements. In this way the same (lower) level of unemployment would exert less upward pressure on wages and prices. The frictional base can be reduced by improvements in the labour market through the more effective dissemination of job information among

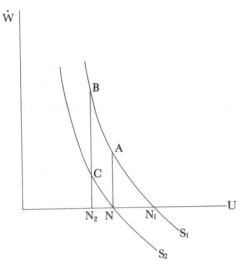

Figure 4.4: *Inflation at the Natural Rate*

employers and workers. The structural base can be lowered by reducing structural imbalance by focusing training and retraining in areas of high prospective labour demand. While Lipsey[36] explains that sectoral structural inbalance may lead to inflationary pressure, even when there is no overall excess demand, the other implicit side of his argument is that there are also sectors which are suffering from a weakness in aggregate demand.

If structural imbalance is reduced, and the labour market improved, the curve not only shifts to the left but also becomes flatter. It becomes flatter because inflationary wage pressure is reduced, there now being fewer sectors of labour shortage in which wages are rising. It shifts to the left because unemployment is lower for any given pressure of demand. That is, inflationary pressure would not begin until overall unemployment is as low as the natural rate, N, instead of N_1. If the goal is to reach N_2 there will be some inflationary trade-off at C, but not as much as there is at the corresponding point on S_1.

Ideally, in a labour market with little friction, structural imbalance, or barriers to mobility, the natural rate would be very low and there would be little motivation to reduce unemployment below this rate. But as a practical matter, Phillips curve analysis leads to a policy of reducing frictional–structural elements as much as possible so as to displace the curve to the left and make it flatter. Then the trade-off no longer becomes a 'cruel dilemma' in that the more successful the frictional–structural cures are, the smaller the stimulus that is required from aggregate demand, and, given the smaller trade-off involved, the lower the resultant inflation.

In the real world there is likely to be some inflation at unemployment rates above the natural rate, indicating that inflation and demand-deficient unemployment can co-exist. For example, if the best that deflationary monetary policy and labour market policy can do is to establish an inflationary unemployment rate at N_1 in Figure 4.5, then clearly movement towards the natural rate N will involve even more inflation, with more still required to move the economy to N_2, which might be the unemployment target.

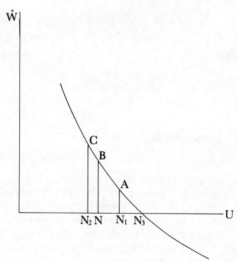

Figure 4.5: *Inflation at the Natural Rate and Demand-Deficient Unemployment*

This result, and the previous analysis of Figure 4.3, lead to different conclusions for the two schools. For the traditionalists, the inflation incurred in achieving lower unemployment at C is the end of the adjustment process. But in the analysis of the natural rate, the movement to N_2 in Figure 4.4, with wage inflation N_2C, is only temporary; accelerating inflation is required to maintain this below the natural rate, since the movement to N_2 is generated only by monetary measures and not by demand stimulation.

The natural rate analysis, no less than traditional Phillips' analysis, recognises the benefits of an improved labour market and the reduction of structural imbalance. But it contributes much more to policy than simply recommending a reduction in the natural rate in order to achieve this. While the conclusion that inflationary monetary policy cannot reduce the level of unemployment in the long run is the important negative aspect of the theory, on the positive side there is the reverse implication that lower rates of inflation can be achieved without increasing the level of unemployment in the long run. The process by which this comes about is described by Figure 4.6.

The conventional graphical treatment of the inflation–unemployment path under the natural rate hypothesis is a loop starting at N and ending at E. In Figure 4.6, A and C are the short-run points A and C of Figure 4.2. The reduction in unemployment collapses at E, when inflation—like a drug to which the economy has become immune—has lost its power to reduce unemployment in the short run because it is

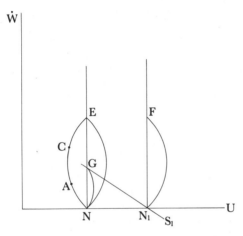

Figure 4.6: *Inflation and Deflation—Unemployment Path under the Natural Rate-Accelerationist Hypothesis*

always fully anticipated by job searchers, and because not even a temporary gap is opened between prices and wages to give employers a short-run incentive to hire more workers. A point worth noting—but one that is not usually made in this standard textbook presentation—is that for the curve to push out in its early stage, and a loop develop, we must assume that from N to A inflation is stronger in succeeding periods under the logical assumption that adaptation to inflation is a continuously improving learning process.

Similarly, there is a downward loop from E to N. On this down side the reduced rate of inflation is not fully anticipated until N. Thus between E and N searchers hold out longer because the same money wage offers now seem like a reduction in real wages, and firms cut back on their workforce if wages fall (rise) relatively less (more) than prices. Another type of trade-off arises in the process of reducing inflation. A wide loop that is traced out rather quickly but is associated with temporarily high unemployment will be the result of strong de-flationary measures,[37] as opposed to a narrow loop which arises over a longer time period but is associated with a smaller short-run increase in unemployment and results from more gentle price depressing measures.[38]

But to imply that the natural rate presents policy-makers with an easy decision simply to deflate the price level until unemployment at N is reached at zero inflation, albeit accompanied by a painful short-term increase in unemployment, is to deny the possibility of demand-deficient unemployment. Consider the presence of Keynesian demand-deficient unemployment and an initial position of stagflation at F, which is at unemployment N_1 at fully anticipated inflation rate N_1F. A downward loop can be generated to N_1 but according to the natural rate hypothesis the new loop could only be the result of an increase in the natural rate, as envisaged by Friedman (see pp.85-6 above). While inflation can be reduced and theoretically eliminated without adding unemployment in the long run, it is often overlooked that the deflationary, or decelerating process does not reduce the unemployment rate.[39] Since N_1 corresponds to unemployment level N_3 in Figure 4.5,[40] any reduction in unemployment towards the natural rate, N, or below it, will require inflation along a Phillips curve as in Figure 4.5.

Note that in Figure 4.6 the policy to reduce inflation, when this co-exists with unemployment above the natural rate, leads to short-run aggravation of the unemployment rate. Modigliani points out that restrictive monetary policy in response to sudden supply shocks on prices and on the demand for money—such as the oil price increases in 1973-5—failed to acknowledge the presence of traditional Keynesian demand-deficient unemployment at the time.[41] In the US, monetary policy was reversed during the Carter administration, and in effect the economy moved back to F. More recently, in both the UK and the US, we seem to have followed the path towards N_1.

Most would argue that the economy is better if it is at N_1 rather than at F, even though the unemployment rate is the same. At N_1, Phillips-type demand expansion can take place without much resulting inflation, and monetary authorities will be less likely to dampen the speed of the recovery by restrictive monetary policy.

Any attempt to reduce unemployment below N_1, without demand stimulation, say, to the natural rate N, would only be achieved by accelerating inflation, as described above. Then N_1 is the unemployment level which can be maintained without inflation, sometimes referred to as the non-accelerating inflation rate of unemployment (NAIRU), which coincides with the unemployment rate on a short-run Phillips curve at zero inflation.[42] Thus, if NAIRU lies above the natural rate, then unemployment at the natural rate can be attained only by accelerating inflation through expansionary monetary policy—assuming there is the possibility for a short-term lag of wage adjustments to price changes—and can be attained more permanently, but at the cost of inflation, through demand stimulation. But then, in theory, deflationary monetary policy can eliminate inflation in the long run at this lower, natural unemployment rate.

In short, a combination of demand expansion and deflationary monetary policy can shift NAIRU to the left, for example, to the natural rate. In Figure 4.6, with Phillips curve S_1 and NAIRU at N_1, demand expansion pushes the trade-off out to G, with deflationary monetary policy reducing the inflationary aspect of the demand expansion on the labour and product markets. A demand loop is generated from G to N until price stability is established at the natural rate. Thus, in the end, Phillips curve analysis would agree with Friedman's famous pronouncement, that 'Inflation is always and everywhere a monetary phenomenon.'[43] But it would suggest that the initiator of inflationary pressures comes from labour and product market tightening, with the degree of consequent inflation *dependent on* monetary policy.

Thus, in theory, NAIRU could be shifted to the left by an expansion in demand when it is above the natural rate, with the inflation eliminated by a concomitant deflationary monetary policy—although in practice negative real elements of monetary restraint might themselves increase unemployment.[44] But of greater importance than the policy of establishing NAIRU at the natural rate through a combination of demand expansion and monetary policy, is the fact that this is not the same thing as saying that there is a natural rate of unemployment towards which the economy gravitates. With demand-deficient unemployment present, more than fully anticipated price stability is needed to bring unemployment down to its frictional-structural base.

Traditional Phillips curve policy is easy in a world with perfectly functioning labour markets and no structural imbalance; all that is required is for demand to be stimulated until the natural rate is reached at zero inflation. The natural rate prescription is also clear in a world in which demand-deficiency can never exist; adopt a non-inflationary monetary policy. In the real world of labour market imperfections, structural imbalances and demand deficiency, policy-makers should realise that they face an inflation–unemployment trade-off while they try to reduce the inflationary cost of the bargain with delicately managed, decelerating monetary measures which do not in themselves generate real, harmful effects on the unemployment rate.

In the extreme position of both theories, their interaction leads to the conclusion that the rate of inflation need not be determined by the level of aggregate demand and the unemployment rate, and that the rate of inflation has no effect on the level of demand and the unemployment rate.

SUMMARY

The two dominant theories of the relationship between unemployment and inflation, the 'traditional' explanation propounded by Phillips and Lipsey and the natural rate hypothesis, are more theories apart than theories in conflict. While the former is concerned about the effects of changes in unemployment on inflation, the latter considers whether monetary expansion and contraction can affect unemployment.

The Phillips curve poses a policy dilemma, involving the choice between low unemployment or price stability, or a lower unemployment–higher inflation trade-off. Until the late 1960s this trade-off hypothesis, apart from some modification and criticism of the simple two-variable relationship, remained unchallenged. But events and theory combined to reduce acceptance of the traditional explanation. First rising prices, then stagflation, served to undermine the trade-off hypothesis. While arguments that the UK and US economies suffered repeated shocks to their price systems which caused unemployment–inflation relationships to become unstable may make theoretical sense, they do underline the difficulty of basing policy on a relationship that is internally weak in its resistance to outside forces.

Proponents of the natural rate agonise over whether there could be short-run gains in lower unemployment from monetary expansion which raises prices before wages. Under the ultimate hypothesis of rational expectations there would be no short-term gains since price increases would be fully anticipated. But apart from this issue of short-term gains, adherents to the natural rate hypothesis see unemployment as basically a supply-side phenomenon, with no role for demand deficiency.

The difference between the two theories is clearly revealed in their treatment of prices. To Phillips curve adherents, price increases are generated by the same forces that reduce unemployment, or they are the result of exogenous factors such as higher import prices. In the latter case, Phillips himself would have agreed with monetarists that the inflation does not lead to, nor is reflected in, reduced unemployment, but results in a point off the Phillips curve; in other words, inflation may be the result of lower unemployment but never its cause.

While the Phillips curve adherents believe that inflation can result from an increase in aggregate demand (which reduces unemployment), this is never argued by the other side. Indeed, it is the different response of prices in the two approaches that may allow a combination of monetary restraint and demand expansion ultimately to reduce unemployment. If, as in the case of stagflation, the non-accelerating inflationary rate of unemployment is above the natural rate, monetary contraction could reduce inflation but not unemployment, while demand expansion could reduce unemployment but raise inflation to even higher levels. Thus in theory, combining monetary restraint with demand expansion it might be possible to bring unemployment down to the natural rate. But this assumes that the instrument of monetary restraint do not themselves reduce aggregate demand. Of course, in a monetarist world in which unemployment is a supply-side phenomenon, this is not a concern.

NOTES AND REFERENCES

1. A. W. Phillips, 'The Relation between unemployment and the rate of change of money wage rates in the United Kingdom, 1861-1957', *Economica* 25, November 1958.
2. ibid., p.283.
3. See Chapter 3 for the discussion of the natural rate hypothesis.
4. Richard G. Lipsey, 'The relation between unemployment and the rate of change of money wage rates in the United Kingdom 1862-1957: a further analysis', *Economica*, 27, February 1960.
5. Empirical support is given to Lipsey's analysis by R. L. Thomas and P. J. M. Stoney, 'Unemployment dispersion as a determinant of wage inflation in the United Kingdom, 1925-66', *Income Policy and Inflation*, ed. M. Parkin and M. Sumner, (Toronto: University of Toronto Press, 1972), pp. 201-35. Thomas and Stoney find that sectoral differences in unemployment rates are a strong contributor to wage inflation and non-linearity in the Phillips curve.
6. While we use the terms frictional–structural and frictional interchangeably simply to imply non-demand deficient unemployment, monetarists or natural rate theorists make a sharp distinction between them. They relate frictional unemployment to search behaviour and structural to market inperfections, such as union wage policy, which prevent market-clearing relative wage movements.
7. For an earlier review of these studies, see Richard Perlman, *Labor Theory* New York: Wiley, 1969), pp.209-10. For a more recent summary of Phillips curve refinements, developments and tests, see Anthony Santamero and John Seater, 'The inflation–unemployment trade-off: a critique of the literature', *Journal of Economic Literature*, 16 June 1978, pp. 500-15.
8. Daniel Hamermesh, 'Wage bargains, threshold effects, and the Phillips curve', *Quarterly Journal of Economics*, 84, August 1970, pp.501-17, finds that bargained wages respond sluggishly to the unemployment rate. For a review of other US and UK studies which also show wages responding weakly to labour market conditions, see David Laidler and Michael Parkin, 'Inflation: a survey', *Economic Journal*, 85, December 1978, p.760. Furthermore D. Purdy and G. Zis, 'Trade unions and wage inflation in the UK: a reappraisal', *Inflation and Labor Markets*, ed. D. Laidler and D. Purdy (Toronto: University of Toronto Press, 1974), pp.1-37, do not find unions an important source of wage inflation in post-war UK.
9. Jim Taylor, *Unemployment and Inflation* (Harlow: Longman, 1974), finds that because of labour hoarding and hidden unemployment of discouraged workers, the official rate often understates labour market weakness or the amount of excess labour. This 'concealed' unemployment makes the

official rate, both in the US and the UK, understate demand deficiency and the volume of involuntary unemployment, thereby weakening the measured Phillips trade-off relationship.

10. This argument is made by Michael J. Piore, 'Unemployment and inflation: an alternative view', *Challenge*, May/June 1978, pp.24–32.

11. Perry, 'Changing labor markets and inflation'. See also Robert J. Gordon, 'Wage price controls and the shifting Phillips curve', *Brookings Papers on Economic Activity*, 1972, pp.385–421. The strongest argument for the Phillips curve shift based on change in the age–sex–colour composition of the workforce in the late 1960s and early 1970s is made by Donald Wise, 'Labour force composition and the Phillips curve', *Economic Inquiry*, 13, June 1978, pp.297–307. The closeness of his adjusted fit to a Phillips curve leads Wise to question the relevancy of the natural rate hypothesis. Support for the view of a shifting Phillips curve because of changes in labour force composition is given by Charles Schultze, 'Has the Phillips curve shifted? Some additional evidence', *Brookings Papers on Economic Activity*, 1971, pp.452–67.

12. But in finding a long-run Phillips relationship for the US over a very long period, Otto Eckstein and James Girola, 'Long-term properties of the price–wage mechanism in the United States, 1891–1977', *Review of Economics and Statistics* 60, August 1978, pp.323–33, maintain that exogenous shocks have simply resulted in a worsening trade-off, evidenced by stagflation.

13. Milton Friedman, 'The Role of monetary policy', and Edmund Phelps, 'Phillips curves, expectations of inflation, and optimal unemployment over time', *Economica*, 34, August 1967, pp.254–281; and S. Phelps, *Inflation Policy and Unemployment Theory* (New York; Norton, 1972), Chapter 2.

14. At this stage the theory is not anti-Keynesian in that it is not that workers are affecting the real wage by their willingness to take a lower money wage, but that they are simply accepting the prevailing real wage. Note also that we call the unemployment 'supply-induced' rather than voluntary. The latter is more of a classical term based on worker reluctance, while in monetarist theory this type of unemployment reflects more on worker ignorance.

15. It appears in many textbooks, and in Santamero and Seater, op. cit., pp.515–17.

16. John Sutton, 'A formal model of the long-run Phillips curve trade-off', *Economica*, 28 November 1981, pp.329–43, develops a short-run Phillips model that does not require money illusion. With downward wage flexibility, excess supply in some sectors finds employment with rising prices which have a strong negative effect on real wages.

17. The workers' error might be in underestimating future price increases. Since firms hire for the future, if they make the same mistake there will be no short-run reduction in unemployment from increased labour demand. On this point see Henryk Kierzkowski, 'Short-run inflation–employment trade-offs and the national level of employment', *Economica*, 27, May 1980, pp.193–9.

18. Robert J. Gordon, 'Can the inflation of the 1970s be explained?', *Brookings Papers on Economic Activity*, 1977, pp.253–77, found that the tendency of inflation to provide weak short-run stimulus in the 1970s was related to the steepness of the short-run Phillips curves that prevailed.

19. This literature is reviewed in Santamero and Seater, *op. cit.*

20. See, for example Thomas Sargent, 'Rational expectations, the real rate of interest, and the natural rate of unemployment', *Brookings Papers on Economic Activity* 2, 1973, pp.729–79.

21. See, for example, Bennett McCallum, 'Price-level stickiness and the feasability of monetary stabilisation policy with rational expectations', *Journal of Political Economy*, 85, June 1977, pp.627–34.

22. Albert Rees, 'The Phillips curve as a menu for policy choice', *Economica*, 37, August 1970, pp.227–37.

23. Orley Ashenfelter, George Johnson and John Pencavel, 'Trade unions and the rate of change of money wages in United States manufacturing industry,' *Review of Economic Studies*, 39, January 1972, pp.27–53.

24. Robert Lucas, 'Expectations and the neutrality of money', *Journal of Economic Theory*, 4, April 1972, pp.103–29; and Thomas Sargent, *op. cit.*, are the chief developers of the rational expectations model of total adjustment within the period of the disturbance.

25. For a negative view on rational expectation and the immediate (intra-period) rationality of the Phillips curve, based on data on employer wage expectation, see Jonathan Leonard, 'Wage expectations in the labor market: survey evidence on rationality', *Review of Economic Statistics*, 64, February 1982, pp.157–61. In a more specific argument against complete intra-period adjustment, Stanley Fischer, 'Long-term contracts, rational expectations, and the optimal money supply role', *Journal of Political Economy*, 85, February 1977, pp.191–205, constructs a model of incomplete adjustment within a period, despite rational expectations, if implicit contracts allow for wage adjustments only after a longer time, or after the second period's monetary change.

26. As Patrick Minford and David Peel, 'The natural rate hypothesis and rational expectations—a critique of some recent developments', *Oxford Economic Papers* 32, March 1980, pp.71–81, point out, there is no role for search theory in a rational expectations model (instantaneous adjustment) in that with full information implied there is no point in search. But perfect knowledge would not reduce 'waiting unemployment', as workers waited for openings in higher-paying jobs if the known probability that they would fill them led to a higher present value than for a job they could take now.

27. In Chapter 3 we criticised Alchian's view that lay-offs represent employers' understanding that workers would not take wage cuts to stay employed, making lay-offs, in effect, a form of worker choice. Alchian's argument is strengthened by implicit contract theory which holds that risk-averse workers exchange a stable wage for lay-offs in slack periods. As expressed by Donald Gordon, 'A neo-classical theory of Keynesian unemployment', *Economic Inquiry*, 12, June 1974, p.456: 'It [contract theory] complements the search theory by specifying something about the things for which the worker is searching'—presumably a job with a wage floor. What is not clear is why risk-averse workers would not trade for job stability rather than wage stability.

28. Phillips, *op. cit.*, p.284.

29. For a post-Keynesian criticism of the natural rate's underlying assumption that the economy tends to be at a natural rate equilibrium, which allows no role for demand-deficiency, see Thomas Tuchscherer, 'The unnatural "natural" rate of unemployment', *Journal of Post-Keynesian Economics*, 4, Fall 1981, pp.25–31.

30. Michael Wachter, 'The changing cyclical responsiveness of wage inflation', *Brookings Papers on Economic Activity*, 1976, pp.115–59.
31. Milton Friedman, 'Nobel lecture: inflation and unemployment', *Journal of Political Economy*, 85, June 1977, pp.451–72.
32. Friedman admits that the changes may be in the opposite direction, to hoard labour.
33. Bennett McCallum, 'Rational expectations and the natural rate hypothesis: some evidence for the United Kingdom', *Manchester School*, 43, March 1975, pp.56–67, finds positive results for the UK.
34. For a review of the results of these tests, see Santamero and Seater, *op. cit.*, pp.525–6.
35. A. P. Thirlwall, 'What are the estimates of the natural rate measuring?', *Oxford Bulletin of Economists and Statistics*, 45, May 1983, pp.173–9.
36. Lipsey, *op. cit.*
37. This answers slower adjustment in expectations to wider price changes. Martin Baily, 'Contract theory and the moderation of inflation by recession and controls', *Brookings Economic Papers*, 1976, pp.585–622, argues that wages will not fall sufficiently during deflation because of contracts. This conclusion is the counterpoint to Fischer's who finds that wages do not rise *pari passu* with prices because of contracts during inflation. Both arguments deny rational expectations, which would be a desirable reaction to deflationary monetary policy.
38. As David Laidler, 'The Phillips curve, expectations and incomes policy', *The Current Inflation*, ed. H. Johnson and A. Nobay (London: Macmillan, 1971), points out, the crucial variable in determining the effect on unemployment is the short-run deviation between expected and actual reduced inflation, which is normally less the smaller the changes in inflation. Laidler does not consider incomes policy, to be discussed in Chapter 10, to be particularly effective in making actual inflation more closely anticipated. But Peter Saunders, 'Inflation expectations and the natural rate of unemployment', *Applied Economics*, 10, September 1978, pp.187–93, finds that incomes policy may lower inflation expectations, which makes the deflationary aspects of these policies dependent on their success, an argument not necessarily contradictory to Laidler's conclusion.
39. Similarly, monetary expansion at N_1 would not, in the long run, strengthen the economy but only lead to inflation. Thus, Keith Carlson, 'Inflation, unemployment, and money: comparing the evidence from two simple models', *Federal Reserve of St Louis Review*, September 1975, pp.2–6, argued against the wisdom of monetary expansion at the time as a means of inducing recovery because it assumed the economic slack in the period would forestall inflation.
40. N_3 may be a theoretical rather than an operational unemployment rate. As Michael Wachter, 'Some problems in wage stabilization', *American Economic Review*, 66, May 1976, pp.65–72, points out, the non-inflationary unemployment rate at any time is difficult to estimate, especially as a goal for monetary policy.
41. Franco Modigliani, 'The monetarist controversy or, should we foresake stabilization policy?', *American Economic Review* 67, March 1977, pp.1–19.
42. NAIRU differs from the natural rate in a disequilibrium situation, such as stagflation, in which workers are not aware of the current real wage range of job offers, etc.

43. Milton Friedman 'What price guideposts?', in George Shultz and Robert Aliber (eds) *Guidelines, Informal Controls and the Market Place* (University of Chicago Press, 1966), pp. 18, 28, 35. Friedman makes the point three times in the same paper. He has, of course, made the same point on many occasions since the publication of this paper.
44. But, as Friedman argues in *The Role of Monetary Policy, passim*, any short-run rise in the interest rate because of, say, reduced money supply, would give way to a decline in the rate as deflationary policy reduced inflationary expectations.

5. Unemployment and Minimum Wage Legislation

INTRODUCTION

Part of frictional unemployment might result as a negative by-product of economic institutions. This unemployment is incidental to the operation of the institutions which, obviously, were not established for the purpose of creating unemployment but to yield positive benefits for workers. Such is the case of the two institutions studied in this and the following chapter—minimum wages and unemployment insurance. The former has been established to raise the income of those at the bottom of the occupational ladder, thereby alleviating poverty. Unemployment insurance reduces the loss of income during unemployment and also allows time for more careful job selection instead of the hasty acceptance of whatever job may be available, something which would tend to occur if unemployment insurance benefits did not exist. But, as we shall argue in Chapter 6, it is doubtful whether this advantage was foreseen at the time it was introduced.

This chapter studies the theoretical basis for the unemployment effects of minimum wage legislation and reviews the findings of the extent to which it contributes to the unemployment level.[1] We begin by discussing basic concepts and then proceed to the simple competitive one-sector model in which all workers are covered by the minimum wage. We then relax the perfect competition assumption before proceeding to a two-sector model which allows for uncovered workers.

Although discussion of a national minimum wage is more applicable to the US than the UK, the UK does have minimum wage-fixing bodies, namely the Wages Councils. These fix wages, hours and other conditions of work in those industries where organisation among employers and workers is not sufficiently developed to sustain voluntary collective bargaining. The Councils have diminished in number in recent years due to abolition and amalgamation, there being 60 in 1959 and only 28 in 1983. The number of workers covered by Wages Council orders was about 2.5 million in 1982, but in fact many of these had their wages determined by voluntary collective agreements. For example, in the early 1970s Metcalf[2] found that over half the males covered by Wages Council orders, and almost half the females, were also covered by collective agreements.

Councils are organised on an industry basis and each takes some account of conditions within its own industry in fixing the minimum rates that are to apply. This being so, the schedule of rates for one Council will differ from that of another. Also, the spread of rates that exists at any point in time will be further widened by the lack of synchronisation in the dates of implementation of the wages orders. However, despite these two factors, over a period of years there is a broad uniformity in the wage increases agreed by the different Councils.

Notwithstanding these institutional differences between the UK and the US, analyses of the unemployment effects of minimum wages will be the same in both countries. However, what needs to be borne in mind is that the proportion of the UK labour force that has its wages fixed in this way is smaller than for the US.

BASIC CONCEPTS

For the institution of a minimum wage, or the raising of an already established one, to have any employment–unemployment impact it must be *effective*. That is, it must set a floor on wages above the prevailing level. In Figure 5.1, the market-clearing wage is W_0 at employment ON_0. If the minimum were set below this level, at W_1, it would be *ineffective* in that it would have no impact on the market wage or employment. In fact, this describes the influence on most workers whose market wage is above the minimum. At W_2 the minimum wage is

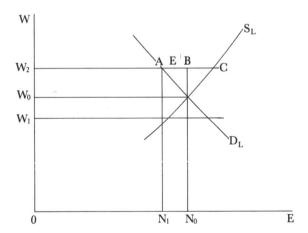

Figure 5.1: *Effective Minimum Wage*

effective in that, at least for some workers, the wage is set above the
market level and an excess supply of labour, AC, is created.

The situation is analogous to an agricultural price support
programme in which a grain surplus is created by the establishment of
a floor above the market-clearing price. There is one big difference,
though, between the two imposed price (wage) minima. In the case of
farm supports, the government stands ready to purchase the surplus
created by its policy, with a resulting unequivocal gain for the covered
farmers. In the labour market, the excess supply resulting from a
higher minimum poses a potential loss of jobs for the covered workers.[3]

The loss in employment is clear. In Figure 5.1 it is measured by AB
or $N_1 N_0$, when profit-maximising firms reduce employment as they
move up their labour demand curve in order to equate once again
labour's marginal revenue product with its marginal cost. But the
effect on unemployment is not so clear. Welch,[4] in noting the more
definite employment effects, writes:

because of the ambiguity of the standard model concerning effects of minimum
wages on unemployment, it is surprising that the majority of empirical
analyses of minimum wage effects have focused on unemployment rather than
on employment, where at least for competitive labour markets, predictions are
unambiguous.

Brown *et al.*[5] also argue that the employment loss is a better measure of
the 'harm' done by a rise in the minimum than is the change in
unemployment. They note that if jobs are lost, and workers leave the
labour force, the harm measured by the change in unemployment is
understated, but if more enter because of the higher wage, the rise in the
unemployment rate overstates the harm. Such an argument is no more
than a variant of the advocacy of the employment ratio as a superior
measure to the unemployment rate as a labour market indicator, an
argument we have criticised in Chapter 1. It also minimises one of the
main psychological costs of unemployment: fruitless job search. We do
not deny that the unemployment effects are less clear than those on the
employment side, but this does not weaken what we think are their
conceptual superiority as a measure of labour market weakness. Also,
we believe that the unemployment effects of a government measure
that interferes with market operation are politically more important
than its employment effects.

Ambiguity over the unemployment effect arises because while AC
measures excess labour supply, part of this represents an increase in
labour supply induced by the introduction, or raising, of the minimum
itself. Assume initially that AB in Figure 5.1 is equal to new
unemployment in that it represents the displacement, $N_1 N_0$, of the
formerly employed workforce. That part of excess supply shown by BC
may represent new entrants into the labour force attracted by the
higher wage, and in this case BC represents additional unemployment.

Thus the total unemployment increase consists of those workers laid off, AB, plus the increase in the labour force, BC.

However, if BC represents workers in uncovered sectors who hold on to their jobs while they apply for the better-paying covered jobs, their frustrated search does not result in additional unemployment, and total unemployment is simply AB. But even this segment of excess supply may overstate the extent of unemployment. Some of the workers laid off might leave the workforce in discouragement, a distinct possibility for low-wage workers in unsatisfying jobs, particularly if they have a tenuous attachment to work. The balance of labour force flows in response to the new (or higher) minimum will therefore determine whether the unemployment increase exceeds the employment decline (AB). If the new entrant component of BC exceeds the discouragement effect among AB workers, then the increase in unemployment will exceed the employment decline, with the reverse holding if new entrants are fewer than the number discouraged. In a quantitative study of these flows, Mincer[6] finds the discouragement effect to be stronger for many demographic groups with a reduction in labour force participation of affected workers. Mincer's findings suggest that the unemployment increase is less than the employment decline.

This can be shown in Figure 5.1 by an adjustment of the supply curve. Note that a supply curve indicates those who are willing to work at a particular wage. If they cannot find jobs at a given wage some will leave the workforce in discouragement. Thus, if at W_2 this discouragement effect is greater than the new entrant effect, BC, then actual supply would be at E, to the left of B, and the unemployment effect, AE, would be less than the employment effect, AB. (This possibility that the labour supply schedule is affected by the state of the labour market is treated in detail in Chapter 3.)

THE BASIC MODEL: STRENGTH OF THE UNEMPLOYMENT EFFECT

For policy purposes, the size of the unemployment effect is of great importance. If the effect is slight, then the benefit of higher wages for the lowest paid can be achieved at little cost, with the small amount of unemployment that results being absorbed through transfers, government jobs, etc. In practice the unemployment effect will depend upon the labour market flows discussed above, and the size of the excess supply gap, AC, in Figure 5.1. The width of the gap, in turn, depends upon how high above the market wage the minimum is set and the elasticities of supply and demand above the market equilibrium wage.

If there are good substitutes for low-wage labour the demand will be elastic. In the service sector where the elasticity of demand for the service and the labour providing it is high the response is likely to be the substitution of a less expensive service. In the extreme, the main substitute for minimum-wage labour in consumer services is not likely to be other labour, but simply doing without. Fast-food places replace more labour-intensive restaurants, motels replace hotels, etc., situations in which the consumer serves himself in response to higher minimum wages. In the industrial sector output may not be severely affected by the displacement of minimum wage labour. The plant may be a little messier, delivery of goods and messages a little slower as minimum-wage labour is displaced rather than replaced.

Apart from simply reducing the demand for output of low-wage services, elasticity of demand for low-wage labour is affected by its substitutability with non-labour factors. Elasticity from this source is also strong, as evidenced by studies showing higher substitutability between capital and unskilled (low-wage) than skilled (high-wage) labour.[7]

On the supply side, short-run increases can take place rapidly and easily. Movement from the uncovered sector requires little or no training or other preparation for entering the covered market. Furthermore, the labour reserve is well stocked with potential workers who may enter the active labour market quickly in response to a higher minimum wage.

The other crucial factor determining the magnitude of the unemployment effect is the degree to which the minimum is raised above the market-clearing level, which depends on how determined the government is to push the floor above that level. If the market wage is above what the government considers adequate in order to eliminate or reduce poverty, a rational government policy would be to leave the minimum unchanged. However, this is unlikely to be the case where the government is committed to tackling poverty caused by low-wage employment.

The main force motivating a rise in the minimum is an increase in the cost of living. For about the first thirty years of US minimum-wage history, after the initial application of the Wage and Hours Law (Fair Labour Standards Act, 1938), increases in the minimum in response to rises in consumer prices posed no serious unemployment problem, since the minimum was not raised much above the market level. This fortunate relationship prevailed because price increases were generally accompanied by strength in the economy, and specifically in the labour market.

It is often argued that in a strong economy a rise in the minimum merely eases a labour shortage and simply reduces excess labour demand. However, this argument has a logical flaw in so far as the basic model applies, if not as a description of the labour market itself. If the minimum is effective, a gap, AC, arises so long as the minimum is set above the market-clearing wage. In good times the floor was probably not pushed very much above the market level since demand for labour was increasing and pulling up the market wage. But as long as it was set above that level, some unemployment should have arisen as a consequence of the higher minimum. If it did not do so this would only mean that the demand-stimulated market wage increase quickly caught up with the minimum, or that there were other employment outlets for displaced workers in uncovered work.[8] But we shall treat the more complex model of a two- (and more) sector labour market in the next section.

While the unemployment effects are likely to be weaker when the minimum wage is raised during prosperous, inflationary periods, since the late 1960s—and especially during the 1970s—inflationary increases in the minimum have not had the supporting presence of prosperity. In this more recent period of stagflation, a given rise in the minimum would tend to push the wage floor further above the market level and lead to greater unemployment than in prosperous periods.

Apart from increases in the cost of living, changes in the minimum have also been affected by the practice of maintaining its relationship with manufacturing wages. Traditionally, the goal has been to peg the minimum at about half the average hourly wage in manufacturing. In recent years the ratio has been a little below 0.5, but as is evident from Table 5.1, the ratio has been very stable during the period 1974–81—a period beginning in a recession year (1974) and characterised throughout by sluggish economic activity and rising prices. Despite all this the minimum was increased six times during the eight-year period.[9] The constancy of the ratio after 1977 is especially noteworthy since the 1977 legislation fixed the increases in the minimum for four years ahead, without, of course, any knowledge of the path of manufacturing wages.

Table 5.1: *Minimum Related to Average Hourly Earnings in Manufacturing, 1974–1981*

Year	Minimum Wage (dollars)	Average Hourly Earnings in Manufacturing (dollars)*	Ratio of Minimum to AHE
1974	2.00	4.42	0.45
1975	2.10	4.82	0.44
1976	2.30	5.22	0.43
1978	2.65	6.17	0.43
1979	2.90	6.70	0.43
1980	3.10	7.27	0.43
1981	3.35	7.38	0.45

*Source: *Monthly Labor Review*, May 1982.

Linking the minimum wage to manufacturing wages poses a greater risk of setting the rate too high above the market level than linking it with the cost of living. This is because, while productivity has been sluggish throughout the US economy, there is reason to believe it advances even more slowly for minimum wage labour than for the workforce as a whole. Although the workforce as a whole is subject to upgrading through human investment, minimum-wage workers are unskilled and not subject to improvement in productivity *in their current jobs* through skill development. The result is that wage increases for a broad segment of the labour force, manufacturing workers, reflect growth in productivity as well as non-competitive forces. With little productivity growth in minimum-wage jobs, the linking of minimum-wage increases to increases in manufacturing wages will result in the minimum wage being set even higher above its market-clearing level than it would otherwise be, with correspondingly greater unemployment effects.

To summarise: under the basic one-sector competitive model the magnitude of the unemployment effect will vary directly with the supply and demand elasticities and the degree to which the minimum is pushed up above the market-clearing wage. An effective minimum will always lead to unemployment effects, even in the best of times. But in a weaker period, the minimum is more likely to have more serious unemployment effects. Thus during the recent period of stagflation, increases in the minimum motivated by inflation are likely to have had more harmful effects than during the first thirty years or so after minimum-wage legislation was introduced, since inflation during this period was a consequence of prosperity. Tying the minimum to average wages in manufacturing adds to unemployment in so far as minimum-wage workers do not achieve the same growth in productivity as do manufacturing workers.

THE MONOPSONY MODEL

In this section we relax the assumption of perfect labour market competition while still considering a one-sector (covered) labour market. The distinguishing feature of the monopsony model, which applies to the less extreme case of monopsonistic competition as well, in which there are a few employers instead of just one, is that the firm is a wage-setter and not simply a wage-acceptor as it is in the perfectly competitive model. As a result, the labour supply schedule facing the firm is not horizontal but upward sloping as the firm must pay higher wages to attract more labour. Thus the firm's marginal cost lies above the wage for any wage, or expressed alternatively, its marginal labour cost curve lies above its labour supply curve, as shown in Figure 5.2.

The firm maximises profits by operating where $MC_L = MR_L$, that is, at employment ON_0 and Wage W_0 in Figure 5.2. At this level of employment the marginal revenue of labour exceeds its wage; that is, *exploitation* occurs and is measured by the gap AB.

The imposition of a minimum wage can reduce and even eliminate this exploitation. Its effect is to create a uniform wage for all quantities to the left of the supply curve, thereby creating identical conditions as under perfect competition in which the firm becomes a price-acceptor, with its $MC_L = W$ over this range. In Figure 5.2, at minimum wage W_1, the new marginal cost curve becomes W_1CEG, with the vertical position CEG representing the movement to the original MC curve once the available supply at the minimum is employed.

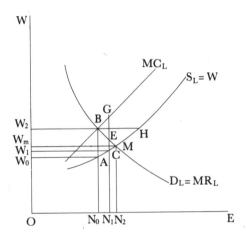

Figure 5.2: *Minimum Wages under Monopsony*

Not only is the wage higher and exploitation reduced to CE, but employment is also increased to ON_1. We have the best of all worlds for the workers, with more jobs, no unemployment and a higher wage. But the employer is not pleased; profits are obviously reduced as a result of having to pay a higher wage. In fact, one risk of setting a minimum wage under monopsony is that it might be set so high as to drive many marginal firms out of business. In these circumstances, Figure 5.2 does not apply; there are not more workers employed in these firms, but no workers.

If the minimum is raised exactly to W_m, the market-clearing wage under perfect labour market competition, exploitation is entirely eliminated and employment is maximised. There is an unequivocal gain to covered workers at this point in that their wage is the highest under the condition of full employment of the workforce. But there are three factors that mitigate against this happy condition arising as a consequence of a minimum wage. First, as already stated, many firms may be forced to close down at this minimum wage. Second, the government would need perfect knowledge of labour supply and demand conditions in the covered sector to locate point M. In practice, it would most likely miss the mark. Furthermore, it might not even wish to set the minimum at this level: the purpose of the minimum is to raise wages, not maximise employment. Thus, in practice, it might set the wage above this level. Third, monopsony is probably not widespread among minimum-wage workers. Unlike the majority of unionised workers, for whom the employment–wage effects under a collectively-bargained, uniform wage are identical to those covered by a government minimum, low-paid workers do not have specialised skills. Thus the thinness of the labour market, a requirement of monopsony or monopsonistic competition, does not arise as it would in the case of even a small employer hiring a specialised type of labour. That is, there is no labour market analogue to product differentiation as a cause of imperfect product market competition among minimum-wage workers. Monopsony can only arise if there is a large employer of minimum-wage labour in a given labour market, such as a large mill in a small town.

If the minimum is set sufficiently above W_m, then unemployment can arise. Suppose it is set at W_2. Although employment is unchanged from its pre-minimum level, there is an excess labour supply, BH. The difference between this monopsony condition and that of the basic model is that here unemployment can arise with no reduction in employment. But again, as under perfect competition, the portion of BH that represents unemployment is uncertain. Some of the covered labour supply represents entrants into the labour force, others are transfers from the uncovered sector. In this simple one-sector model—or, to be more precise, a model in which we ignore the repercussive effects of the minimum on non-covered markets, we assume that potential transfers do not find work in the covered sector and keep their old jobs.

In the monopsony case, the net effect on unemployment is simply the difference between the inflow into the labour force and the discourage-ment effect. Note that it would be illogical to argue that the latter might be larger even if we allow for the displacement of covered workers by the new entrants—and we must allow for this possibility because, unlike unionised workers, minimum-wage workers have no institutional control over their jobs. The argument is illogical because, if the discouragement effect were greater, there would be a labour shortage at the minimum wage, and it makes no sense to speak of workers being discouraged to the degree that part of the discouraged group is in strong demand by employers.

Much of the analysis of the unemployment effect of a minimum wage can be applied to bargained wages in a trade union setting. Referring to the monopsony model, if a union gains a wage increase above W_0 in Figure 5.2—and it would be a weak union indeed that did not set its wage goal above the level that would prevail in its absence—it would have the same wage range up to W_m before excess labour supply develops. But those factors that lead to a large excess supply of minimum wage labour—high elasticity of labour demand and supply—tend to be absent in the case of uncovered labour, making for a smaller unemployment effect.

The elasticity of demand for union labour will tend to be lower than that for minimum-wage labour, particularly in the case of skilled workers who cannot be substituted so readily in the production process. Furthermore, a union can create barriers to substitution by preventing the replacement of its own workers by other workers through closed shop agreements and agreements that ban sub-contracting. In addition, a union can forestall lay-offs by severance pay provision. The short-run supply elasticity for union labour tends to be lower wherever unions are successful in lengthening periods of training and introducing other barriers to entry.

As for the bargained wage itself, unions are more likely to have more detailed knowledge of the product market situations in which they operate than does the government when it sets a minimum for a large group of workers cutting across many firms and industries. The union can therefore avoid bargaining for a wage that would result in too wide an excess supply gap developing. About the only factor operating in the direction of a stronger unemployment effect for union labour, as compared to minimum wage labour, is the absence of a discourage-ment effect which mitigates the impact of a higher minimum on the measured unemployment of low wage labour.

THE EXTENDED MODEL: UNCOVERED WORKERS

Up to this point in the analysis the presence of an uncovered sector has only lurked in the background, as a source of labour to the covered sector when the minimum is raised, and as an employment oppor-tunity of last resort for displaced minimum-wage workers. In this section we consider the interaction effects on the two sectors of a rise in the minimum.

Despite the expansion of coverage in the minimum, there still remains a sizeable, uncovered sector. While there has been a strong increase in the percentage of workers covered, there nevertheless remains a smaller percentage of low-wage earners covered, and this is the more relevant statistic.[10] With the upward trend in skill development of the workforce as a whole, the potential base of minimum-wage workers has undoubtedly shrunk. Thus, it is not inconsistent for the percentage of uncovered low-wage workers to have declined proportionately less than the low-wage labour force as a whole.[11]

One limitation to the reduction in the uncovered sector is that federal law allows only the control of firms engaged in inter-state commerce, and while the scope of such commerce has received broad interpretation from the courts, there are still many establishments which do not fit this description. Although in many cases state and local laws have filled the gap in federal law by instituting their own minima, it is just those areas with the lowest prevalent wages which remain uncovered.

The fact that minimum wages are set by law, under arbitrary limitation to their application, leads to an important condition for analysing the unemployment effects in the two sectors. That is, we can assume that there is no difference in skill requirements (or the lack of them) for low-wage jobs between the two sectors, and, for simplicity, it is reasonable to assume that all workers in either sector can qualify for any job in either of them.[12] Further, we can assume that the workers in the covered sector do not control their jobs, since their higher pay is not protected by exclusive barriers to entry such as a union might impose,[13] but by arbitrary legislation that makes the position more attractive without making the claim to it by one worker stronger than that of any other. In effect the job is covered, not the worker.

This does not imply that at a given moment uncovered workers will displace workers who held covered jobs, but that in the flux of the labour market, with quits, lay-offs, etc., and with some firms expanding and then contracting, the employment mix in the covered sector is not determined by the earlier location of the worker, whether in the uncovered or covered sector.

A graphical approach to the analysis of the unemployment effects of a minimum in a two-sector model is presented in Figure 5.3. Before the imposition of the minimum, wages are equal in the two sectors. An effective minimum raises the wage level to $W_{c(1)}$ in the covered sector. To simplify the analysis, let us assume initially that there are no new entrants into the labour force and that all the adjustments take place among the workers already employed in the two markets. Then, as before in our discussion of the basic model, in the left panel of Figure 5.3, AB represents the displaced workers in the covered sector, and BC the transfer from the uncovered market.

The displaced workers, AB, will transfer to the uncovered sector where they will be absorbed into employment without causing any unemployment of uncovered workers—but only at the cost of a lower wage in the uncovered sector. Earlier we assumed that potential transfers from the uncovered sector, BC, could not find work in the covered sector and would therefore hold on to their original jobs. But under the assumptions of this section—identical workforces in the two sectors with respect to productivity and other aspects of labour supply—it really makes no difference whether the BC workers become employed in the covered sector, replacing some of the $ON_{c(0)}$ workers

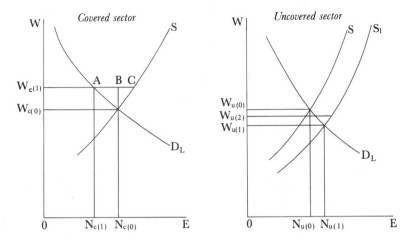

Figure 5.3: *Effect of Minimum Wage on Covered and Uncovered Sectors*

in the process, or not. If they do, then, under our assumptions, those that they displace in the covered sector can move to the uncovered sector for employment, and they would do so.

Therefore, the raising of the minimum has no effect on unemployment, although it will be accompanied by redistributional effects as those moving from the covered to uncovered sector will end up with lower wages, while those moving in the opposite direction will end up better-off. Although there is no unemployment, the economy as a whole suffers because national product falls as a direct consequence of the inability of the market to equalise the marginal products of equally productive labour.

Given the assumption of inter-sectoral equality in demand and supply elasticities, it should be noted that the impact on wages in the two sectors will be symmetrical, with the increase in the minimum being offset by the same percentage decline in the uncovered sector. This follows because the net movement into the uncovered sector is always equal to the reduction in employment, AB, in the covered sector. This remains true irrespective of whether the net transfer consists entirely of workers displaced in the covered sector, or whether it includes some who originated from the uncovered sector and are returning there, having failed to get a job in the covered sector. The final result has wage $W_{c(1)}$ and employment $ON_{c(1)}$ in the covered sector, and wage $W_{u(1)}$ and employment $ON_{u(1)}$ in the uncovered sector, with $N_{u(1)}N_{u(0)} = AB$.

For this neutral unemployment result to occur, we have made the explicit assumption that there would be no addition to the labour force attracted by the higher minimum. We should note four other assumptions implied in the analysis. These are:

(i) Labour moves willingly from covered sector unemployment to uncovered job opportunities, at reduced wages.

(ii) Wages in the uncovered sector can fall freely, and sufficiently, to absorb the expanded labour supply there.

(iii) There is no discouragement effect.

(iv) There is no interaction with other labour sectors.

Allowing for new entrants into the labour force and relaxing these four assumptions one by one makes the analysis more complex, but leads to the result that a rise in the minimum does increase unemployment among low-wage labour.

If the low-wage labour force expands as workers are attracted by the higher minimum, then part of BC represents new entrants. Relaxing this one assumption, relating to new entrants, changes the conclusion of our previous analysis of zero unemployment effects. To some degree the new entrants will displace some $ON_{c(0)}$ workers, who in turn will shift to the uncovered market with the same effects as before. But to the extent they do not do so, they will search for a job only in the covered sector. Unlike the BC workers who are transfers from the uncovered sector, they are unlikely to return, or in this case transfer to the uncovered market with its depressed wage. Since it was the high wage in the covered sector that attracted new entrants in the first place, they are not going to move to the uncovered sector where even lower wages than previously prevail.

Thus, unemployment arises whenever new entrants do not find jobs. But whenever they are successful in finding jobs the workers that they displace will look to the uncovered sector. The increase in labour supply to that sector will therefore be greater than the decline in employment in the covered sector and, as a consequence, the decline in wages in the uncovered sector will be greater than the increase in the minimum wage. An extreme possibility would be that all BC workers are new entrants who find jobs and displace some $ON_{c(0)}$ workers who seek jobs in the uncovered sector. Although there would be no unemployment effect, the increased supply of workers to the uncovered sector would be at a maximum and so too would be the negative wage effect. At the other extreme, where all new entrants become unemployed, the negative wage effect on the uncovered sector is minimised—that is, the percentage reduction in it is just equal to the percentage increase on the minimum wage.

(i) No easy movement. The extreme possibility referred to above, in which there is no unemployment, cannot arise if we relax the first implied assumption concerning the easy (and willing) movement of

workers from the covered to uncovered sector, irrespective of whether they are displaced directly as a result of the minimum, or indirectly by new entrants.

We do not know who these displaced workers are with respect to their position on the labour supply curve to the covered sector. If only those who were on the lower end of the supply schedule were displaced, specifically those willing to accept the depressed wage that their movement to the uncovered sector would induce, then the extreme possibility mentioned above would be realised; new entrants BC would displace a like number of $ON_{c(0)}$ workers who would move to the uncovered sector, with zero unemployment effect but with maximum impact on the wage differential. However, as long as some of those displaced have a higher reservation wage than that which they would have to accept if they moved into the uncovered sector, they would behave in the same way as the new entrants in that they would hold out for higher wages and remain unemployed rather than transfer. There is one difference in their attitudes, if not their behaviour, which does not alter this conclusion but underlines the labour market disruption caused by the legal minimum. While the new entrants will only work for wages above $W_{c(0)}$, there is a range below this level and above the depressed wage in the uncovered sector at which the displaced labour *would* work, but because of the minimum that wage is not offered.

Similar responses are likely from transfers among BC workers. They would return to the uncovered sector if the former wage prevailed because they were willing to work at that wage previously.[14] But they might not be willing to work at a lower wage so they remain unemployed in the covered sector.

Thus, once we allow new entrants into the analysis and drop the assumption of full movement of displaced workers to, and transferred workers back to, the uncovered sector, unemployment effects arise.

(ii) Inflexible wages. These effects become stronger once we relax the assumption that uncovered wages can fall freely in response to increased supply. In reality, although there is no legal minimum wage in the uncovered sector, wages for any position confront what Reder[15] calls a *social minimum*, established by custom if not by law. In general, the social minimum refers to a base subsistence wage. Workers are not expected to work for less, and if they can only earn less in some jobs these jobs tend to be eliminated. In the US, for example, hardly any workers are employed just to open elevator doors, and very few people shine shoes for a living any longer.

As a result of this social minimum there is a limit to how far down $W_{u(1)}$ can be pushed. This means that if the movement from covered to uncovered sector is large, some unemployment will appear in the uncovered sector itself as well as in the covered. In this way, the tendency for unemployment to result from the imposition of the minimum is increased.

The process of unemployment in the uncovered sector begins with a surplus of labour at the social minimum. Whether the affected workers themselves would be willing to work at a lower (real) wage is immaterial; there are simply no jobs available to them at a lower wage, so that they are unemployed, not only in a practical sense, but also in conformity with official measurement criteria. They are willing to work at the going wage—which cannot fall—but there are no jobs available for them.

Downward wage inflexibility is the basis of the contention of Levitan and Belous[16] that teenage unemployment that seems to rise as a result of a higher minimum wage is actually, in large part, the consequence of an increased supply of labour being unable to drive down the wage. They argue, in effect, that even if the minimum had not been imposed, or raised, the growing supply of teenage labour would give rise to increased teenage unemployment because their wages could not adjust downward to this increased supply.

In addition, there is the possibility already alluded to (see note 14) that the wage aspirations of those displaced in the covered sector, and those induced into it by higher wages but unable to find a job there, have been raised. If so, then these two groups might prefer to remain unemployed in the covered sector in the hope of finding a job that pays the new minimum. Alternatively, they could transfer to the uncovered sector and search for a job that pays a wage in excess of $W_{c(0)}(=W_{u(0)})$. Both of these possibilities would seem likely if one of the effects of raising the minimum is that it raises the wage aspirations of those previously employed at, or seeking, wages within the vicinity of the old minimum. In both cases there would be higher unemployment and, irrespective of whether it occurred in the covered or un-covered sector, this would tend to offset the decline in wages in the uncovered sector. In the extreme, where fewer workers compete for uncovered jobs, uncovered wages would rise as well as those in the covered sector.[17]

(iii) Discouragement. In relaxing another implicit assumption, we allow for discouragement. If we follow the logical method of analysis of the basic model, then discouragement must come from unemployment.[18] Thus, discouragement, represented by departure from the labour force, would reduce the unemployment effects resulting from the higher minimum. Discouraged new entrants would leave the work-force; we have already concluded that they would not move to the uncovered sector, but after the discouragement effect there would still be net unemployment from those searching for minimum-wage jobs. The same result applies to the displaced workers, AB, except that some of them will move over to the uncovered sector.

In the uncovered sector itself there can also be some discouragement among EF workers, who are unemployed because of the social minimum of $W_{u(2)}$, a group comprising those who never left the sector and those returning from search in the covered sector. But again, if discouragement is less than the unemployment that motivates it, the impact of an effective social minimum will be to add to unemployment. Thus, the effect of the minimum will be to increase unemployment despite the mitigating factor of discouragement which dampens its effect on the official unemployment statistics.

(iv) Interaction. Relaxing the last assumption, or omission of interaction with other labour market sectors, adds to the unemployment effect of the minimum wage. Although new entrants into the labour force will tend to depress the wage in the uncovered sector by more than the rise in the minimum, several other factors will tend to mitigate the decline in the uncovered wage. These factors include: discouragement; downward wage inflexibility, strengthened by the existence of a social minimum wage; lack of transferability of workers between sectors; and the tendency of displaced workers to engage in job search. On balance, therefore, it seems highly likely that uncovered wages will fall less, proportionately, than the increase in the minimum wage, and could conceivably rise. Thus the average wage for low-wage labour will tend to rise. In so far as demand and factor substitution takes place, demand will shift away from goods and services employing a heavy concentration of low-wage labour, and other factors, including workers who receive above minimum wages, will be substituted for low-wage labour in production. Thus, the existence of interaction effects will add to the unemployment of low-wage labour, even though they might reduce the impact of the minimum wage on overall unemployment as the demand for higher-wage labour rises. Labour mobility to other sectors cannot take place because the minimum directly affects those at the bottom of the wage-skill occupational distribution. If demand expands in other job sectors, they cannot move to them.

THE SPECIAL CASE OF TEENAGE LABOUR

Because of the chronically high unemployment among teenagers, an amendment was proposed to the Minimum Wage Act 1977, making provision for the establishment of a lower minimum rate for teenage labour. That this amendment failed by a single vote suggests just how finely balanced the arguments are concerning the introduction of a lower teenage rate. Against the move is the effect that a lower minimum would have on teenage income. The purpose of a minimum is to raise income, not to reduce it, even for a sub-group of the population. Also, there is the fear that any reduction in teenage unemployment will simply be at the expense of older workers, the more important contributors to family income.[19] Weighed against these negative factors is the one obvious positive outcome of a lower unemployment rate for teenagers, the population sub-group with the highest incidence of unemployment.

In this section we focus on the issue of the impact of a differential minimum on overall unemployment, although we touch upon the other aspects of the debate noted above. At the outset it should be emphasised that in comparing the teenage labour force with other groups, for simplicity referred to as older workers, compositional differences should not be ignored. Of necessity the teenager will be less trained and less experienced, and therefore the group will have a much higher concentration of unskilled, low-wage workers than other groups.

To demonstrate the type of logical error that can arise if compositional differences are ignored, the fact that demand elasticity is greater for teenage labour than for older workers would mislead policy makers to an easy but deceptive solution of the problem of high teenage unemployment. Lower the minimum for teenagers and the increase in their employment will outpace the decline in employment of their close substitute, older workers. But as we have noted before, the elasticity of demand for low-wage labour is high, and it is the concentration of low-wage workers among teenagers that explains the group's high demand elasticity. Thus the issue is whether low-wage workers among teenagers and the relatively few low-wage workers among older workers have different demand elasticities, and *prima facie* there is no reason why they should have.

We should also examine closely the respective productive attributes of teenage and older low-wage workers, for it is those attributes that determine their demand schedules. Here we are really addressing the question of whether the demand schedule is higher for older low-wage workers than younger ones. It is the difference in these schedules which determines the degree of employment transfer from older to younger low-wage workers that will result from a higher effective minimum for the older workers. Of course, the impact on unemployment is not that clear, depending on labour market inflows (of teenagers because of greater job opportunities) and outflows (of discouraged older workers).

As a matter of policy though, the overall merit of these offsetting changes is uncertain. On the one hand, the unemployment rate of a visibly high-incidence group could be reduced substantially, while that of a relatively low-incidence group, older workers, would not experience an appreciable rise in its rate. There is more than deception in this favourable outcome, based as it is on the relatively high and low concentration of low-wage workers among teenagers and older workers, respectively. It would probably be socially beneficial to spread more equally among definable groups such a negative attribute as unemployment. On the other hand, unemployment would be transferred to a group that on balance contributes a higher share to family income. A concomitant rise in the poverty rate, based as it is on household income, would be a highly undesirable consequence of the transfer.

In theory, if young and old are of equal efficiency—translated in more precise economic terms as being homogeneous factors of equal marginal productivity at all levels of input—then any wage differential which paid the young less would result in total substitution in production.[20] There would be no older workers hired at all until all the available younger ones were employed. Clearly, the result is more complex when the two factors are imperfect substitutes. If, as is generally thought, older workers are more productive, then setting the wages equal would lead to more older than younger workers being hired as employers equate the marginal productivity of each with the uniform wage. But if the (effective) minimum for younger workers were lowered, then to equalise the ratio of their marginal products to their wages for each group, younger workers would be substituted for older ones.

In theory, the relative minima could be set to equalise the employment of both. However, it is uncertain whether the number of younger workers hired would exceed the number of older ones displaced. It depends on the elasticity of substitution of the two factors, which in turn depends on the general shape of their marginal productivity schedules. What can be said for certain is that if the older workers are more efficient, a lower minimum for teenagers would result in some employment transfers to them: how much is an empirical question.

It remains to consider the relative efficiency of the two groups. The main determinants of relative productivity are training, or skill development, and experience. But unskilled work, almost by definition, requires little or no training, and job duties are so routine that experience in them teaches very little. In order to explain differences in efficiency one has to resort to such characteristics as motivation and sense of responsibility, attributes which are less measurable than training or experience. While we might agree that necessity would make these qualities stronger among older workers, sometimes these subjective traits can be seen only in the eye of the employer. In other words, preference and prejudice (i.e. discrimination) play a role in the hiring of unskilled workers; it does not matter whether a given older job seeker is more motivated and responsible than a teenage applicant, as long as the employer thinks that he is the older worker will get the job.[21]

Thus, on relative productivity grounds alone, a slightly lower minimum for teenagers—nothing like the two-thirds or 50 per cent ratio suggested—is probably justified to equalise employment prospects and the unemployment impact of an effective minimum. Any larger difference would represent an accommodation to the realities of discrimination. A socially more acceptable solution would be an extension of age discrimination legislation to younger as well as older workers. If this is done, and the law rigorously applied, employment opportunities would be more randomly distributed and the impact of the minimum on unemployment among low-wage workers in the two groups would be much the same. There would be less pressure for a lower teenage minimum except for those who wanted to see the teenage unemployment rate lowered even at the cost of a more or less equivalent cut in employment of older workers.

EMPIRICAL STUDIES

There have been many studies on the quantitative effects of minimum wages on the employment-unemployment of affected workers, particularly teenagers.[22] It is interesting to note that such studies indicate that, for teenagers, a rise in the minimum has a much stronger employment effect than unemployment effect.

These results reflect the tendency for teenagers to drop out of the labour force when jobs are scarce for them.[23] Consequently, if a lower minimum for teenagers improves job opportunities for them, the increase in teenage employment would probably be greater than the reduction in teenage unemployment. For older workers who can less easily afford to be discouraged and to quit job search,[24] a lower teenage minimum which reduced their job opportunities would have a larger impact on their unemployment. Thus, the overall effect of a differential minimum would be a tendency for the unemployment rate to increase because of the different pattern of labour market flows exhibited by teenagers and older workers.

As for the effect of the minimum on teenage unemployment itself, because of labour force withdrawals that accompany the resulting unemployment, empirical studies do not show a substantial impact. In their summary of these studies, Brown *et al.*,[25] conclude that a 10 per cent rise in the minimum leads to 1-3 per cent reduction in teenage employment, while in ten of the twelve studies reviewed the corresponding increase in the teenage unemployment rate was less than 1 per cent, and usually substantially less. They confirm this result in their own study of the teenage labour market.[26] Thus, while withdrawals undoubtedly reduce the impact on teenage unemployment, there is nothing to be complacent about in a situation in which unemployment is mitigated by discouragement.

The studies summarised by Brown *et al.* show some slight reduction in unemployment for the 20-4 year age group as a result of a rise in the minimum. This suggests employer preference for this group and some substitution of it for teenagers, a pattern that would tend to reverse itself if a differentially lower teenage minimum were established. Although this result is not surprising, what is surprising, or at least contrary to expectations, is that there appears to be no differential impact on black teenage unemployment as a result of a rise in the minimum. The black teenage unemployment rate is much higher than the white—a subject that we look at in Chapter 8—but not because of the existence of minimum wage laws. The absence of a differential impact on unemployment for black teenagers casts serious doubt on the policy argument in support of a lower minimum for teenagers, namely that it would be especially helpful in lowering black teenage unemployment.

SUMMARY

While the minimum wage is instituted for the beneficial purpose of raising the earnings of low-wage workers, it has the harmful side-effect of increasing unemployment. This unemployment effect results regardless of the degree of labour market competition, although it is likely to be greater the more competitive the labour market. Under imperfect labour market conditions there is a greater range for the minimum to rise without generating excess labour supply, but the low-wage markets covered by minimum wage legislation are less likely to be imperfectly competitive than the market for labour in general.

In any case, excess labour supply is not equivalent to increased unemployment since some of the excess supply might have transferred from the uncovered sector, and might return to their old jobs, if indeed they ever left them. Also the fact that some workers are unable to find work will discourage them into leaving the labour force, though against this will have to be offset any new entrants. However, the tendency of discouraged workers to exceed new entrants for some groups, especially teenagers, leads to an increase in unemployment that is much smaller than the decline in employment.

A lower minimum for teenagers would certainly reduce the teenage unemployment rate, but the price for this would be not only lower earnings for individual teenagers, but also a reduction in employment for older workers. However, in so far as the productivity of older and younger unskilled workers is more or less equal, a lower teenage minimum would help to counter labour market discrimination against them.

One of the factors which will have made for a stronger unemployment effect in recent years is the traditional linkage of the minimum to the price level, which in a period of stagflation will have tended to push the minimum further above the market clearing level than in the past. Despite this, empirical studies show that the effect on unemployment, as opposed to employment, has not been all that great.

NOTES AND REFERENCES

1. Study of the unemployment effect of the minimum wage begins with George Stigler, 'The economics of minimum wage legislation', *American Economic Review*, XXXIV, June 1946, pp.358–65. The effect of unemployment insurance on unemployment has its origins in the more recent literature on job search.
2. David Metcalf, *Low Pay, Occupational Mobility, and Minimum Wage Policy in Britain* (Washington and London: American Enterprise Institute, 1981).
3. Welfare payments, unemployment insurance and a rise in public employment serve as inferior counterparts to government grain purchases in offsetting this loss.
4. Finis Welch, 'Minimum wage legislation in the United States', *Economic Inquiry*, 12 September 1974, p.29.
5. Charles Brown, Curtis Gilroy and Andrew Kohen, 'The effect of the minimum wage on employment and unemployment', *Journal of Economic Literature*, XX, June 1982, p.487.
6. Jacob Mincer, 'Unemployment effects of minimum wage changes', *Journal of Political Economy*, 84, August 1976, pp.87–104.
7. David Hamermesh and James Grant, 'Econometric studies of labor–labor substitution and their implications for policy', *Journal of Human Resources*, 14, Fall 1979, pp.518–41. They conclude that 'the more human capital embodied in a group of workers, the less substitutable are members of that group with capital; indeed, it seems possible that . . . the more highly skilled . . . are complements with capital and are jointly substitutable with capital for less skilled labor' (p.537).
8. Thus Labor Department Studies of the rise in the minimum to $0.75 per hour in 1950, US Department of Labor, *Results of the Minimum Wage Increase of 1950* (Washington, 1954) and to $1.00 in 1956, US Department of Labor, *Studies of the Economic Effects of the $1.00 Minimum Wage* (Washington 1957), concluded that the unemployment effects of the increases were negligible. Our argument is that the strength of the economy made the rises shortly *ineffective*, or unnecessary: that is, the market wage for low-wage labour soon caught up with the minimum
9. It is interesting to note that, in contrast, in the 36-year period, 1938–74, there were only nine increases in the minimum.
10. Brown *et al., op cit.*, p.490, cite recent statistics which show that while 84 per cent of all workers are covered, only 80 per cent of low-wage workers are employed in covered establishments.
11. Of course, this argument reflects the reduction in the overall unskilled (low-wage) share of the workforce, with the implication that the influence of a minimum wage on the overall unemployment rate will diminish over time even though it has the same relative impact on unskilled unemployment. But in this chapter we discuss the nature of the unemployment effect, as well as its magnitude.
12. Describing workers in the secondary sector of a dual labour market, which would include minimum-wage workers, Peter Doeringer and Michael Piore, *Internal Labor Markets and Manpower Analysis* (Lexington, Mass.:

Heath, 1971), p.168, write, 'Many employers do not appear to draw distinctions between one secondary worker and another . . . and almost seem to be hiring from an undifferentiated labor pool.'

13. One would have to search long to find a unionised worker at the minimum wage.

14. A complicating possibility is that this behaviour (supply) might change once they had the prospects for higher paid work, even if there were no current openings. This possibility is discussed below. See p.118.

15. Melvin Reder, 'The theory of occupational wage differentials', *American Economic Review*, LXV, December 1955.

16. Sar A. Levitan and Richard S. Belous, *More than Subsistence: Minimum Wages for the Working Poor* (Baltimore: Johns Hopkins Press, 1979), pp.93-6.

17. This argument is advanced by Robert Flanagan's comment on Edward Gramlich, 'Impact of minimum wages on other wages, employment and family income', *Brookings Papers on Economic Activity*, 2, 1976, p.455.

18. Throughout we are referring to additional effects resulting from a minimum so that more precise language would require expressions such as *additional* discouragement from *additional* unemployment, etc.

19. Gramlich, *op. cit.*, pp.444-5, finds that the median family income of low-wage teenage workers is almost twice as high as that of low-wage adult workers. That the results show that families are more dependent on the earnings of adults is not surprising; nor is it surprising, given the magnitude of the difference, that policy-makers are reluctant to initiate measures that weaken the labour market position of adults.

20. In fact, Philip Cotterill, 'Differential legal minimum wages', in *The Economics of Legal Minimum Wages*, ed. Simon Rottenberg (Washington: American Enterprise Institute, 1981), pp.296-316, argues that it is just this similarity in productivity, or large range of overlap in individual productivity for those of different age groups, which would make for severe negative effects on older worker employment if a lower teenage minimum was introduced.

21. In this connection the findings of James F. Ragan, Jr, 'The effect of a legal minimum wage on the pay and employment of teenage students and nonstudents', in *The Economics of Legal Minimum Wages*, pp.11-41, that job loss from a (higher) minimum is much more pronounced among black than white teenagers indicates that there is also discrimination *within* the low-wage, low-productivity teenage labour market itself.

22. These studies are summarised by Brown *et al*, *op. cit.*, pp.502-8, and in Gramlich *op. cit.*, and Robert Goldfarb, 'The policy content of quantitative minimum wage research', *Industrial Relations Research Association Proceedings*, December 1974, pp.261-8.

23. Jacob Mincer, 'Unemployment effects of minimum wages', *Journal of Political Economy*, 84, August 1976, pp.87-104; and Douglas Adie, 'Teenage unemployment and real federal minimum wages', *Journal of Political Economy*, 81, April 1973, pp.435-41, find substantial labour market withdrawal by teenagers when a rise in their minimum wage weakens their job opportunities.

24. Mincer, *op. cit.*, finds no tendency for labour force withdrawal of older (25 and over) males as a result of a rise in the minimum.

25. Brown *et al.*, *op. cit.*, p.508. Further, Goldfarb, *op. cit.*, argues that some of the measured impact on teenage unemployment is really attributable to

the recent growth in the teenage labour force than to a rise in the minimum wage.
26. Charles Brown, Curtis Gilroy and Andrew Kohen, 'Time series evidence and the effect of the minimum wage on teenage employment and unemployment', *Effect of the Minimum Wage on Employment and Unemployment*, Vol. V (Washington, 1981), pp.103–27.

6. Unemployment Insurance and Unemployment

UK AND US SYSTEMS COMPARED

Unemployment insurance (UI) was instituted in the UK with the passing of the National Insurance Act 1911, and in the US was introduced at the national level under the Social Security Act 1935. In the UK the system is administered nationally, while in the US it is administered by individual states according to the guidelines set by the federal government. Over the years since it was introduced, the coverage of UI has increased in both countries. In the UK almost all adult males were covered by the late 1940s, whereas in the US it was not until the late 1970s that several million employees in state and local government were brought within scope of the UI laws. Legislation introduced in the UK in 1977 has also resulted in an increase in coverage among married females.

From the outset in the US the employment benefit paid under UI was earnings-related, subject to both a minimum and a maximum. In the UK benefit is paid at a flat rate, although an earnings related supplement (ERS) was introduced in 1966, only to be phased out again in 1982. In both countries, individuals who quit their jobs voluntarily are subject to a period of disqualification before they are entitled to receive benefits. Whereas in the US, UI is financed by a percentage tax on employers' payrolls, with employees contributing nothing, in the UK both employers and employees contribute. However, in the UK the contributions for UI are not separable from the contributions that finance other National Insurance benefits, (e.g. retirement pensions, sickness benefits). Since 1975 the total system has been funded by contributions from both employers and employees that are proportional to earnings, subject to both a minimum and a maximum earnings limit.

In both countries, eligibility for UI benefits depends on the contribution record. In the US, this usually means one year's employment in a covered industry, with the duration of benefits lasting up to 26 weeks, according to the time spent in covered employment. In the UK, in order to be eligible for maximum benefit, an individual has to have a minimum of 50 weekly contributions in the appropriate year.[1] Furthermore, in the UK benefit is payable for a continuous period up to one year, although for this purpose two spells of unemployment that are separated by less than six weeks are counted as a single spell. Until it was phased out in 1982 the ERS was payable for a period of up to six months, beginning two weeks after the commencement of the spell. While in operation, the number in receipt of ERS never usually exceeded 20 per cent of those unemployed at any particular time.

In order to qualify for UI benefit, unemployed workers in both countries have to be available for work, with the added requirement in the US that there must be some evidence of search activity. In both countries an individual is deemed not to have demonstrated availability if 'reasonable' offers of work are turned down, 'without good cause', and in the UK if unreasonable restrictions are placed on the location and type of work that is being sought. However, what constitutes reasonable and good cause is open to interpretation and may well differ from one official to another, from one town to another, or, in the case of the US, from one state to another. The *de facto* position is therefore that the availability test is often not enforced. The same is true of the requirement in the US to demonstrate search activity, since not all states require individuals to visit local offices on a regular basis, and many make benefit payments through the post. In the UK, although demonstration of search activity was never a formal requirement, the incentive to engage in job search has probably been blunted by the development of similar practices, and is likely to be further eroded by the relaxation, in late 1982, of the registration requirement in order to qualify for benefit.

One important difference between the UK and the US systems of UI is in the method of financing. In the US, not only is the cost borne exclusively by employers, but the tax varies with an individual employer's record on unemployment. Thus the employer with a good record on terminations and lay-offs, whose workers will benefit relatively little from the UI fund, will be exempted from payment of the tax, or part of it, once his tax payments have built up to a certain level relative to the benefits paid out. In this sense, as Becker[2] has pointed out, experience rating has the effect of making 'unemployment benefits an extension of the wage system, a regular cost of doing business'.

Although UI clearly redistributes income to those currently unemployed, it is nevertheless only concerned with relatively short and limited periods of time during the normal working life. In neither the UK nor the US—and particularly in the latter—were the UI schemes that were introduced conceived as programmes that were fundamentally concerned with redistributing income, although in both countries elements of income equalisation arise given their minimum and maximum benefit provisions.[3]

In effect, the worker—to an indeterminate degree—pays for his own UI, either directly through his own contributions, or indirectly through his employer's. That part that is funded by employers (all of it in the case of the US) constitutes a labour cost that would otherwise be available for wages. But apart from extra governmental support which in the US particularly occurs during times of cyclical recession, the indeterminacy of the cost to the employee arises from the fact that the term unemployment insurance is a misnomer.

Insurance is a payment for protection against a loss with a *predictable* probability—that is, it is risk and not uncertainty protection. The chance of being unemployed for any worker is uncertain, depending on personal characteristics, the type of job he holds and the type of industry in which he is employed. But even if workers could be grouped in a large pool which would have a somewhat predictable unemployment rate, given the state of the economy, it would still be impossible to arrive at a correct (i.e. competitively profitable) premium. This is because economic conditions generally (i.e. the state of the economy), which are the major influence on the overall rate of unemployment, are so unpredictable.[4] However, even if this were not the case, those with high probabilities of unemployment would still be excluded from the market, either because they are not offered insurance cover on the grounds that they constitute a bad risk, or because the premium is set so high that they are unable to meet it. Thus market failure occurs and there is a need for the state to intervene.

In short, in the absence of government management and finance as a source of funding of last resort, the system of UI could not operate. Expressed differently, the worker or his employer could not buy private unemployment insurance, at least, certainly not at the low rates now paid to the fund. Thus, in a system of public unemployment insurance, there is an implicit but indeterminate subsidy to the worker, and/or his employer, leading to indeterminacy of the worker's contribution to his own insurance.

In addition to replacing income—albeit only partially—UI permits the unemployed time for more selective job search, thereby reducing the necessity to accept first, or early, job offers, and enhancing the probability that they will eventually find jobs that are more suited to their capabilities. If this occurs, their subsequent income will be raised, along with national output, although the duration of current unemployment will be extended. However, these effects of UI were not foreseen at the time the programmes were enacted, even though by 1955 the Department of Labor in the US was able to claim that the prevention of 'the sacrifice of skills'[5] was one of the objectives of UI, thereby granting public recognition to the fact that it allows for more—and hopefully more productive—search time. Of course, the economy was much stronger in 1955 than in 1935 and the Labor Department no doubt felt safe in claiming as an advantage of UI an aspect that, despite its benefit, does raise the unemployment rate.

In this chapter we examine this relationship between UI and the unemployment rate.[6] Specifically, we study the effect of UI on the duration of job search and its consequent effect on the unemployment rate. We then focus on the question of whether UI leads to optimum search time, following this with a review of the results of empirical studies that investigate the impact of UI on unemployment. We conclude with a brief section on the impact of UI on labour demand.

UNEMPLOYMENT INSURANCE AND JOB SEARCH

Search can be considered an investment, since it is characterised by costs and, later, returns.[7] The costs, for unemployed searchers, are measured mainly by the length of time they go without earnings while seeking a job, plus the other outlays involved in search itself—transportation costs and, more importantly, the cost of using private labour market intermediaries to help in job placement. Where public employment services are available the worker might be able to avoid this latter type of cost.

UI offsets lost earnings to some extent and thus reduces the main ingredient of search cost. Therefore UI reduces the cost of search for any length of time required to find an acceptable job. But in so far as its impact on unemployment is concerned, UI reduces the unit time cost involved in search and, assuming that the other non-time costs of search remain constant, or at least do not increase, it will result in more time being spent on search. And the longer the average time spent on search by the unemployed, the higher the unemployment rate will be.

UI is not a minor contributor to the reduction of search costs. The benefit received while unemployed relative to net earnings while employed, referred to as the benefit–earnings ratio, or the replacement ratio, is discussed below, and again in Chapter 9 when we deal with the private costs of unemployment. For the moment it is sufficient to note that the interaction of the UI and tax systems, in both the UK and the US, is such as to give rise to replacement ratios which are typically within the 60–70 per cent range and, for some groups, are higher still. Thus the loss of earnings from unemployment becomes quite manageable for job searchers—provided that it does not have to be endured for too long.

On the other hand, two other forms of unemployment insurance in the US—supplementary unemployment benefits (SUB) paid by employers, and extended benefits paid under the public programme—are unlikely to be important contributors to search unemployment. SUB, for which provision is made in collective bargaining agreements, reduces still further the earnings loss from unemployment although such payments are regarded as taxable income. However, those unemployed workers in receipt of SUB payments are on temporary lay-off from good jobs and, since their principal employment goal is to be called back to the jobs they have temporarily lost, they are unlikely to remain unemployed after the point of recall searching for a better job.

Extended benefits take the form of a lengthening of the benefit period, usually from 26 to 39 weeks, but exceptionally to 65 weeks as during the recession of 1975. Such benefits are usually triggered when the unemployment rate reaches a certain level, and they will certainly ease the hardship caused by long-term unemployment. But it is extremely doubtful whether this emergency measure contributes much to search unemployment. The long-term unemployed are not likely candidates for search unemployment for two reasons; first, even with extended benefits their financial resources become strained after a long period of unemployment, and they cannot hold out for a better job. Second, after a long period of unemployment, they become much more knowledgeable about the wages that attach to particular jobs and they adjust their reserve wages accordingly; expressed differently, their wage aspirations fall in response to the realities of the labour market. We discuss changes in the aspiration level over time more fully in the following section on optimal search.

UNEMPLOYMENT INSURANCE AND OPTIMAL SEARCH

For unemployed workers UI allows time for more selective search by reducing the major component of search costs, the lost earnings that result from unemployment. From the individual worker's point of view, any improvement in benefits is an unmitigated gain.[8] It can lead to more productive search time, and result in a job offer at a higher wage. Alternatively, it can increase the leisure component of unemployment.

Taking the latter point first, improved UI may result in more desultory job search effort; the greater the degree of income offset, the less hurry the worker is in to take a particular job. Thus he will take longer to accept a particular job than he would have done had UI benefit been lower. Such an outcome is no more than that of the usual income effect. The effect on the individual is to make him take more leisure and work less or, in this particular case, to postpone work.[9]

Thus, if the effect of improved UI benefits is more desultory search, with the final outcome being the same job attained but with longer search time, this represents a gain to the optimal decision-making worker. He has purposely chosen the benefits of leisure over quicker return to work, and in accordance with traditional labour supply theory, he chooses a combination that makes both his income and leisure higher (both being normal goods). That is, he does not lengthen his period of search to the extent that he incurs a greater net financial loss from unemployment than he would have incurred with lower benefits.

The investment aspect of search also influences the length of search time that will be undertaken by the rational job searcher. Higher UI benefits reduce the cost of search and thus increase the rate of return on investment in search for any given job that is attained after a given period of search time. Assuming that an individual is initially equating the marginal benefit from search with the marginal cost of search time, he will no longer be in equilibrium if UI benefit is raised, and he will therefore increase the time spent in search.

Despite its basic investment qualities, investment in search has an imputed aspect that differentiates it from other human investments. Fruitless search time is mostly unproductive so that returns on search are not continuous as they are in other investments. For example, two years at college involve a cost and a return. As an investment, the decision to continue until graduation is based on *incremental* costs— more or less the same as in the first two years--and incremental returns—much higher than in the first two years. Thus, for those who have successfully completed the first two years, the decision to continue is an easy one, based as it is on a high rate of return on the additional investment.

In job search, though, there is no return on, say, the first two months of unsuccessful search. In fact, the failure to find a job that matches the worker's aspirations is an element in reducing these aspirations. This is the main factor that tends to put a practical limit on search time; another is the strained financial resources of the unemployed worker. But even if there were a capital market to finance search investment, the rational borrower for job search would lower his sights over time as a result of the information he acquires through testing the market; that is the realisation that he is unlikely to get a job at his original wage goal.

A closer look at the investment aspects of job search gives us a clearer explanation of how higher UI benefits lengthen job search, which consequently raises the unemployment rate. The unemployed job seeker faces a probability distribution of attainable wages, or *wage offers* (WO), with the probability of getting an offer declining the higher the wage. Search is required in order to translate these potentially attainable wages into actual wage offers, and the longer the worker searches, the higher his WO will be. The rational job seeker will optimise his job search by taking a job when the expected present value of the marginal returns (in a stream of higher future earnings) to a higher-paying job, obtained through further search, just equals the marginal cost of additional search. This becomes his *acceptance wage* (AW).

Time plays an important role in establishing the equilibrium position at which AW = WO. AW declines over time for two reasons: first, the worker's subjective probability distribution of wages will shift downward as unsuccessful search leads the worker to lower what he thinks his probability will be of getting a given higher wage. In Holt's[10] terminology, the worker has an adaptive aspiration level. That is, he adjusts his sights downwards as his period of unemployment, searching for jobs within a given wage expectation range, lengthens. There is evidence, both in the US and in Britain, in support of the adaptive aspiration hypothesis. For the US, Barnes[11] found that the reservation wage declines with extended search during a spell of unemployment, as expectations are revised downward in the light of unsuccessful search. In a British study, Nickell[12] found that higher UI had much less effect in increasing search time for the unemployed worker the longer he had been unemployed. Cooke[13] found that when the unemployment rate was high, the reduction in search that accompanied the decline in the reservation wage outweighed the effect of extended weeks of UI eligibility in lengthening search, leading to a net reduction in search time. This result supports our argument, presented above, that extended benefits would have little effect on increasing search time, since benefits tend to be extended in periods of high unemployment. Second, on the cost side, subjective non-monetary factors may raise the marginal cost of additional search. For example, depleted resources may create an uneasiness that raises the subjective cost of further search. As for monetary costs, after a time borrowed funds may be required to sustain spending power during further search and, in general, more expensive funding sources must be used.

A declining AW meets a rising WO and equilibrium is established at optimal search time. Introduction of UI into the worker's decision on search lengthens search time by raising AW. Its impact is not on the wage probability distribution, but on reducing the marginal cost of search.

The analysis of the effect of UI on AW and on search unemployment is shown graphically in Figure 6.1. AW is a function both of the probability of getting a job at the wage sought, and the cost of further search. WO has been drawn with a slightly declining positive slope, reflecting the assumption that more search time leads to decreasingly better offers.

Now, if UI increases, AW will move outwards to AW_1, reflecting an increase in the acceptance wage for any given amount of search. The higher UI will mean that additional search costs are lower and, therefore, for each duration of search the individual will hold out for a higher wage, with a lower probability of it being offered (e.g. for OA search, C rather than B). With the wage offer curve given by WO_0, equilibrium will shift from B to E. The worker will now search OG instead of OA and will attain a higher wage offer of W_1 instead of W_0.

If greater search time beyond OA does not lead to better offers, then WO_0 will become horizontal after B and, assuming the same shift in AW to AW_1, equilibrium will be achieved at D, with greater search time OF, but the same wage offer W_0. Thus the higher UI has reduced the cost of further search but, when accompanied by no improvement in job offers resulting from further search, the movement from B to D does not involve a better job. The only difference between B and D is that at D the worker is more certain of his wage potential, which is no greater than it would have been with less search. The price that he has had to pay for this greater knowledge is greater search time and, if search time is as time consuming and as strenuous and stressful as work,

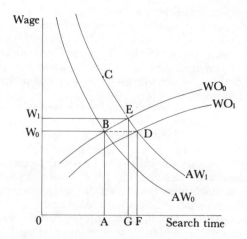

Figure 6.1: *Search Time and Job Acceptance*

he has gained nothing from deferring work in order to search longer. On the other hand, if we begin as before with equilibrium at B, but assume that an increase in UI is accompanied by desultory search, this can be shown by a shift in the wage offer curve from WO_0 to WO_1, indicating that with desultory search a lower wage offer is obtained for any given duration of search. If as before greater search beyond OA does not lead to better offers, then the new equilibrium will be at D where WO_1 meets with AW_1. D lies on the horizontal dotted line extension of W_0 at B, indicating a situation in which wage offers cannot be attained above W_0. The result will be longer search for the same wage, W_0, as existed before UI was raised. However, with desultory search some of the search time, OF, will represent additional leisure.

But a rising WO curve, describing a situation in which longer search can lead to a better (paying) job, is more realistic given the individual (non-homogeneous) characteristics of the worker which make specific jobs vary in the degree to which they fit his capabilities. From the point of view of the worker, he has a range of potential productivity depending on the specific job he finds. In such situations the higher UI leads both to more search, and to higher paid and more productive work.

In a study of post-unemployment wages, Ehrenberg and Oaxaca[14] find that a rise in UI leads to productive job search in the form of higher wages. In particular, they find this tendency more pronounced for prime age and older workers. For young women they find no rise in post-unemployment wages, rather, a tendency for them to drop out of the labour force, indicating to the writers that these women take added UI in the form of leisure. (If such is the case, the unemployment effect of higher UI is mitigated by this movement out of the labour force.)

Ehrenberg and Oaxaca also find no post-unemployment gain for young men, but this group do not tend to drop out of the labour force. The implication is that either they take the benefits of added UI in the leisure of desultory search, or that more extensive job search is fruitless for them—Ehrenberg and Oaxaca do not measure the intensity of search.[15] Thus we have evidence of all three cases—more productive search (higher post-unemployment wage), more leisure, and fruitless search.

The analysis so far can therefore be summarised as follows: regardless of the post-unemployment outcome—that is, regardless of whether wages rise or not, of whether search is fruitful or fruitless, intensive or desultory—higher UI results in longer optimal search time, and consequently higher unemployment. All of this stems from the fact that higher UI raises the AW curve. However, there are two theoretical arguments against the inevitability of longer search as a consequence of higher UI. The first is related to the change in the AW curve; the second to the effect on the WO curve.

As for the first argument, Mortensen[16] suggests that a rise in UI provides an incentive to those who are not eligible for UI—because they have exhausted benefits, have quit their previous jobs without good cause, have not worked before, etc.—to accept job offers that they would not otherwise have accepted. The reason for this is that higher UI benefit makes a given job offer more attractive since it confers eligibility to these benefits in the future. While not disagreeing with this theoretical possibility, we believe that increased employment among this ineligible group does not depend upon its incentive to work being raised. The same result would arise if the individuals in the group face a more favourable distribution of job (wage) offers as a result of employers' responses to the recipients of UI increasing their reservation wages. In short, it is possible that some of the non-recipients of UI will step into some of the jobs that would have gone to the recipients of UI, had they not extended their period of search, and this possibility is not dependent on an increase in the incentive for the former group. Both this and the Mortensen effect will tend to depress the AW curve, thus offsetting any outward shift caused by the reduction in the cost of search time for those covered by UI. Thus the final outcome depends upon the relative magnitude of these two opposing tendencies. The duration of job search and aggregate unemployment could therefore conceivably fall after an increase in UI, or at least remain unchanged. However, Barron and Gilley[17] have tested Mortensen's argument and find that it is not supported by the behaviour of the unemployed. Although, as expected, an increase in UI increases the search time of those eligible for UI, it has no effect on the behaviour of ineligible job seekers.

As for the effect of higher UI on the WO curve, increased benefits not only strengthen the ability to withstand the loss of job earnings, they might also stimulate more intensive and extensive search. That is, greater resources may allow the use of more expensive—and productive—search aids such as private employment agencies and better travel facilities. As a consequence the individual searcher is brought into contact with a greater number of job openings and a better (paying) job can be secured with the same search time. The effect is to raise the WO curve.[18] The overall result of these shifts in the AW and WO curves—which, as yet, has not been tested—could be that higher UI leads to a (much) higher post-unemployment wage, a lower duration of search and lower unemployment.

Thus, in most circumstances, an increase in UI leads to a gain for the individual recipient. Only in the case where active search is pursued with no improvement in job opportunities will an increase in UI not result in benefits, since in this case the worker simply engages in longer fruitless search. However, while the gains to the recipient are clear, this is not always the case for society as a whole. Where the recipient responds to the increase in UI by engaging in desultory search there is no source of social gain; there is simply a transfer of tax funds to pay for the leisure of a particular group, the job seekers. If search is fruitless, there is a clear social loss. Tax funds are used with no benefit to the recipient, and none to society.

The only possible source of social gain occurs when active search results in higher wage offers that reflect higher productivity. But while this wage–productivity gain is beneficial to the workers, and even to society, it may not represent the optimum use of public funds. Investment principles must be applied in evaluating the merits of an increase in UI. What is the cost of the rise in benefits for a given period of added unemployment per worker? What is the shape of the WO curve? That is, how much search time does it take (how long must the benefits per worker be applied) to attain a given higher-wage job? What is the average length of time this better paying job will be held? The rate of return to additional outlays on UI benefits—derived from these considerations—must then be compared with that on alternative public investment in order to decide whether investment in UI 'pays'.

Even if the current level of UI represents a good public investment, in that the rate of return on the higher post-unemployment earnings attributable to productive search, measured against the cost of UI (money outlay plus increased unemployment), exceeds that on alternative public investments at the margin, investment policy requires careful consideration of a *rise* in UI. We can expect diminishing returns from increased search effort so that a point must be reached at which the cost of higher benefits exceeds the gain from increased search.[19]

Of course, the decision process is clouded by the fact that UI is not just, nor even primarily, an investment. We should not lose sight of its basic purpose as a mitigator of the hardship caused by unemployment. Therefore, as a matter of public policy, the decision to raise UI will not be made mainly on its investment aspects, but it will certainly be politically helpful to policy-makers to know the magnitude of the gains, even if they are but a by-product of higher UI.

UNEMPLOYMENT INSURANCE AND LABOUR DEMAND

UI can influence the unemployment rate in its effect on labour demand as well as on labour supply. Its effect on the demand side operates through the payment structure, as contrasted with the effect of benefits on labour supply. In this brief section we look at two aspects of the US payment structure, experience rating and the maximum payment associated with it.

Experience Rating
In the US, payment schedules into the UI fund have been changed many times but the constant principle determining a firm's position in the range of payment rates charged is the firm's experience rating, its unemployment level over time. A lower unemployment experience results in a lower tax, and the cost difference to the firm can be substantial. Thus, there is an incentive to have a stable workforce. The easiest way to achieve this goal is to reduce the probability of unemployment by reducing the work force susceptible to lay-offs. An incentive is created to encourage overtime work instead of an expanded workforce; in short, the experience rating system reduces the net cost of overtime. To the extent that overtime becomes institutionalised, that is built into normal labour requirements, the effect is to raise the unemployment rate.

At the other extreme, experience rating encourages firms to put their workforce on reduced hours, rather than lay off workers in slack periods. This has a dampening effect on measured unemployment, but results in an equivalent amount of underemployment. Therefore, on balance, experience rating has an uncertain effect on unemployment. To the extent that the incentive to overtime is balanced by the incentive to expand part-time work, total hours worked are the same but there has been a rearrangement of work patterns such that, by reference to standard schedules, some employees are overworked and others under-worked.

Payment Limits
There are limits to the experience rating range. Firms in industries where the sporadic nature of production leads to frequent periods of lay-off tend to have to pay the maximum rate. For such firms, there is no added cost for making unemployment even more frequent. Therefore, such firms will tend to have a more casual workforce, not to see how high they can raise their unemployment frequency without added cost, but to take advantage of the experience rating limit by

hiring lower-paid casual labour. The effect of the limit is therefore to motivate employers to gear production to the use of casual and temporary workers, with a consequent rise in the unemployment rate as the number of temporary lay-offs rises.

This argument is advanced by Feldstein,[20] who supports his theory with an empirical study[21] which finds a significant effect of UI on the volume of temporary lay-offs. These findings lead Feldstein to the policy recommendation of shifting the basis of experience rating from the firm to the worker. Higher wages would then have to be paid for temporary, casual jobs, since workers would need to be compensated for the higher risk of unemployment that they face as this would disadvantage them with a high experience rating. Faced with higher wages in these jobs, employers would then have an incentive to organise production differently, away from methods which rely largely on temporary and casual labour that is now much more expensive.[22]

Quite apart from its impact on the frequency of unemployment spells, a high incidence of temporary lay-offs tends to raise the unemployment rate because those on lay-off—and especially those with good prospects of early recall—have less incentive than the average to search for other jobs. Reduced search time[23] lowers the probability that workers on lay-off will find temporary employment elsewhere during lay-off, and this raises the unemployment rate at any time.

IMPACT OF UI ON UNEMPLOYMENT: EMPIRICAL STUDIES

There have been a large number of studies investigating the impact of UI on the unemployment rate. The magnitude of the effect depends on the degree to which UI lengthens search and increases the flow into unemployment. These studies reflect not only differences in approach (e.g. as between time series studies and cross-sectional studies), but also differences in the way the effect is measured. Some measure the effect of absolute changes in the replacement ratio, others percentage changes. Sometimes the impact of these changes is measured on the duration of unemployment, sometimes on the percentage change in unemployment. Sometimes the results are presented in terms of an elasticity measure, which shows the percentage change in unemployment with respect to a 1 per cent change in the replacement ratio.

Results for UK
The replacement ratio increased dramatically in 1966 following the introduction of the ERS, thus providing an ideal opportunity to try and capture the effect of UI on unemployment. One of the earliest studies for Great Britain was that undertaken by Maki and Spindler.[24] Using time series data, they estimated that the elasticity of male

unemployment with respect to the replacement ratio was 0.68, and that the introduction of the ERS increased male unemployment by 33 per cent over the period 1967-72. The major criticism of this particular study is that the theoretical basis which underlies it is weak, and does not specify whether the increase in unemployment has resulted from an increased inflow into the stock, or from an increase in the average duration of those in the stock, or some combination of the two. However, as Nickell[25] has pointed out, the flow into male unemployment changed little over the period under study suggesting that, whatever they had intended, Maki and Spindler were capturing the effect on duration. This interpretation is reinforced by the fact that voluntary quitters are penalised by loss of UI benefit, and therefore it seems unlikely that this group will have accounted for much of the observed increase in unemployment.

But the Maki-Spindler study is open to even more serious criticism, as Nickell has pointed out. First, since it is a time series study, much of the 'apparent' impact of the rising replacement ratio on unemployment can be explained by rising unemployment itself. Secondly, the use of a replacement ratio that is computed for a married man with two children, on the assumption that he is drawing ERS, grossly exaggerates the benefit actually received; during the period covered by the study less than 20 per cent of the unemployed were in receipt of ERS. As a consequence the Maki-Spindler estimate of unemployment induced by ERS is upwardly biased, as is evidenced by the fact that for most of the period covered by their study their estimate of the absolute number induced is greater than the actual total number of unemployed in receipt of ERS. As Atkinson[26] has pointed out, the Maki-Spindler results imply that ERS accounted for about 110,000 of male unemployment at the end of 1966. MacKay and Reid[27] investigated the unemployment experience of over 600 engineering workers who were declared redundant in 1966-8, and found that the average duration of the average wage-earner in the sample was increased by 20 per cent as a result of ERS. On this basis they estimated that male unemployment nationally would have increased by only 12,000. However, MacKay and Reid included the intensity of job search as a separate variable and, as Atkinson has observed, since the effect of higher UI benefits is supposed to operate partly through reduced search activity—what we have called desultory search—the total impact of ERS on unemployment 'may be understated by the coefficient on their benefit variable'.

Nickell, using a cross-section study consisting of 426 males from the GHS, estimated that the elasticity of duration of unemployment with respect to the replacement ratio was about 0.6, and that the ERS increased the average duration of those in receipt of it by 27 per cent, thus adding about 10 per cent to male unemployment. The impact of the ERS was largely confined to those unemployed for less than 26 weeks and, therefore, Nickell concludes that the efficiency losses that would result from increasing the benefits of the long-term unemployed would be negligible. Nickell's study is based upon a model that tests the probability of leaving unemployment and adopts a more extensive measure of the replacement ratio. His results are generally regarded as being more realistic than those of Maki and Spindler.

A DE study[28] in 1976 suggested that if the ERS caused all of those claiming it to double their average duration of unemployment—which is very strong assumption compared with the findings of Mackay and Reid, and Nickell—then during the period 1966-70 this would only have resulted in an increase in unemployment of about 50,000, or 0.2 per cent of the 1970 labour force.

Therefore, although we can be fairly certain that there was some ERS-induced unemployment after 1966, the exact magnitude of this effect is still uncertain. Nickell's estimates suggest that it might have added between 60,000 and 70,000 to the male unemployment total for 1972, compared with the DE figure of 50,000 for total unemployment in the late 1960s. What we can be certain of is that given the decline in the replacement ratio after 1971, there would have been no further *increase* in this type of unemployment after that date.

Results for the US

In reporting their results for GB, Maki and Spindler make the point that they compare favourably with results obtained by Grubel and Maki for the US. This latter study[29] includes both a time series analysis for the US for the period 1951-72, and a cross-section analysis of 48 states in the year 1971. Instead of using the overall unemployment rate as the dependent variable in their regression model, they use the unemployment rate among workers insured against unemployment. Furthermore, in addition to the replacement ratio (or benefit income ratio, as they call it) they also include independent variables that capture ineligibility to benefits and the percentage of the civilian labour force covered by UI.

From the time series data they estimated the elasticity of the insured unemployment rate with respect to the benefit-income ratio to be 6.0, and conclude from this that if the insurance-related variables had been at their 1955 levels the insured unemployment rate would have been only 2.5 per cent in 1972, instead of the 3.5 per cent actually observed. In terms of overall unemployment they conclude that raising UI benefits above the 1955 level meant that in 1972 this was about 11 per cent higher than it otherwise would have been—i.e. 5.6 per cent instead of 5.0 per cent. The elasticity estimate for cross-section data was much lower at 0.9, suggesting that in 1971 overall unemployment would have been only 1.5 per cent lower (i.e. 0.1 percentage points). They admit that this reflects more accurately (than the time series estimate) the pure induced effect of UI in 1971, attributing the difference to changes in attitudes to work, better chances of getting a job, and better welfare. However, while admitting that their 'cross-section results indicate that there are probably other important conditions and social policies [other than UI-related variables, that is] which would have to be kept at their 1955 levels to achieve the suggested reduction in 1972 unemployment', Grubel and Maki nevertheless still persist in arguing that 'the conclusion drawn from the time series results that unemployment in 1972 would be 11 per cent lower if all of the insurance related variables were at their 1955 levels, remains valid.' Clearly, both statements cannot be true, and we are inclined more to the cross-section estimate, which shows only a small effect.

Most other studies find relatively small effects, and can be summarised briefly. Classen[30] found that in 1975 a $10 increase in UI benefit increased duration, on average, by one week, raising the overall rate by 0.4 percentage points. Assuming that the average benefit level was $100 in 1975 and, given that the overall rate of unemployment was 8.5 per cent, Classen's results suggest an elasticity of about 0.5. An even smaller effect for the period 1962–7 was found by Chapin.[31] He estimated that raising UI benefits relative to average wages by 10 per cent led to a 1.3 per cent increase in duration, which in 1967 amounted to just one day.

In contrast, Barron and Mellow,[32] adopting a transition probability approach, estimate that in 1976 receipt of UI benefit increased the average duration of unemployment by eight weeks, thereby raising the overall rate by 1.6 percentage points. This result is partly explained by the fact that this study did not exclude those who had exhausted their benefits because they had been unemployed for more than a year from its sample, nor did it exclude those who ended their unemployment by leaving the labour force. On this latter point, the study found that the impact of UI in reducing labour force withdrawal was about equal to its impact in reducing employment probability. Thus, about half of the overall impact found in this study arises because it takes account of the fact that recipients of UI have a lower probability of leaving the labour force than non-recipients. In other words, it counts as unemployment periods of 'idleness' that other studies have regarded as taking place outside the labour force.

Similarly, a small elasticity is implied by Marston's[33] finding for 1969—when the overall rate was 3.5 per cent. Measuring the impact of UI on D_2, one of the measures of completed spells discussed in Chapter 2, he concluded that the unemployment rate in 1969 would have been lower by 0.2–0.3 percentage points. This, according to Marston, is 'not a figure that supports the notion of armies of unemployed malingerers and chiselers'.

Adopting a somewhat different approach, in which they tested a model of benefit liberality across states for 1971, Holen and Horowitz[34] came to the opposite conclusion. In their model, benefit liberality is not determined by the benefit–earnings ratio, but by other factors, including the denial rate (i.e. the rate at which UI claims are denied).

Although they found that variations in the benefit–earnings ratio across states had 'virtually no influence on unemployment', they did find that the denial rate had a significant impact. This led them to conclude that if UI eligibility standards relating to job search and voluntary job quitting had been more rigorously enforced, so as to achieve a doubling in the national denial rate, the 1971 unemployment rate (5.9 per cent) could have been cut by 1.4 percentage points.

We can conclude from this brief survey of the UK and US literature that the evidence from cross-sectional studies indicates that UI benefits do have a significant, but relatively small effect on measured unemployment. However, as Katz[35] has pointed out, this impact might be non-linear with respect to the overall level of unemployment. Thus at higher levels of unemployment a given increase in UI would lead to less of an increase in unemployment. The relatively small increases in UI-induced unemployment in the late 1960s and early 1970s might therefore be smaller still in the 1980s. As Atkinson has so aptly put it: 'there is at present no strong evidence that there is a large proportion of volunteers among the unemployed watching the monetarist experiments of the 1980s. It does indeed appear to be a "conscript" army.'[36] If it is not a conscript army but a voluntary one, then the abolition of ERS in the UK in 1982 should soon begin to manifest itself in a reduction in UI induced unemployment.

NOTES AND REFERENCES

1. The word 'maximum' needs some explanation. Prior to 1975 the requirement was at least 50 weekly contributions in the appropriate year. However, after 1975 the requirement has been that the value of contributions must be equal to at least 50 times the weekly rate for those on the lower earnings limit. As Disney has pointed out, this means that the system is regressive because those with incomes above the lower earnings limit need fewer than 50 weeks of employment in order to qualify for maximum benefits. See R. Disney, 'Unemployment insurance in Britain', in John Creedy (ed.), *The Economics of Unemployment in Britain* (London: Butterworth, 1981).

2. Joseph M. Becker, *Unemployment Insurance Financing: An Evaluation* Washington and London: American Enterprise Institute, 1981), p.63.

3. Disney, *op. cit.*, stresses that in the UK the desire to limit the redistributive aspects of National Insurance was made explicit on several occasions during the legislative development of the scheme.

4. Sherwin Rosen, 'Comment' on Dale Mortensen, 'Unemployment insurance and job search decisions', *Industrial and Labor Relations Review*, 30, July 1977, speaks of the 'covariance' that arises during bad times when unemployment is high almost everywhere so that the insurance principle of risk diversification is impossible to apply for such conditions. Rosen

(p.519) also notes that the 'moral risk' in UI in which the insurance risk (unemployment) can be controlled by the potential beneficiary makes unemployment not truly insurable. He points out that 'insurance companies do not write bankruptcy insurance or have suicide clauses in life insurance policies.'

5. Cited in William Haber and Merril Murray, *Unemployment Insurance and the American Economy* (Homewood, Ill.: Irwin, 1966), p.26.

6. Our treatment confines itself to the overall rate.

7. For the earliest treatment of job search as an investment in labour market information, see George Stigler, 'Information in the labor market', *Journal of Political Economy*, 70, Supplement, October 1962, pp.94–105. J. J. McCall, 'Economics of information and job search', *Quarterly Journal of Economics*, 84, February 1970, pp.113–26, expanded Stigler's analysis into a fully-structured theory of search.

8. The exception to this result, when future intensive search does not lead to job offers at higher wages, is described below. See pp.133–4.

9. In support of theoretical conclusion that UI will lead to more leisure during a spell of unemployment, see John Barron and Wesley Mellow, 'Search effort in the labor market', *Journal of Human Resources*, XIV, Summer 1979, pp.389–404, who find that UI significantly reduces the search time per unit of time of the unemployed.

10. Charles Holt, 'Job search, Phillips' wage relation and union influence: theory and evidence', *Microeconomic Foundations of Employment and Inflation Theory*, ed. Edmund Phelps (New York: Norton, 1970), pp.61ff. Revision of expectations, which Lippman and McCall describe as *adaptive search policies*, plays a central role in their job search model. Steven Lippman and John McCall, 'The economics of job search: a survey', *Economic Inquiry*, 19, January 1974, pp.155–88.

11. W. F. Barnes, 'Job search models, the duration of unemployment and the asking wage: some empirical evidence', *Journal of Human Resources*, X, Spring 1979, pp.230–40.

12. S. J. Nickell, 'The effect of unemployment and related benefits on the duration of unemployment', *Economic Journal*, 89, March 1979, pp.34–49.

13. William Cooke, 'The behavior of unemployment insurance recipients under adverse market conditions', *Industrial and Labor Relations Review*, 34, April 1981, pp.386–95.

14. Ronald Ehrenberg and Ronald Oaxaca, 'Unemployment insurance duration of unemployment and subsequent wage gain', *American Economic Review*, 66, December 1976, pp.754–66.

15. Elsewhere they speculate that young men might take post-unemployment jobs that pay less but have good on-the-job training opportunities. 'Impacts of unemployment insurance on the duration of unemployment and the duration of unemployment on the post-unemployment wage', Industrial Relations Research Association, *Proceedings of 28th Annual Winter Meetings*, pp.234–41. If this is the case the immediate post-unemployment wage becomes a poor measure of the benefits of higher UI for young men.

16. Dale Mortensen, 'Unemployment insurance and job search decisions', *Industrial and Labor Relations Review*, 30, July 1977, pp.505–17.

17. John Barron and Otis Gilley, 'The effect of unemployment insurance on the search process', *Industrial and Labor Relations Review*, 32, April 1979, pp.563–6. Related to Mortenson's argument, but operating against it,

Daniel Hamermesh, 'Entitlement effects, unemployment insurance and employment decisions', *Economic Inquiry*, 17, July 1977, pp.317–32, finds that for *married* women, an increase in UI raises their labour force participation.

18. As an analogue to this argument, note that in Figure 6.1, when search is desultory, optimum search time of OF is greater than under normal search, OG.

19. A similar point has been made by Herbert Grubel, Dennis Maki and Shelley Sax, 'Real and insurance-induced unemployment in Canada', *Canadian Journal of Economics*, 8, May 1975, pp.174–91. (See p.188.)

20. Martin Feldstein, 'The unemployment caused by unemployment insurance', *Industrial Relations Research Association, Proceedings of the 28th Annual Meetings*, 1975, pp.228–40. For a more rigorous treatment of this issue, see M. Feldstein, 'Temporary lay-offs in the theory of unemployment', *Journal of Political Economy*, 84, June 1976, pp.937–58.

21. Martin Feldstein, 'The effect of unemployment insurance on temporary lay-off Unemployment', *American Economic Review* , LXVIII, December 1978, pp.834–46.

22. Martin Feldstein, Statement at Hearings, Joint Economic Committee, US Congress, October 1972, *Reducing Unemployment to 2 Per Cent*, p.28.

23. Barron and Mellow, *Search Effort in the Labor Market*, find this reduction in search time during lay-off.

24. Dennis Maki and Z. A. Spindler, 'The effect of unemployment compensation on the rate of unemployment in Great Britain', *Oxford Economic Papers*, Vol.27, November 1975, pp.440–54.

25. S. J. Nickell, 'The effect of unemployment and related benefits on the duration of unemployment', *Economic Journal*, Vol.89, March 1979, pp.34–49.

26. A. B. Atkinson, 'Unemployment benefits and incentives', in John Creedy (ed.), *op. cit.*

27. D. I. MacKay and G. L. Reid, 'Redundancy, unemployment and manpower policy', *Economic Journal*, Vol.82, December 1972, pp.1256–72.

28. Department of Employment, 'The changed relationship between unemployment and vacancies', *Department of Employment Gazette*, October 1976, pp.1093–9.

29. Herbert G. Grubel and Dennis R. Maki, 'The effects of unemployment benefits on US unemployment rates', *Weltwirtschaftliche Archiv*, 2, 1976, pp.274–99.

30. Kathleen Classen, 'The effect of unemployment insurance on the duration of unemployment and subsequent earnings', *Industrial and Labor Relations Review*, 30, July 1977.

31. Gene Chapin, 'Unemployment insurance, job search, and the demand for leisure', *Western Economic Journal*, 9, March 1971, pp.102–7.

32. John Barron and Wesley Mellow, 'Unemployment insurance: the recipients and its impact', *Southern Economic Journal*, 47, January 1981, pp.606–16.

33. Stephen Marston, 'The impact of unemployment on job search', *Brookings Papers on Economic Activity*, 1975, pp.13–48.

34. Arlene Holen and Stanley Horowitz, 'The effect of unemployment insurance and eligibility enforcement on unemployment', *Journal of Law and Economics*, 17, October 1974, pp.403–31.

35. Arnold Katz, '"Overview" of the economics of unemployment insurance, a symposium', *Industrial and Labour Relations Review*, 30, July 1977, p.433.

36. Atkinson, *op. cit.*

7. Unemployment in the UK and US since the Second World War

During most of the post-second world war period, governments in both the UK and the US have been committed to the pursuit of policies aimed at ensuring that there would be no return to the unemployment levels of the 1930s. In this chapter we touch briefly on the nature of these commitments, outline the main fluctuations and trends in unemployment in both countries, and indicate the main dimensions of unemployment in both. We also look at the underlying flows that are important determinants of the actual rates.

THE 1944 WHITE PAPER IN THE UK

During the inter-war period, 1921–38, unemployment among the uninsured workforce of the UK fluctuated between 9.7 and 22.1 per cent, averaging 14.2 per cent for the period as a whole. The rate came down to negligible proportions during the second world war, averaging only 0.5 per cent for 1944, which amounted to only 90,000 people. Towards the end of the war it was widely felt in influential quarters that the success of employment policy in the post-war period could determine the fate of democracy.[1] Therefore, it is not surprising that in May 1944 the wartime government published a White Paper, *Employment Policy*,[2] in which it accepted that after the war one of the 'primary aims and responsibilities' of government would be 'the maintenance of a high and stable level of employment'. According to the White Paper this was to be achieved by the pursuit of policies that would ensure

(i) that there was a sufficient mobility of workers between occupations and localities to ensure that structural unemployment did not become a severe problem; and

(ii) that total expenditure on goods and services did not fall to a level that would give rise to general (i.e. cyclical) unemployment.

It was made clear in the White Paper that a condition for the attainment of these objectives was reasonable stability in the level of wages and prices. It was, of course, the coalition government's acceptance of (ii) above which reflected its conversion to the Keynesian thesis of demand management, and which marked its break with the old Treasury orthodoxy that predominated during the inter-war period. Indeed, it was the recognition of the need to move towards a Keynesian policy of demand management that marked a radical change—if not a revolution—in official economic thinking. However, while accepting the political significance of the White Paper, some recent commentators have suggested that it was far from radical in its economic outlook. For example, Deacon[3] has suggested that it was 'relatively conservative on economic policy'; while Showler[4] has asserted that 'contrary to popular opinion, the 1944 White Paper on Employment Policy was less than complete endorsement of Keynesian interventionism.' While these commentators have the benefit of hindsight, the same cannot be said of Beveridge,[5] who at the time felt that the White Paper did not go far enough. This in itself reflected a fundamental shift by Beveridge who was somewhat dubious about the message contained in the *General Theory* when it first appeared.[6]

The White Paper committed the government to a 'high and stable level of employment', but did not specify a target rate of unemployment. In his famous report, also published in 1944, Beveridge argued that the government ought to commit itself to full employment—a situation that he defined as occurring when there are 'more vacant jobs than unemployed men, not slightly fewer jobs'.[7] He went on to assert that full employment 'means that the jobs are at fair wages, of such a kind, and so located, that the unemployed men can reasonably be expected to take them; it means, by consequence, that the normal lag between losing one job and finding another will be very short.'[8] Translating this into a single statistic, Beveridge argued that full employment implied 'a reduction of unemployment to not more than 3 per cent'. At the time Keynes regarded Beveridge's 3 per cent as too optimistic. In a 1942 Treasury Memorandum he had argued that the minimum level of unemployment in the post-war period would more likely be of the order of 5-6 per cent, and when he wrote to Beveridge in 1944 to compliment him on his book, he included the comment: 'No harm in aiming at 3 per cent unemployment, but I shall be surprised if we succeed.'[9]

THE UK RECORD: 1948-82

Over the nineteen-year period 1948-66, the unemployment rate averaged 1.7 per cent according to the definition then prevailing—only 1.6 per cent if, according to current practice, the temporarily stopped are excluded. As Table 7.1 shows, in only five years—1952, 1958, 1959, 1962, and 1963—did the average monthly unemployment rate exceed 2 per cent; and in only one of these years did it reach 2.6 per cent. However, since 1966 the official unemployment rate has never

The Economics of Unemployment

Table 7.1: *Unemployment in the UK: 1948–82*

	Total		Males		Females	
	No (000s)	*% rate*	*No (000s)*	*% rate*	*No (000s)*	*% rate*
1948[1]	334.4	1.6	251.7	1.8	82.7	1.2
1949	338.0	1.6	249.9	1.8	88.1	1.3
1950	341.1	1.6	241.1	1.7	100.0	1.4
1951	281.4	1.3	182.3	1.3	99.1	1.4
1952	462.5	2.2	254.7	1.8	207.9	2.9
1953	380.0	1.8	245.5	1.8	134.5	1.8
1954	317.8	1.5	208.2	1.5	109.6	1.5
1955	264.5	1.2	169.5	1.2	95.0	1.2
1956	287.1	1.3	191.0	1.3	96.1	1.2
1957	347.2	1.6	241.9	1.7	105.3	1.3
1958	500.9	2.2	351.5	2.4	149.4	1.9
1959	512.1	2.3	369.6	2.5	142.5	1.8
1960	392.8	1.7	283.9	1.9	108.9	1.3
1961	376.8	1.6	275.4	1.9	101.4	1.2
1962	499.9	2.1	370.3	2.5	129.6	1.5
1963	612.3	2.6	468.3	3.1	143.9	1.7
1964	413.4	1.7	309.7	2.0	103.6	1.2
1965	359.7	1.5	272.7	1.8	87.0	1.0
1966	390.9	1.6	307.8	2.0	83.1	0.9
1967	599.1	2.5	478.7	3.2	120.4	1.4
1968	601.3	2.5	501.5	3.4	99.9	1.1
1969	597.1	2.5	505.1	3.4	92.0	1.0
1970	639.8	2.7	542.1	3.7	97.8	1.1
1971	848.6	3.7	713.5	4.9	135.0	1.5
1972[2]	964.7	4.2	735.6	5.1	149.9	1.7
1973	630.3	2.7	522.8	3.7	107.5	1.2
1974	631.0	2.7	523.8	3.7	107.2	1.2
1975[3]	1013.7	4.3	798.8	5.6	214.9	2.3
1976	1359.4	5.7	1023.5	7.1	336.0	3.5
1977	1483.6	6.2	1069.2	7.4	414.3	4.3
1978	1475.0	6.1	1040.2	7.2	434.8	4.4
1979	1390.5	5.7	963.9	6.7	426.5	4.3
1980	1794.7	7.4	1233.6	8.7	561.1	5.7
1981	2733.8	11.4	1944.3	13.7	789.5	8.1
1982[4]	3126.8	13.3	2223.3	15.9	903.5	9.4
1982(III)	3275.6	13.9	2298.4	16.1	977.2	10.1

Notes: [1] The figures for 1948 are based upon the average of the six months, July to December.

[2] Up to and including 1972 the total figures include the temporarily stopped; thereafter they are excluded. The male and female figures include the temporarily stopped up to and including 1971 only.

[3] Up to and including 1975 adult students are included in all figures; thereafter they are excluded.

[4] The figures for 1982 are based upon the average of the first ten months only. The percentage rate is based upon the estimated number of employees, both employed and unemployed, in June 1982; it is subject to revision. (The June estimate of employees is from *Employment Gazette*, (November 1982).

Source: Department of Employment, *Yearbooks* and *Employment Gazettes*.

been below 2 per cent. After 1966 it remained around 2.5 per cent for the rest of the decade, increasing to an average of 3.5 per cent for the period 1971–5, and 5.9 per cent for the period 1976–9. Thereafter, it rose dramatically, from 7.4 per cent in 1980 to 11.4 per cent in 1981; by the third quarter of 1982 it averaged 13.9 per cent, having reached 14 per cent in September of that year.

Clearly, 1966 marks some sort of watershed as far as the UK labour market is concerned. However, even before that date there is evidence of a gradual and long-term increase in the unemployment level. Analysing troughs and peaks in unemployment for Great Britain, Brittan[10] observed a tendency for the seasonally-adjusted rate to rise from the early 1950s to 1966, after which there was a 'noticeable leap'. The reason for this was, as Blackaby[11] has pointed out, that there was a major shift in unemployment triggers for reflationary action between the late 1950s and the early 1970s. Whereas at the beginning of this period governments reflated when the seasonally adjusted rate reached 2 per cent, during the winter of 1971–2 the trigger had increased to about 3.6 per cent. Since then the reflationary trigger has increased still further and, in late 1982, with the unemployment rate around 14 per cent, it was nowhere in sight.

Until 1966 the economy therefore performed better, in terms of the recorded unemployment rate, than Keynes predicted. This was largely because he exaggerated the importance of the non-demand-deficient categories of unemployment. Beveridge, though he still overestimated the importance of these categories, proved to be more realistic in his estimates than Keynes. In a study spanning the period 1948–66, Thirlwall[12] regressed vacancies against unemployment and estimated that the amount of non-demand-deficient unemployment for Great Britain averaged 1.6 per cent. This was also the average total rate of unemployment for the period as a whole, suggesting that full employment was the norm, with zero demand-deficient unemployment.

Taking the period 1948–81 as a whole, the absolute fluctuation from year to year in the UK unemployment rate has not been great, averaging only 0.6 percentage points (ignoring the direction of change). However, this average figure masks a change that occurred after 1970. During the period up to 1970 the change from one year to the next never exceeded 1 percentage point, and typically was about 0.3 per cent. From 1970 onwards, more often than not, the change from one year to the next exceeded a percentage point and typically was of the order of 1.2 percentage points. Thus the rate of unemployment not only increased after 1970, it also became more volatile.

That the British economy experienced full employment up until 1966 is accepted by all commentators. In analysing why this was so, Matthews[13] has argued that the main reasons were the strength of private investment demand, together with foreign demand for exports;

Keynesian deficit financing played no direct role. However, such a view ignores the role played by public investment in house building, and overlooks the importance that the commitment to full employment had on business confidence and, therefore, its indirect effect on private investment. Furthermore, as Scott[14] has commented:

Given the government's commitment to full employment, if private investment had not increased as compared with before the war, some other component of final demand could have taken its place. Private consumption could have been stimulated by tax cuts, or public consumption or investment could have been increased further. The fact that these additional sources of demand were not needed was evidence, perhaps, of the responsiveness of private investment to high demand.

However, taking the post-war period as a whole, the absolute level of unemployment in late 1982 was about ten times the level for the period 1948–50, while the percentage rate had increased to about 8.5 times its earlier level. For those brought up in the Keynesian tradition the unthinkable has happened as the prosperity and confidence of the first two post-war decades, backed up by the political commitment to full employment, has given way to unemployment on a similar scale to that experienced during the inter-war period. Indeed, the rate of 13.9 per cent that was recorded for the third quarter of 1982[15] compares unfavourably with the adjusted average rate of 10.9 per cent for the period 1921–38.[16] It remains to be seen whether the early 1980s were an aberration, or whether they turn out to be typical of the last two decades of the present century.

THE CAUSES OF HIGHER UNEMPLOYMENT IN UK SINCE 1966

The immediate cause of the break in 1966 was a savage deflation of aggregate demand in July of that year, prompted by a sterling crisis which reflected an underlying weakness in the balance of payments, and intensified by a seven-week-long seamen's strike, which began in May. However, there was also an increase in the underlying structural–frictional component of unemployment in the late 1960s and early 1970s which resulted in an outward shift of the UV curve. Several explanations have been advanced for this break in the unemployment–vacancy relationship, including the increase in replacement ratios that was discussed in Chapter 6. Other potential explanations on the supply side include the introduction of the Redundancy Payments Act 1965; changes in the employment service; and changes in the characteristics of the unemployed. On the demand side, the explanations include technological change; changes in labour hoarding; and such policy changes as the introduction of the Selective

Employment Tax (SET) and the Regional Employment Premium (REP).

Redundancy Payment Act 1965

As a result of this legislation a worker is compensated for his loss of job according to his age and length of service, provided that he has been with the same employer for two years or more. After the 1966 downturn in the labour market, some redundant workers therefore received lump sum payments on severance from their job, and these could conceivably have had an income effect on the work-leisure trade-off, encouraging those who became involuntarily unemployed to take a short holiday or search the labour market a little longer than they otherwise would before taking another job. However, the evidence in support of such an increase in voluntary unemployment is not strong, suggesting that the Redundancy Payments Act had a negligible effect on the observed increase in unemployment after 1966.

Changes in Employment Service

According to Layard,[17] a small but unquantifiable proportion of the increase in unemployment since 1973 has been caused by institutional changes in the employment service. In particular, he cites the separation of the two basic functions—the matching of workers with jobs, and the payment of benefits—both of which had, until 1973, been carried out under one roof in the old employment exchanges. Post-1973 they have been carried out under separate roofs in Job Centres and benefit offices. In the former, there was not only a shift towards self-service, but also a change in the nature of the service offered. Whereas previously the emphasis of the service had been on placing the unemployed, since 1973 it has been on attracting and filling vacancies. This change in emphasis has militated against the interest of the long-term unemployed who, as a result of the changes, only have to visit the benefit offices once a fortnight, but are under no compulsion to visit a Job Centre at all unless they wish to do so. The result of all this has been that active job search among the long-term unemployed has been discouraged, and the rate at which the employment service submits them for jobs has tended to decline. As a consequence of both of these factors, unemployment has increased.

Characteristics of the Unemployed

Surveys by the DE into the characteristics of the unemployed were carried out in 1961, 1964, 1973 and 1976.[18] These surveys identified those who had poor prospects of obtaining work and the absolute numbers placed in this category increased from 141,000 in 1961 to 186,000 in 1964, 320,000 in 1973, and 539,000 in 1976. Thus, during 1964–76 the number with poor prospects had increased by 353,000, that is, about 1.5 per cent of the 1976 labour force. Although some commentators have suggested that this increase represents an increase in the number of unemployables, or in the irreducible minimum of unemployment, it seems highly plausible that the number falling into this category will be cyclically sensitive. Furthermore, the assessment made by DE employment officers responsible for identifying those with poor prospects is unlikely to have been independent of the state of the local and national labour markets. Thus the increase in the number categorised as having poor prospects cannot be regarded as representing the quantitative change in the number of unemployables. Nevertheless, given that prolonged unemployment is likely to lead to an erosion of skills, incentives and job motivation, the increase in the number might be taken as indicative of some degree of supply-side change which might take both time and resources to eliminate. Also, to the extent that individuals are classified as having poor prospects because they seek only part-time work, this might be regarded as a shift in attitudes away from full-time work towards a more casual type of employment, and, as such, might be responsible for an increase in unemployment.

Labour Hoarding

It is sometimes suggested that the acceleration in productivity growth during the period 1965–74 reflected a quickening in the pace of technological change which caused structural imbalances within the labour market to increase and, with it, structural unemployment. While there is no evidence to support this view, the acceleration in productivity growth in the late 1960s is consistent with a shake-out of labour and a reduction in labour hoarding. Why should this be so? Why should firms have adjusted their employment relative to output more after 1966 than before that date? The answer lies in rising quasi-fixed costs of employment, coupled with a widespread belief among employers that the recession was going to last longer and that demand would therefore be much slower to pick up. Taylor[19] found that labour hoarding declined sharply in 1967–8 when a recovery of output was accompanied not by an increase in employment, but by firms raising the utilisation rate of their existing labour force. He found that, expressed as a percentage of the labour force, the aggregate rate of labour hoarding for sixteen British industry groups declined from 9.3 per cent in the fourth quarter of 1966 to only 2.3 per cent in the fourth quarter of 1968. It was this simultaneous fall in the rate of labour hoarding and in the level of employment that suggested a deliberate shake-out of labour during this period, although, as Taylor points out, the term shake-out might not be an accurate description of what was happening in the labour market at the time because it

implies that employers were discharging workers in order to prune their workforces. But the 'shake-out' might simply have taken the form of reluctance by employers to take on workers even though there was a recovery in demand during 1967–8. In view of the extreme pessimism in the British economy during 1966, employers may have consciously decided to play a waiting game in the 1967–8 recovery.

Indeed, the rise in unfilled vacancies during the period June 1967 to December 1968, while registered unemployment remained unchanged, suggests that employers were keen to take on more workers but that they were becoming more selective for the reasons already given.

Technological Change
More generally it can be argued that technological change has resulted in higher unemployment. The decline in traditional production industries, coupled with the introduction of new technology, has led to a marked decline in employment in manufacturing and production industries. The spread of new technology to the service sector has meant that employment has not grown sufficiently in services to absorb those displaced in the industrial sector. And if the growth in aggregate demand is slow, or restrained (see below), then the more likely will these sectoral shifts leads to unemployment.

Other Policy Changes
A number of other policy changes that were introduced in 1966–7 might have contributed to greater labour market imbalances and higher unemployment, though there is little hard evidence to support this. Included in this list are the introduction of SET, REP and the 14.3 per cent devaluation of sterling that occurred in November 1967. SET was designed to stimulate employment in manufacturing at the expense of the service and distributive trades; REP was intended to give a further stimulus to manufacturing employment in the depressed regions; and devaluation favoured employment in export- and import-substituting industries. However, since both SET and REP were abandoned during the 1970s, their effects are unlikely to have been permanent.

Taking account only of the supply-side changes, including the effect of the earnings related supplement (ERS), Laslett[20] has estimated that by 1973 the frictional–structural component had increased by 0.6 per cent over the average level for the period 1948–66. Since this was assumed to be a period of full employment, with a frictional rate of 1.1 per cent, the corresponding frictional rate for 1973 was therefore 1.7 per cent out of a full employment rate of 2.3 per cent. According to Laslett, frictional unemployment increased by a further 0.7 per cent between 1973 and 1976, thus giving rise to a full employment rate of 3.0 per cent in 1976.

Using the Wharton method of fitting trends from peak to peak, Taylor[21] has estimated that between the late 1950s and 1973 frictional unemployment increased by 2.3 per cent, thus accounting for the whole of the trend increase in registered unemployment during this period. However, as Worswick[22] has noted, use of the Wharton method involves making a judgement about the level of frictional–structural unemployment and there is a tendency for increases in this component to be built into the model. Thus, Taylor's estimate of the increase in frictional–structural unemployment is almost certainly an overestimate.

Most estimates of the natural rate are in line with these more conventional measures of non-demand-deficient unemployment. Parkin, Sumner and Ward[23] estimated that the natural rate was around 1.7 per cent for the period 1956–71. Flemming[24] put it a little higher for the period 1952–65, somewhere between 1.75 and 2.0 per cent. For the later period, 1968–78, Sumner[25] estimated it to be 3.2 per cent. However, according to Minford,[26] the rate was as high as 7.25 per cent in 1979, and increased still further to between 8 and 10 per cent by 1982.

Therefore, on the basis of the evidence presented above, the full employment level of unemployment increased from around 1.7 per cent in the first two post-war decades to around 3 per cent by the mid-1970s. If this figure is taken to be correct, it implies that in 1977 about half of registered unemployment was attributable to a deficiency in aggregate demand. Assuming no further increase in the frictional–structural component (natural rate) between the mid-1970s and the early 1980s, demand deficiency accounted for between 10 and 11 per cent of the unemployment in late 1982. On the other hand, accepting Minford's estimate of the natural rate implies that demand deficiency accounted for only 4–6 per cent of unemployment in 1982.

We believe that the level of demand-deficient unemployment was nearer to the upper estimate (10–11 per cent) because, as Thirlwall[27] has pointed out, estimates of the natural rate, such as Minford's, capture cyclical demand influences and thus do not measure Friedman's concept of the natural rate.

That demand-deficient unemployment was nearer to this upper estimate is suggested by Figure 7.1, which shows the seasonally adjusted series of unemployment and vacancies for the UK. For October 1982 seasonally adjusted unemployment was 3.29 million, while vacancies stood at 0.11 million. However since, according to the DE, notified vacancies only amount to about one-third of the total, total vacancies were probably about 0.34 million. Given that demand-deficient unemployment is equal to the difference between total unemployment and total vacancies, this suggests that demand-deficient unemployment was as high as 2.9 million in October 1982, that is, about 12.4 per cent of the labour force. Thus, our estimate of something within the range 10–11 per cent looks reasonable.

One other point that is clearly borne out by Figure 7.1 is that the last time the unemployment and vacancies series came near to crossing was in 1966. However, since reported vacancies need to be multiplied by a factor of three in order to obtain the true level of

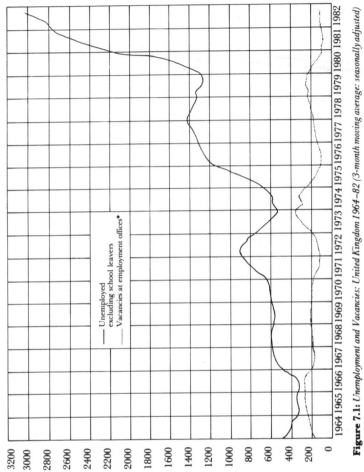

Figure 7.1: *Unemployment and Vacancies: United Kingdom 1964–82 (3-month moving average: seasonally adjusted)*

*Vacancies at employment offices are only about a third of total vacancies

Source: Employment Gazette, November 1982.

vacancies, the true vacancy series would have crossed the unemployment series some time during 1973, when the former was rising and the latter falling. The graph also suggests that the adjusted vacancy series would have crossed the unemployment series again at the end of 1974, or early in 1975, as the economy moved downwards into recession. The level of unemployment at which the two series crossed was, in both cases, about 650,000—that is, about 4.5 per cent of the labour force. This is somewhat higher than the 3 per cent mentioned above, but even if this is taken to be the full employment rate of unemployment it would still imply that demand deficiency accounted for over 9 per cent of unemployment in late 1982.

That demand has been deficient since 1974 is not really in dispute; however, the reasons for this deficiency need some explanation. In short, the explanation is that successive governments have placed more emphasis on curbing inflation and less on securing full employment. Inflation—or rather its avoidance—has overtaken full employment as the primary goal of economic policy and, as a consequence, governments have abandoned the traditional Keynesian techniques of demand management that worked so well during the first two post-war decades.

Inflation in the UK accelerated in the late 1960s and early 1970s. The most plausible explanation is that trade unions exerted a greater wage push, not because of any sudden increase in their monopoly power, but simply because they became more conscious of the power that they had possessed for some time. The devaluation of 1967 also contributed to this cost-push pressure. This acceleration in wage demands continued into the 1970s despite the fact that, apart from the period of rapid expansion in 1972–3, output growth was fairly stagnant, especially after the first oil price crisis in late 1973. Also, the acceleration in productivity growth that occurred from 1964 onwards came to an end after 1973 and the failure of trade unions to adjust their real wage aspirations resulted in both accelerating inflation and rising unemployment. To the extent that these aspirations were translated into higher real wages, unemployment increased; to the extent that they were thwarted by producers marking up prices, inflation resulted. A passive monetary policy was therefore required in order to prevent unemployment from increasing further. In fact, the opposite happened; the government engineered a further increase in labour market slack in order to dampen down wage aspirations and bring them into line with slower output growth.[28]

The growth in real wages relative to output is best seen by considering the real product wage which shows the total labour cost per worker relative to value added per worker. For manufacturing industry the real product wage increased from 95 in the 1960s to 105 in the 1970s (1970 = 100), while manufacturing employment declined by about 9 per cent over the same period.[29]

In addition to wage-push pressures, the deterioration in the terms of trade and the consequent rise in import prices that occurred during 1972-3,[30] coupled with the quadrupling of oil prices in late 1973, meant that inflation was imported into the UK. Allen[31] found that the contribution of rising import prices to inflation increased throughout the period 1972 to 1974, for much of the period at an accelerating rate. The upshot of all this was that during 1975 the annual rate of inflation exceeded 25 per cent. At the same time the balance of payments deteriorated, and between 1971 and 1974 a record surplus on current account of £1.1 billion was transformed into a record deficit of £3.5 billion. The deterioration in the visible balance was even more dramatic, the deficit increasing by almost £2.8 billion between 1973 and 1974 as the value of imports increased by about 50 per cent, giving a deficit of £5.2 billion for 1974. In the absence of a dramatic improvement in exports, a deficit of this magnitude could only be rectified by reducing domestic consumption which, during a period of stagnant or slowly rising output, was bound to have an adverse effect on employment.

Therefore, given record rates of inflation and record balance of payment deficits, it is not surprising that successive governments turned away from full employment in the hope of securing both greater price stability and external balance. Increasingly they relied upon monetarist prescriptions, coupling this with attempts to control the growth in public expenditure. Although external balance was restored in 1977, and the rate of inflation was reduced to about 8 per cent by the end of 1978, the price of this success was a rising level of unemployment. And, after the winter of 1978-9, the rate of inflation turned upwards once again and the new Conservative government pursued even more rigorously the deflationary demand policies of the outgoing Labour government.

Scott[32] has suggested a somewhat different explanation for the decline in demand for labour since 1966, although it is not unrelated to the rapid growth in real wages and the rise in the real product wage that has been discussed above. Both these factors have been associated with a decline in the share of profits which, together with a weakening of business confidence—caused by the acceleration of inflation and the decline in the prospects for growth—resulted in a decline in investment, particularly of the labour-using type. The growth in manufacturing investment that has occurred has therefore been of the labour-saving variety, and the balance between labour-using and labour-saving investment that is vital for ensuring that economic progress is achieved, with the growth in jobs matching the growth in labour force, has been absent. Thus manufacturing employment has declined. As noted in Chapter 2, Scott refers to the unemployment arising from this deficiency in the demand for labour caused by an insufficiency of labour-using investment, as structural unemployment. However, the estimates of the increase in the frictional–structural component of unemployment that have been discussed so far in this chapter have not included this particular species of structural unemployment.

A further refinement to Scott's argument is that put forward by Jordan[33] who points out that, given the UK's low rate of growth and profitability, there have been few opportunities for investment in recent years outside of North Sea oil and gas. As a consequence, British multinational companies have tried to offset rising wage costs by automation (i.e. labour-saving investment), while investing their surplus profits abroad where productivity has been growing more rapidly and/or labour costs have been lower. Thus, Britain has become 'more attractive as a market for foreign exports than . . . as a location for multinational investment.'

THE 1946 US EMPLOYMENT ACT

In the US unemployment exceeded 25 per cent in 1933, the most depressed year of the inter-war period, and it still stood at around 19 per cent in 1938. During the war it had fallen to 1.2 per cent by 1944 and, fearful that the full employment of wartime might give way to the mass unemployment of the 1930s, Congress passed an Employment Act in 1946. This emerged as a compromise between the Senate and the House of Representatives after the latter had failed to ratify a Full Employment Bill that had been passed by the Senate in 1945. The goal of full employment was replaced by one of high employment and the Act, which has been described as the 'economic Magna Carta'[34] of the US, commits the federal government 'to promote maximum employment, production and purchasing power', and in so doing provide 'useful employment opportunities for those able, willing, and seeking to work'. Under the Act the Council of Economic Advisers was established and charged with the responsibility of reporting annually on 'current and foreseeable trends in the level of employment production, and purchasing power', and to make recommendations that will create the conditions necessary for the fulfilment of the Act's objectives. Although the Act did not itself specify a target rate for unemployment, the Council of Economic Advisers suggested 'a moderate range around 4 per cent' in its early reports. Thus, although a single rate was not made explicit, between 1946 and 1961 there was tacit acceptance on the part of official policy-makers of a target goal in the neighbourhood of 4 per cent.[35] During the administration of President Kennedy, this target became more explicit as the Council of Economic Advisers accepted 4 per cent as an interim goal, expressing the belief that it would be possible to achieve even lower rates.

THE US RECORD: 1947-82

Table 7.2 summarises the US record for the post-war period. Closer examination of the table reveals that unemployment in the US is more volatile than in the UK. In thirteen of the post-war years that are shown, the fluctuation in the unemployment rate exceeded 1 percentage point, and in five of these years it exceeded 2 percentage points. Taking the period as a whole, the typical fluctuation from year to year was about 0.9 percentage points, with no tendency for this to increase in the 1970s. However, the fluctuation in the unemployment rate was untypically low during the period 1962-9, particularly in the later years. The greater volatility of US unemployment suggests that aggregate demand fluctuates more in the US than in the UK, or that unemployment in the US is more responsive than in the UK to changes in aggregate demand.

During the eleven-year period 1947-57, the annual unemployment rate exceeded 5 per cent in four years and the overall average for the period was between 4 and 4.5 per cent. In terms of the implicit goals set by the Council of Economic Advisers the period can therefore be regarded as one of full employment. But whether or not full employment would have been achieved had it not been for the post-second world war boom in 1947-9 and the expansionary effects of the Korean War, 1950-3, is another matter. However, after 1957 there was rather a dramatic increase in unemployment and for the period 1958-64 the rate averaged almost 6 per cent. During this period there was a heated debate between the structuralists and the demand-deficient school about the underlying causes of the unemployment increase, and the uncertainty that this generated impeded the implementation of a full employment policy.[36]

After 1964 the unemployment rate declined under the stimulus of the Kennedy-Johnson tax cuts of 1964 and the escalation of the war in Vietnam, which resulted in a large increase in federal government expenditure and the absorption of many young people into the armed forces. For the period 1966-9 the rate averaged about 3.7 per cent, falling as low as 3.5 per cent in 1969, thereby confirming the belief of the Council of Economic Advisers that 4 per cent was not a floor below which the rate could not fall. However, in 1970 the economy once again moved away from full employment, and since then a rate below 5 per cent has been recorded in only one year, 1973. Furthermore, the average rate increased from 5.4 per cent in 1970-4 to 6.5 per cent in 1975-9, increasing still further to over 7 per cent in 1980-1. Between July 1981 and July 1982 the rate increased from 7.2 to 9.8 per cent, and in August 1982 the psychological 10 per cent barrier—'the threshold of genuine depression'[37]—was passed for the first time since the second world war. It meant that over 11 million Americans were out of work.

Therefore, unlike the UK, the post-war experience of the

Table 7.2: *Unemployment in the US: 1947–82*

	Total		Males		Females	
	No. (000s)	% rate	No (000s)	% rate	No (000s)	% rate
1947	2311	3.9	1692	4.0	619	3.7
1948	2276	3.8	1559	3.6	717	4.1
1949	3637	5.9	2572	5.9	1605	6.0
1950	3288	5.3	2239	5.1	1049	5.7
1951	2055	3.3	1221	2.8	834	4.4
1952	1883	3.0	1185	2.8	698	3.6
1953	1834	2.9	1202	2.8	632	3.3
1954	3532	5.5	2344	5.3	1188	6.0
1955	2852	4.4	1854	4.2	998	4.9
1956	2750	4.1	1711	3.8	1039	4.8
1957	2859	4.3	1841	4.1	1018	4.7
1958	4602	6.8	3098	6.8	1504	6.8
1959	3740	5.5	2420	5.2	1320	5.9
1960	3852	5.5	2486	5.4	1366	5.9
1961	4714	6.7	2997	6.4	1717	7.2
1962	3911	5.5	2423	5.2	1488	6.2
1963	4070	5.7	2472	5.2	1598	6.5
1964	3786	5.2	2205	4.6	1581	6.2
1965	3366	4.5	1914	4.0	1452	5.5
1966	2875	3.8	1551	3.2	1324	4.8
1967	2975	3.8	1508	3.1	1468	5.2
1968	2817	3.6	1419	2.9	1397	4.8
1969	2832	3.5	1403	2.8	1428	4.7
1970	4093	4.9	2238	4.4	1855	5.9
1971	5016	5.9	2789	5.3	2227	6.9
1972	4882	5.6	2659	5.0	2222	6.6
1973	4365	4.9	2275	4.2	2089	6.0
1974	5156	5.6	2714	4.9	2441	6.7
1975	7929	8.5	4442	7.9	3486	9.3
1976	7406	7.7	4036	7.1	3369	8.6
1977	6991	7.1	3667	6.3	3324	8.2
1978	6202	6.1	3142	5.3	3061	7.2
1979	6137	5.8	3120	5.1	3018	6.8
1980	7637	7.1	4267	6.9	3370	7.4
1981	8273	7.6	4577	7.4	3696	7.9
1982	10678	9.7	—	9.9	—	9.4

Sources: Employment and Training Report of the President, 1982, Table A–28, for years 1947–81.
    Monthly Labor Review, February 1983, Tables 2 and 4, for 1982.

US cannot be characterised as two decades of full employment followed by almost two decades of high and rising unemployment. Instead, there was a decade of fairly full employment, followed by a 7-8-year period of relatively high unemployment, which in turn was followed by a second, but shorter, period of full employment. Since 1970 the economy has moved further away from the goals of the 1950s. However, compared with the average level of unemployment that prevailed during this first post-war decade, the increase since 1970 has been less dramatic than has been the case in the UK. Thus, whereas for the US unemployment in 1982 was about 2.5 times its earlier level, the corresponding figure for the UK was 8.5. That the increase in the US has been less dramatic than the increase in the UK also emerges if one compares the 1982 experience with that of the inter-war period. Whereas for the UK 1982 compared unfavourably with the average experience of the inter-war period as a whole, for the US the 10 per cent rate experienced in the second half of 1982 compared favourably with the 1930s, when the rate never fell below 14.3 per cent, and for the period 1931-9 averaged over 19 per cent.

Until the mid-1960s, the US full-employment policy had not been as successful as that in the UK, and this was due largely to the greater emphasis that was placed in the US on the attainment of the other macroeconomic goals (inflation control and balance of payments equilibrium), coupled with a fiscal conservatism and a dislike of government intervention. After 1964 the relative importance attached to these changed somewhat, as they did in the UK. During the early 1980s both governments have attempted to roll back the size of the state and to get to grips with inflation, and in both countries the mood is one of fiscal conservatism and tight monetary control.

1958-64: STRUCTURAL TRANSFORMATION OR INADEQUATE DEMAND

The Bureau of Labor Statistics estimated that for the period 1955-7 normal frictional unemployment accounted for 2.5 per cent of the total, although given changes in the composition of the labour force they expected this to rise to about 3.0 per cent by 1975.[38] Assuming this figure for the mid-1950s to be correct, almost 3.5 per cent of the unemployment during 1958-64 must have been attributable either to structural factors or a deficiency in aggregate demand. Indeed, concern over the higher unemployment rates after 1957 gave rise to two opposing views, those of the structuralists and the aggregate demand school. The former assumed that structural transformation rather than a deficiency in aggregate demand was the main cause of the higher unemployment, and that the structural transformation arose for two reasons—the relative decline of goods producing industries, and a quickening in the pace of technological change resulting from automation. The decline of traditional industries employing blue-collar workers, coupled with the relative growth of service industries such as education, health, finance and public services, in which employment tends to be biased towards white-collar workers, including technicians and professional workers, had resulted in a twist in the pattern of labour demand in favour of the latter. A further twist was added by the acceleration of automation in the 1950s which reduced the number of simple and repetitive jobs involving unskilled or semi-skilled labour. Instead there was a growing demand for engineers, technicians, designers and workers with the education and knowledge to develop and administer the new systems. In short, the twist in the pattern of demand resulted from an increase in the demand for better-educated and more highly-skilled workers. All of this would not have mattered had the workforce been able to adapt to the changing requirements of the labour market, but since it was unable to do so the result was an increase in labour market imbalance and unemployment. Furthermore, greater geographical imbalances compounded the problem.

In support of this thesis, Killingsworth[39] cited the fact that between 1950 and 1962 (when unemployment was respectively 6.0 and 6.2 per cent) the only group which experienced a reduction in unemployment was that at the top of the educational ladder—college graduates. In addition, he noted that those at the bottom of the educational ladder had also suffered a decline in labour force participation, while those at the top had increased their participation. Killingsworth therefore concluded that more investment in human beings was required in order to break the bottlenecks for skilled and educated manpower. This could take the form of more and better schooling at all levels; more manpower training and retraining; and better labour market counselling for the young and other disadvantaged groups. In addition, regional development policies to improve the infrastructure of depressed regions, together with assistance for the relocation of workers, would help correct geographical imbalances.

In the absence of such structural cures, Killingsworth argued that any attempt to expand aggregate demand would result in the economy facing severe shortages of skilled and educated manpower long before the unemployment rate fell to 4 per cent. Indeed, in the absence of manpower training and retraining policies, he doubted whether it would be possible to get much below 5 per cent.

The opposite view was held by the Council of Economic Advisers.[40] While not denying that some structural changes had occurred, or that some unemployment was structural, the Council argued that there was no evidence of an *increase* in structural unemployment after 1957. It pointed out that while disadvantaged groups, e.g. teenagers, unskilled workers, blacks, etc., share more than proportionately in increases (and decreases) in unemployment, the true test of the structural hypothesis is whether there has been a change in the relationship between the total unemployment rate and the rates of sub-groups. The Council found that the relationship had, in fact, been remarkably stable. Furthermore, although the Council admitted that since the war there had been an increase in the educational requirement of jobs, relative to supply, it argued that this change occurred prior to 1957 and that it had not prevented the economy from operating at around the 4 per cent level in the mid-1950s. Changing educational requirements could not, therefore, explain the higher unemployment after 1957. Similarly, the change in the help-wanted index during 1955–7, and again in 1960–2, did not suggest an underlying increase in structural unemployment.

The Council therefore advocated the expansion of aggregate demand through fiscal measures as the 'crucial central element' in the attack on unemployment. However, it accepted that even though structural unemployment had not increased, its very existence gave rise to a 'human and an economic problem' that needed to be attacked 'by any means possible', and that a simultaneous attack on structural unemployment and demand deficiency would be 'mutually re-inforcing'. Indeed, the Council acknowledged that after a period of prolonged slack, such as occurred after 1957, 'there is more need than in the usual cyclical recovery for an effective programme of specific labour market policies to assist demand stimulating policies in tailoring men to jobs and jobs to men.'

Although by dint of argument and of numbers the demand-deficient school seemed to have the edge, the debate was rather inconclusive due largely to the lack of information on job vacancies, which made it impossible to be sure whether there existed a large number of jobs for which qualified applicants could be found. However, in retrospect, the evidence seems to support the demand-deficient side since, after the 1964 tax cuts and the subsequent growth in government expenditure resulting from the escalation of the war in Vietnam, the unemployment rate eventually fell below 4 per cent for four successive years, and the rates of the disadvantaged groups cited by the structuralists declined. The price that had to be paid for this was accelerating inflation, and when unemployment levels began to increase again in the 1970s the rates for the disadvantaged groups once again increased disproportionately.

It is obvious from the position adopted by the Council of Economic Advisers and the statements quoted above that the debate between the structuralists and the demand-deficient school was not one about absolutes, but rather about the relative usefulness of aggregate demand policy on the one hand, and manpower policies on the other, in combating higher unemployment. This being so, it is not surprising that a whole series of retraining measures and job programmes, administered by the Department of Labor, were introduced during the 1960s and continued through the 1970s and into the 1980s. All have—or had—unemployment, or underemployment, as one of the eligibility criteria and some, such as the Job Corps, and Neighbourhood Youth Corps, were directed towards the young. One of the earliest and most important of these manpower programmes was the Manpower Development and Training Act 1962, which provided training in a skill centre or school and was later extended to include on-the-job training. The Job Corps, introduced in 1965, provided training away from home for the young, and placed great emphasis on the provisions of remedial skills and services. In addition, special programmes for public employment were introduced, and in 1973 the Comprehensive Employment and Training Act (CETA) brought all training and employment programmes together for funding purposes. However, while providing greater financial rationalisation, CETA allowed greater decentralisation in the management and administration of the programmes, thereby facilitating greater cooperation between them. The total budget for CETA during fiscal year 1980 was $8.26 billion, while the number of first-time beneficiaries under the various schemes was expected to be 2.61 million.[41]

HIGHER UNEMPLOYMENT IN THE 1970s

The US economy, like that of the UK, experienced accelerating inflation during the 1970s and attempts to bring it under control resulted in higher unemployment. So much so that one critic, Leon Keyserling,[42] Chairman of President Truman's Council of Economic Advisers, and principal author of the 1946 Employment Act, described the increase in unemployment after 1978 as the result of the 'most flagrant, complete, unjustified, deliberate and explicit violation of law' in the history of the US during the twentieth century. The significance of 1978 is not that there was no deliberate creation of unemployment before the date, but that this only involved a violation of the law—at least according to Keyserling—after the passing of the Humphrey–Hawkins Full Employment and Balanced Growth Act in that year.

The decade began with a sharp increase in unemployment in 1970–1, as the Nixon administration traded off unemployment in pursuit of greater price stability. Despite this deliberate deflation of demand, coupled with the de-escalation of the war in Vietnam, inflationary pressures accelerated again after 1973. This was the result of the devaluation of the dollar, rising food prices, the OPEC oil price increases and the lifting of wage and price controls imposed in 1971 in the guise of President Nixon's 'New Economic Policy'. The inflation rate exceeded 12 per cent in 1974, with the result that aggregate demand was syphoned off, GNP declined, and the economy moved into recession in late 1974. This proved to be the most serious recession since the 1930s, with the unemployment rate exceeding 9 per cent in 1975, and averaging 8.5 per cent for the year as a whole. It remained above 7 per cent during the two years that followed.

This recession of the mid-1970s was allowed to develop without any attempt to combat it. Despite a period of reckless monetary growth in 1972, a presidental election year, monetary policy had become tight by 1974 and the government's fiscal stance amounted to a policy of neglect.[43] In short, according to Blinder[44] 'policy-makers sat idly by as the worst recession of. . . post-war history gathered momentum.' Thus the period 1973-6 was characterised by the absence of stabilisation policy; it was as though Keynes had never lived.

Under both the Nixon and the Ford administrations, the 4 per cent target goal for unemployment was abandoned. Three main reasons were advanced to justify this:

(i) earlier increases in UI benefits had eroded the incentive to work;
(ii) increases in the national minimum wage had resulted in adverse employment effects for low-productivity workers, especially teenagers; and
(iii) the composition of the labour force changed towards teenagers with above average rates of unemployment.

All three arguments suggest an increase in the frictional–structural component of unemployment, alternatively called the natural rate. Points (i) and (ii) have been dealt with at length in Chapters 5 and 6; (iii) is taken up again in Chapter 8, but here we give some idea of the suggested magnitude of this effect. Wachter,[45] assuming a full employment rate for prime age males of 2.9 per cent, has estimated that for the labour force as a whole the full employment rate increased from around 4.0 to 4.2 per cent in the 1950s, to 5.5 per cent in the period 1975-7. These estimates are derived from past relationships of the unemployment rates of fourteen different age-sex groups and that for prime age males. Apart from the fundamental criticism of this approach (see Chapter 8), estimates based upon it are sensitive to the assumption that is made concerning the 'normal' or full employment rate of unemployment for prime age males. If it is too low, or if it increases throughout the period under study, then this could clearly bias the overall estimates downwards.

However, Wachter's estimates are very close to Gordon's[46] estimates of the natural rate. According to him, the natural rate increased from 4.4 per cent in 1960 to 5.4 per cent in 1973, and remained at this level until 1978. Although more recent estimates have not been published, President Reagan's Council of Economic Advisers appear to have been working on the assumption that it was in the range 6.0-6.5 per cent during 1982-3[47]—that is, double the rate that Martin Feldstein,[48] Chairman of the Council, thought was attainable in the early 1970s. It is also considerably higher than the 4 per cent target goal of the early 1960s, a target that was also enshrined in the Humphrey-Hawkins Full Employment and Balanced Growth Act 1978. According to the Act this goal—which in an earlier version of the Bill preceding the Act had been set as low as 3 per cent—represents the minimum level of frictional unemployment consistent with efficient job search and labour mobility. Although it was originally intended that this goal be reached by 1983, this was subsequently amended to 1985. Clearly, with unemployment exceeding 10 per cent in early 1983 it still seems unlikely that the target will be met by this later date. Indeed, the expansion in output and employment that would be necessary to ensure that the target is reached by 1985 would probably be too great for the economy to sustain without triggering a new wave of inflation.

Despite the 4 per cent goal of the Humphrey–Hawkins Act, this brief survey of evidence suggests that by the late 1970s the full employment level of unemployment might well have increased to around 5–6 per cent. Assuming that no further increase occurred between the late 1970s and the early 1980s, this would imply that by the end of 1982 4–5 per cent of US unemployment was attributable to a deficiency in aggregate demand.

UNEMPLOYMENT FLOWS

For any period, the average stock of unemployment is dependent on the number of people who become unemployed during that period and the average time that each spends unemployed. Thus, in a steady state, the stock of unemployment will be equal to the rate of inflow into the stock times the average duration of unemployment. In a non-steady state, changes in the stock will reflect either a change in the rate of flow or a change in the average duration, or both.

Although flow statistics are not available for the whole of the post-war period for the UK, they are available from 1972 onwards for Great Britain. Table 7.3 shows the magnitudes of the three-monthly average flows on to and off the unemployment register over the period 1978–82. Inflows of around 280,000 per month during 1978 were accompanied by outflows of around 287,000 and, therefore, the level of unemployment declined. Thereafter, the rate of inflow increased rapidly so that by January 1981 it stood at 360,000 per month and, given that the rate of outflow was still only 276,000, the unemployment stock increased at a rate of about 100,000 per month (the discrepancy between the net flow figure and the average change in the unemployment stock arises because the coverage of the flow statistics does not coincide exactly with that of the wholly unemployed). Although the rate of inflow declined after January 1981, the rate of outflow increased considerably. As a result there was a declining monthly rate of increase in unemployment during 1981–2.

It is clear from the table that the flows through the unemployment register are large relative to the unemployment stock, and even larger when compared to changes in that stock. For example, for Great Britain the inflow of wholly unemployed, excluding school leavers, on

Table 7.3: *Unemployment Flows: Great Britain, 1978–82*

	Average flows for 3 months ended (000s)			Wholly Unemployed, seasonally adjusted	
	Inflow	Outflow	Excess	Level (m)	Average change over 3 months ended (000s)
1978 January	283	288	-5	1.362	-0.5
April	282	289	-7	1.340	-7.4
July	280	286	-6	1.307	-10.8
October	276	286	-10	1.286	-7.1
1979 January	275	282	-7	1.271	-5.1
April	270	271	-1	1.253	-6.0
July	266	276	-11	1.228	-8.0
October	269	270	-1	1.221	-2.5
1980 January	280	267	13	1.261	13.4
April	303	267	36	1.380	39.6
July	320	263	58	1.538	59.2
October	348	270	78	1.814	85.6
1981 January	360	276	84	2.119	101.5
April	343	277	66	2.327	69.5
July	331	274	57	2.491	54.7
October	312	266	46	2.625	44.6
1982 January	340	321	19	2.708	27.7
April	333	324	9	2.744	12.1
July	350	324	26	2.816	24.0
October	354	323	31	2.945	42.9

Source: Employment Gazette, December 1982, Tables 2.2 and 2.19.

to the register amounted to about 3,347,000 in 1978, which was 2.54 times the average stock for that year. In 1981 the inflow had increased to about 4 million, but since the average stock had also increased to almost 2.5 million the corresponding ratio had fallen to 1.62, an indication that the average duration of unemployment had increased. When expressed as a percentage of the labour force, the inflow during 1981 was 17.2 per cent, a figure not too dissimilar to the 1966 male inflow rate of 15.3 per cent estimated by Cripps and Tarling,[49] although for the male age groups 18-24 years and 50-9 years they estimated the rate to be 30 per cent and 10 per cent respectively.

Although there is some variability in the gross flows through the register, they remain substantial irrespective of whether unemployment is high or low, rising or falling.[50] Table 7.3 suggests that the variability in inflows is greater than that for outflows; this was also true of the longer period, 1972-82, when the range in variation of inflows was around 105,000, and that for outflows 73,000. The inflow series tends to be more sensitive (i.e. responds more quickly) to changes in labour market conditions than does the outflow series. Thus, an increase in the rate of inflow tends to be accompanied by a fall in the rate of outflow, but only after a lag. Similarly, when unemployment is about to fall, the inflow series is the first to reflect this.[51]

A sample[52] of males joining the unemployment register in the autumn of 1978 shows that a high proportion were young and unmarried, and that they were more likely to have held semi-skilled or unskilled manual jobs with earnings far below the national average (50 per cent had earnings in the bottom 20 per cent of the earnings distribution). Furthermore, a high proportion had had recent experience of unemployment, half of them in the previous year and three-quarters some time in the previous five years. This confirms the findings of Creedy and Disney,[53] who investigated changes in labour market states in the early 1970s and found that individuals are more likely to experience sickness and unemployment in any one year if they have experienced sickness and unemployment in the previous year. Similarly, they found that individuals were 'more likely to return to full employment, following a year in which they experienced some unemployment, if they were previously fully employed.' Finally, the 1978 survey suggests that married males who become unemployed are less likely to be supported by a working wife than in the population at large —only one-third of the wives of the unemployed in the sample were working, whereas over 50 per cent of married females do, in fact, work.

A further analysis of the same data was undertaken by Stern,[54] who found that monthly male unemployment inflow rates, by socioeconomic group, varied from 0.4 per cent for senior and intermediate non-manual personnel, to 4.4 per cent per month for unskilled manual workers, and 8.4 per cent for personal service workers. He also found that monthly inflow rates varied with age, being 3.0 per cent for those under 20, 2.7 per cent for those aged 20–4, and about 0.6 per cent for those aged 40–59 years. However, these age differences largely reflect the effects of different job experience. Comparing men over and under 30, each group had an inflow rate in excess of 5 per cent where their previous job experience was less than 12 months. For those with 1–3 years of job experience the rates were 0.9 and 0.8 per cent for the under 30 and over 30-year age groups respectively, and these rates declined even further to 0.3 and 0.2 per cent for those with 5–10 years' job experience. Thus the inflow into the stock of unemployed is, as economic theory predicts, much higher for the unskilled and those who have only been in their jobs for a relatively short time.

Although gross flow data are generated in the US in the monthly CPS, they have not been published since 1952 because of inherent deficiencies. The Gordon Committee recommended that a programme of research be undertaken in order to correct for these deficiencies, with the resumption of publication as soon as possible

Table 7.4. Reasons for Unemployment, 1973–81

	1973		1975		1979		1981	
	% share of total unemployment	Unem-ployment rate	% share of total unemployment	Unem-ployment rate	% share of total unemployment	Unem-ployment rate	% share of total unemployment	Unem-ployment rate
All Unemployed								
All unemployed	100.0	4.9	100.0	8.5	100.0	5.8	100.0	7.6
Job losers	38.7	1.9	55.4	4.7	42.8	2.5	51.6	3.9
Job leavers	15.7	0.8	10.4	0.9	14.3	0.8	11.2	0.8
Re-entrants	30.7	1.5	23.8	2.0	29.5	1.7	25.4	1.9
New entrants	14.9	0.7	10.4	0.9	13.4	0.8	11.9	0.9
Adult males								
All unemployed	100.0	3.2	100.0	6.8	100.0	4.2	100.0	6.3
Job losers	59.1	1.9	75.0	5.1	63.6	2.5	71.0	4.5
Job leavers	15.9	0.5	8.5	0.6	14.1	0.6	9.9	0.6
Re-entrants	21.6	0.7	14.5	1.0	19.3	0.8	16.4	1.0
New entrants	3.4	0.1	2.1	0.1	3.0	0.1	2.8	0.2
Adult females								
All unemployed	100.0	4.8	100.0	8.0	100.0	5.7	100.0	6.8
Job losers	34.6	1.6	50.0	4.0	37.4	2.1	45.4	3.1
Job leavers	18.6	0.9	13.9	1.1	16.3	0.9	14.0	1.0
Re-entrants	41.5	2.0	31.9	2.6	40.0	2.3	35.3	2.4
New entrants	5.3	0.3	4.2	0.3	6.3	0.4	5.2	0.4
Teenagers								
All unemployed	100.0	14.5	100.0	19.9	100.0	16.1	100.0	19.6
Job losers	17.2	2.4	25.6	5.0	20.5	3.3	21.9	4.3
Job leavers	11.8	1.7	8.7	1.7	11.8	1.9	9.2	1.8
Re-entrants	29.5	4.3	29.9	6.0	29.0	4.7	27.6	5.4
New entrants	41.5	6.0	35.8	7.1	38.6	6.2	41.3	8.1

Source: *Employment and Training Report of the President*, 1982 (and earlier issues) Table A-36.

thereafter. To date, these recommendations have not been implemented. However, in a background paper for the National Commission on Employment and Unemployment Statistics, Smith and Vanski[55] provide useful summary statistics for 1976. In that year, the average size of the labour force was 94.8 million and in a typical month 3.7 million workers withdrew, while 4.5 million entered. Thus, the gross monthly turnover of the labour force in 1976 was 8.2 million, or 8.6 per cent. The average level of unemployment during the year was 7.3 million, and nearly 40 per cent of these left unemployment each month, either because they had found a new job or because they left the labour force, their place in the stock being taken by an equivalent number of newly unemployed. For unemployed teenagers the corresponding proportion was even higher—53 per cent of them found a job or left the labour force in a typical month.

Despite the lack of regular data on gross flows, US data on the reasons for unemployment are published regularly and this throws some light on the extent to which unemployment is associated with labour force entry and re-entry. The data are summarised in Table 7.4, which shows that unemployment following re-entry into the labour force is more important for adult females and teenagers than for adult males. For adults, re-entry unemployment tends to decline relatively as unemployment increases, but even in 1975—a deep recession year—it still accounted for about 32 per cent of adult female unemployment. For teenagers it accounted for a fairly constant 28–30 per cent of unemployment irrespective of the overall teenage rate. However, the re-entry rate of teenage unemployment (i.e. unemployed teenage re-entrants expressed as a percentage of the teenage labour force) varied between 4.3 and 6.0 per cent—that is, about twice the corresponding female rate.

Entry into the labour force for the first time occurs almost exclusively among teenagers, and accounts for about 40 per cent of all teenage unemployment. Indeed, in each of the nine years 1973–81, the new entrant rate of teenage unemployment (i.e. unemployed teenage new entrants expressed as a percentage of the teenage labour force) was higher than the overall unemployment rate for adult males.

Table 7.4 also shows that voluntary job leaving declines as a reason for unemployment as unemployment increases. However, the voluntary job-leaving rate, which is highest for teenagers and lowest for adult males, is fairly constant through time for all three groups. As might be expected, involuntary job losers dominate changes in unemployment for all groups. Both the percentage share of job losers in unemployment and the job-loser rate increase as unemployment increases. In 1981 it accounted for over 70 per cent of adult male unemployment, about 45 per cent of female unemployment, and less than 25 per cent of teenage unemployment. Despite this, the job-loser rate for teenagers was, more often than not, still higher than that for adult males, though clearly not in 1981.

Similar data on the reasons for unemployment are not available for the UK.

THE DURATION OF UNEMPLOYMENT

In addition to the flow of people into unemployment (i.e. the number of spells), the unemployment rate will be influenced by the duration of each spell. Since the official statistics on duration relate to interrupted spells of unemployment, they tell us nothing about the length of completed spells. Nevertheless, they can be used to calculate minimum

Table 7.5: *Long-Term Unemployment in Great Britain: Mid-Year 1950–82 (% of unemployed)*

Year	26 weeks and longer	52 weeks and longer	Year	26 weeks and longer	52 weeks and longer
1949	26.5	15.3	1971	29.5	15.9
1951	27.4	16.9	1972	37.7	20.4
1953	24.6	12.3	1973	40.9	26.9
1955	24.1	13.1	1974	33.7	21.6
1957	23.4	10.6	1975	26.4	13.7
1959	32.6	15.6	1976	33.8	16.4
1961	31.5	18.7	1977	35.4	19.8
1963[1]	33.8	17.0	1978	37.8	21.7
1965	31.4	19.1	1979[2]	39.8	24.6
1967	29.2	13.2	1980	34.4	19.2
1969	30.9	17.5	1981	46.1	22.0
1970	30.6	17.6	1982	54.8	33.6

Notes: [1] From 1963 onwards estimates relate to July of each year; prior to 1963 the estimates are for June of each year.

[2] Prior to 1979 the estimates are for GB. From 1979 onwards they are for the UK.

Source: Department of Employment; *Yearbooks* and *Employment Gazettes*.

estimates of long-term unemployment, provided that some arbitrary dividing line between short- and long-term unemployment is adopted. As Sinfield[56] has commented, although long-term unemployment in the UK is now regarded as lasting longer than 12 months, in the late 1960s—and even as late as the early 1970s—a 6-month cut-off point was widely accepted as the appropriate dividing line. Table 7.5 shows that whichever definition is adopted, the UK has experienced not only an absolute increase in long-term unemployment, but a relative increase too. For example, whereas about 21 per cent (i.e. 39,200) of the unemployed in June 1956 had been unemployed for longer than 26 weeks, the corresponding percentage for July 1982 was almost 55 per cent (i.e. 1.75 million). In other words, the number who had been out of work for 26 weeks or longer in mid-1982 was 44 times as great as it had been 25 years earlier. But everything is relative: by mid-1982, 1.07

million people had been unemployed for 12 months or more—a staggering 52-fold increase on the 1956 level.

Long-term unemployment poses particular problems because the longer an individual has been unemployed the less likely is that individual to find another job. This is largely because employers tend to use unemployment experience as a screening device, eliminating those with longer spells of unemployment irrespective of their other

Table 7.6: *Long-Term Unemployment in US: Annual Averages 1948–82 (% of unemployed)*

Year	27 weeks and over	Year	27 weeks and over
1948	5.1	1966	8.3
1949	7.0	1967	5.9
1950	10.9	1968	5.5
1951	6.7	1969	4.7
1952	4.5	1970	5.7
1953	4.3	1971	10.4
1954	9.0	1972	11.6
1955	11.8	1973	7.8
1956	8.4	1974	7.3
1957	8.4	1975	15.2
1958	14.5	1976	18.3
1959	15.3	1977	14.8
1960	11.8	1978	10.5
1961	17.1	1979	8.7
1962	15.0	1980	10.8
1963	13.6	1981	14.0
1964	12.7	1982	16.6
1965	10.4		

Sources: Employment and Training Report of the President, 1981, Table A-35 for years 1948–80.
Monthly Labor Review, February 1983, Table 7, for years 1981 and 1982.

attributes. Of course, this will be reinforced if prolonged unemployment saps the will and the initiative of the unemployed. Thus, if the economy is operated at a high level of unemployment over a prolonged period of time, long-term unemployment is likely to become a serious problem requiring more than just expansionary demand policies to combat it.

For the US, data are only available for those whose unemployment lasts 27 weeks or longer; this is summarised in Table 7.6. According to this definition, the proportion of long-term unemployment increased during 1981–2 as overall unemployment increased, but it was no higher in the 1980s than it had been in 1975–7, although it was higher than it had been in the 1950s and 1960s, with the exception of the period 1958–63.

Comparing the US and UK data reveals that the proportion of unemployment that is long-term is not as great in the US, and never has been, as it is in the UK. Indeed, the absolute number unemployed for six months or more in the US in 1982 was about the same as in the UK. Thus, on the basis of this evidence alone, it seems likely that the average duration of unemployment is less in the US than in the UK.

A more detailed analysis of the duration of interrupted spells of unemployment shows that males have a higher proportion of long-term unemployment than females. For example, in 1982 the proportions of males and females who had been out of work for six months or more in the UK were about 59 and 45 per cent respectively. Although comparative statistics are not available, the same is true for the US where in 1980 males accounted for about 65 per cent of long-term unemployment, even though they only accounted for about 56 per cent of total unemployment.

In Chapter 2 we discussed duration measures for completed spells of unemployment. The terminations weighted average duration (D_2) measures the average duration of all spells that terminate within a given period of time, while the experience weighted average duration (D_3) measures the average length of spell experienced by those who are unemployed at a particular point in time. It was stressed in Chapter 2 that since D_2 gives undue weight to shorter spells its welfare implications can be quite misleading. Therefore D_3 is the preferred measure.

Table 7.7 compares D_2 for the two countries. It shows that for Great Britain the average duration of male unemployment spells terminating within each year of the mid-1960s was around 7–8 weeks, and that by the end of the 1970s this had increased to around 17 weeks. For the US, the corresponding figure, for males and females, was about 6 weeks in the early 1960s, increasing to around 9 weeks in the high unemployment year of 1975, but falling back to 6–7 weeks during 1977–8. Thus, while there has been a marginal increase in D_2 in the US over the last two decades, this has not been anything like as marked as the increase in the UK. (It should be remembered, however, that if females have lower durations of unemployment than males, this will tend to depress the US figures in Table 7.7 compared with those of the UK.)

One of the problems of estimating the duration of unemployment spells by measures such as D_2 is that individuals who experience multiple spells of unemployment within the observation period will bring down the average (see next section). Another is that if the period of unemployment is preceded, or followed, by a period out of the labour force, the duration figure will understate the time spent between jobs, and will not reflect accurately the ability of the labour market to generate jobs for those who want them. In the US context, failure to search for a job in the four weeks preceding the count will mean a break in an individual's spell of unemployment. Where the reason for the withdrawal is the desire to pursue non-work activities,

Table 7.7: *Comparison of Measures of Duration GB and US, 1961–79*

| | D_2 | | D_3 | |
	GB	US	GB	US
1961	—	7.2	—	31.2
1962	—	6.2	—	29.4
1963	8.7	6.4	54	28.0
1964	8.4	5.8	58	26.6
1965	7.6	5.2	61	23.6
1966	7.1	4.2	59	20.8
1967	9.7	5.0	55	17.6
1968	10.4	4.5	57	16.8
1969	10.8	4.6	60	15.8
1970	10.1	5.4	61	17.4
1971	11.3	6.8	61	22.6
1972	12.8	6.2	71	24.0
1973	10.1	7.0	76	20.0
1974	9.0	5.6	72	19.4
1975	14.1	9.1	62	28.2
1976	15.5	8.0	70	31.6
1977	17.0	7.2	78	28.6
1978	17.2	6.3	81	26.2
1979	17.0	—	88	—

Sources: Data for GB from Brian G. M. Main, 'The length of employment and unemployment in Great Britain', *Scottish Journal of Political Economy*, Vol.28, No.2. June 1981, Table 1. Data for the US from G. A. Akerlof and B. G. M. Main, 'Unemployment spells and unemployment experience', *American Economic Review*, December 1980, Table 1.

the unemployment spell is not biased in any way. However, if withdrawal is the result of genuine discouragement the recorded duration will give a false picture and, as Akerlof and Main[57] point out, will understate the impact of bad labour market conditions. Akerlof and Main report that for the US one-third of all male spells of unemployment end in withdrawal from the labour force; for women the corresponding proportion is greater than one half. Clark and Summers[58] confirm that for 1974–5 about 45 per cent of all unemployment spells end in withdrawal. On the other hand, about 40 per cent of all spells begin from outside of the labour force, and not as a result of an individual losing or leaving his job.

Clark and Summers also point out that 46 per cent of those who withdrew from the labour force in 1977 claim to have done so because of failure to obtain a regular job, but only a third of these (i.e. 15 per cent of total) were officially classified as discouraged. Furthermore, they stress that withdrawal is often very brief, and cite the fact that one-third of those who withdrew from the labour force in June 1976 re-entered the next month, with 44 per cent re-entering within two months. They estimate that in 1974 the typical unemployed person spent one month outside the labour force even though he was desirous of obtaining work. This lends support to the view that 'many of those classified as not in the labour force are functionally indistinguishable from the unemployed'.[59]

When the effects of withdrawal are excluded from estimates of duration such as D_2, Clark and Summers found that average duration increased by 74 per cent in 1974, and 90 per cent in 1975. For women over 20 years of age they found that average duration more than doubled.

In addition to the measurement problems associated with withdrawal, re-entry and multiple spells, D_2 gives undue weight to shorter spells and thus does not capture the effect of the concentration of unemployment among a relatively small group. That this is a problem in the US is highlighted by Clark and Summers, who found that in 1974 only 2.4 per cent of the labour force experienced a total of more than 26 weeks of unemployment, but nevertheless accounted for 41 per cent of all unemployment during that year. For male teenagers, 8.4 per cent accounted for almost 54 per cent of unemployment. Given that unemployment is so heavily concentrated upon a relatively small number of workers who are out of work for such a large part of the time, the experience weighted measure of duration, D_3 is more appropriate.

For Great Britain, D_3 has always been longer than a year—at least since 1963. Furthermore, it has increased gradually throughout the period, falling back in the mid-1970s but increasing rapidly towards the end of that decade. Unemployment is therefore typically being spent in ever longer spells. As Main[60] points out, the fact that D_3 has not increased as rapidly as D_2 may reflect the fact that 'spells have lengthened more than proportionately at the short end of the spell distribution than at the long end.'

In the US, taking the period as a whole, there has been no increase in D_3, although comparing the late 1960s and the late 1970s suggests almost a doubling in spell length. However, in the US those who are unemployed during the week of the count are typically unemployed for a much shorter period than their counterparts in GB. In 1977–8, D_3 was almost three times as high in GB as in the US. Part of this difference could be explained by a greater tendency to withdraw temporarily from the labour market in the US, as discussed above. It could also be explained if those who experience unemployment in the US incur a higher incidence of multiple spells. Of course, the tendency to withdraw and the incidence of multiple spells will not be unrelated. For example, if an individual withdraws from the labour force after a short period of unemployment and then re-enters, experiencing a further short spell of unemployment, the official statistics will capture two relatively short spells rather than one long spell. It is to the problem of repeated spells that we now turn.

REPEATED SPELLS OF UNEMPLOYMENT

The evidence on recurrent spells of unemployment is rather fragmentary for both the UK and the US, although in the former periodic surveys into the characteristics of the unemployed provide intermittent evidence. In mid-1961, when the overall unemployment rate was 1.3 per cent, 43 per cent of the male unemployed and 40 per cent of females had suffered two or more spells of unemployment in the previous year. In contrast, 28 per cent of unemployed men had held no job in the previous year, while 26 per cent had held two or three jobs.[61] In June 1973, when the overall unemployment rate was 2.4 per cent, 28 per cent of the unemployed had suffered two or more spells of unemployment in the previous year, while 3.5 per cent had suffered four or more.[62] Compared with 1961, recurrent unemployment had therefore declined, but only at the expense of more people not having held a job in the previous year. In the 1973 survey, 44 per cent of the males and 38 per cent of the females were in this category.

The major problem with this type of survey, as Disney[63] has commented, is that it contains 'a preponderance, relative to the average, of individuals with low probabilities of leaving unemployment. If such individuals also have low probabilities of leaving employment, the sample survey will underestimate the extent of repeated spells of unemployment.' The DHSS cohort study,[64] carried out during 1978–9, does not suffer from this defect. In this sample 35 per cent of the unemployed males (interviewed in the autumn of 1979) had had more than one spell of registered unemployment during the previous twelve months. This survey also reveals that 13 per cent of the unemployed had spent some time of the previous year in unregistered unemployment. Disney himself, analysing a cohort of unemployed for the period 1971–3, found that for those who were 28 years of age and unemployed in 1971 the risk of incurring a second spell of unemployment during the two-year period that followed was greater than the average probability of becoming unemployed in the first place. In other words, for this particular age group, Disney concluded that 'unemployment breeds unemployment'. Although his study did not specify what proportion of the cohort experienced multiple spells, his analysis did, nevertheless, enable him to conclude that spell recurrence accounted for 'much of the high concentration of unemployment among a small number' of each age group studied over the three-year period.

To enable these figures to be seen in their true perspective it might help to quote yet further statistics. Writing in 1977, Metcalf and Nickell[65] commented that given the then rates of flow into and out of unemployment, and given an equitable distribution of spells, individual workers could expect, on average, to experience one spell of unemployment every six years. Translated into expectations over a normal working life of 42 years, each individual faces an average of seven spells of unemployment. Clearly, from the evidence of the surveys quoted above, a significant proportion of the unemployed in the UK experience far more than their fair share of unemployment spells. The corollary is, of course, that many do not experience their fair share, as is evidenced by Daniel's[66] 1973 finding that 61 per cent of the over 55 age group who were unemployed had never been out of work before experiencing their current spell. This is a somewhat surprising result given that in 1973 many of the youngest in this age group would have entered the labour force 41 years earlier, that is, in 1932. Indeed, assuming that they had all left school at the minimum school leaving age (then 14 years), all in this age group would have entered the labour force between 1923 and 1932, and would have had up to sixteen years in the labour force before the outbreak of the second World War. Nevertheless, taken at its face value, Daniel's result shows that even when one considers such a lengthy period of time (i.e. up to 41 years), unemployment spells are still very unequally distributed.

For the US, such evidence as there is tends to confirm the UK picture. Akerlof and Main report that 34 per cent of all those who experienced unemployment in 1976 had more than one spell, and that this group was responsible for more than half of all the spells in that year. Construction workers were particularly badly affected, with 18 per cent of those with three or more spells provided by this group, even though construction workers accounted for less than 6 per cent of workers generally.

SUMMARY

Judged by the targets that policy-makers set for themselves immediately after the second world war, the UK enjoyed greater success in achieving full employment than did the US until the mid-1960s; thereafter the US achieved full employment for four or five years too. During the 1970s unemployment increased in both countries, and by the 1980s it had passed 10 per cent in both. Part of this increase in both countries is the result of an increase in the frictional-structural component of unemployment, but by far the largest part of the increase is attributable to a deficiency in aggregate demand.

Unemployment is heavily concentrated in both countries as a result of long duration, or repeated spells. Evidence on the former suggests that this is greater in the UK than in the US, but the incidence of the latter may well be higher in the US and may often be associated with temporary withdrawal from the labour force. It seems likely that the full employment rate of unemployment in the UK is now somewhere in the range of 3–4 per cent, while the corresponding rate for the US is in the 5–6 per cent range. To bring the rates down below these levels would require sustained periods of expansion in both countries, particularly in the UK. But demand expansion would also need to be coupled with labour market policies, and perhaps a reduction in unemployment benefit too. However, in the UK at least, it seems unlikely that the economy will return to full employment in the foreseeable future.

NOTES AND REFERENCES

1. A. Deacon, 'Unemployment and politics in Britain since 1945', in B. Showler and A. Sinfield (eds), *The Workless State* (Oxford: Martin Robertson, 1981).
2. *Employment Policy*, Cmnd 6527 (London: HMSO, 1944).
3. Deacon, *op. cit.*
4. Brian Showler, 'Political economy and unemployment', in Showler and Sinfield, *op. cit.*
5. William H. Beveridge, *Full Employment In a Free Society* (London: Allen & Unwin, 1944).
6. Richard Kahn, 'Unemployment as seen by Keynesians', in G. D. N. Worswick (ed.), *The Concept and Measurement of Involuntary Unemployment* (London: Allen & Unwin, 1976).
7. Beveridge, *op. cit.*
8. Ibid.
9. Kahn, *op. cit.*
10. S. Brittan, 'Full employment policy: a reappraisal', in Worswick, *op. cit.*
11. F. T. Blackaby, 'The target rate of unemployment', in Worswick, *op. cit.*
12. A. P. Thirlwall, 'Types of unemployment: with special reference to non demand-deficient unemployment in Great Britain', *Scottish Journal of Political Economy*, Vol.16, No.1, February 1969.
13. R. C. O. Matthews, 'Why has Britain had full employment since the war?', *Economic Journal*, September 1968.
14. M. Scott (with R. A. Laslett), *Can We Get Back to Full Employment?* (London: Macmillan, 1978).
15. The rate of 13.9 per cent refers only to the third quarter of 1982. Since the basis of the count changed in October of that year it is not possible to quote an annual average rate that is calculated on the old basis.
16. The official unemployment statistics for the inter-war period are based only on the insured working population. When they are adjusted to take account of unemployment among non-insured workers the average rate for the period 1921–38 was 10.9 per cent. C. H. Feinstein, *National Income, Expenditure and Output of the United Kingdom, 1855–1965* (Cambridge: Cambridge University Press, 1972), Table 58.
17. R. Layard, 'Unemployment in Britain: causes and cures', Discussion Paper No.19, Centre for Labour Economics, LSE.
18. A useful summary of the surveys is to be found in the chapter by R. A. Laslett entitled 'A measure of the full employment rate of unemployment in the UK', in Scott, *op. cit.*
19. Jim Taylor, *Unemployment and Wage Inflation: With Special Reference to Britain and the USA* (Harlow: Longman, 1974).
20. Laslett, *op. cit.*

21. Jim Taylor, 'The unemployment gap in Britain's production sector', in Worswick, *op. cit.*
22. G. D. N. Worswick, 'Summary of the discussion', in Worswick, *op. cit.*
23. J. M. Parkin, M. T. Sumner and R. Ward, 'The effects of excess demand, generalised expectations and wage–price controls on wage inflation 1956–71', in K. Brunner and A. Meltzer (eds), *The Economics of Price and Wage Controls* (New York: North Holland, 1976).
24. J. S. Fleming, *Inflation* (London: Oxford University Press, 1976).
25. M. T. Sumner, 'Wage Determination', in J. M. Parkin and M. T. Sumner (eds), *Inflation in the United Kingdom* (Manchester: Manchester University Press, 1978).
26. Patrick Minford, *Unemployment: Cause and Cure* (Oxford: Martin Robertson, 1983).
27. A. P. Thirlwall, 'What are estimates of the natural rate of unemployment measuring?', *Oxford Bulletin of Economics and Statistics*, Vol.45, No.2, May 1983.
28. Layard, *op. cit.*
29. D. Metcalf, 'Unemployment: history, incidence and prospects', *Policy and Politics*, Vol.8, No.1, 1980.
30. This resulted from the fact that most advanced industrial countries were expanding their economies during 1972–3. It was exacerbated by the depreciation of sterling that followed the decision to float in mid-1972.
31. R. G. D. Allen, 'The immediate contributors to inflation'. *Economic Journal*, Vol.85, September 1975.
32. Scott, *op. cit.*
33. B. Jordan, *Mass Unemployment and the Future of Britain* (Oxford: Basil Blackwell, 1982).
34. Betty G. Fishman and Leo Fishman, *Employment, Unemployment and Economic Growth* (New York: Thomas Y. Crowell, 1969).
35. R. A Gordon, *The Goal of Full Employment*, (Chichester: Wiley, 1967).
36. Ibid.
37. Robert Lekachman, 'Unemployment in America', *New Society*, 20 April 1975.
38. Otto Eckstein, 'Aggregate demand and the current unemployment problem', in Arthur M. Ross (ed.), *Unemployment And The American Economy* (New York: Wiley, 1964).
39. C. C. Killingsworth, 'Automation, jobs and manpower', in W. G. Bowen (ed.), *Labor and the National Economy* (New York: Norton, 1965).
40. Council of Economic Advisers, 'Structural unemployment', in Bowen, ibid.
41. *Employment and Training Report of the President*, 1981.
42. Leon Keyserling, 'The Humphrey–Hawkins Act since its 1978 enactment', in David C. Colander (ed.), *Solutions to Unemployment* (New York: Harcourt, Brace, Jovanovich, 1981).
43. Alan S. Blinder, *Economic Policy And the Great Stagflation* (London: Academic Press, 1979).
44. Ibid.
45. Michael Wachter, 'The changing cyclical responsiveness of wage inflation', *Brookings Papers on Economic Activity*, 1, 1976.
46. Robert J. Gordon, *Macroeconomics*, (Boston: Little-Brown. 1978).
47. This was mentioned to one of the authors during discussion with a staff member of the Council of Economic Advisers in April 1983.

48. Martin Feldstein, 'The economics of the new unemployment', *Public Interest*, No.33, Fall 1973.
49. F. Cripps and R. Tarling, 'An analysis of the duration of male unemployment in Great Britain', *Economic Journal*, Vol.84, June 1974.
50. *Employment Gazette*, June 1980.
51. Ibid.
52. S. Moylan and B. Davies, 'The Disadvantages of the unemployed', *Employment Gazette*, August 1980.
53. John Creedy and Richard Disney, 'Changes in labour market states in Great Britain', *Scottish Journal of Political Economy*, Vol.28, No.1, February 1981.
54. J. Stern, 'Who becomes unemployed?', *Employment Gazette*, January 1983.
55. Ralph E. Smith and Jean E. Vanski, 'Gross change data: the neglected data base', in National Commission on Employment and Unemployment Statistics, *Counting the Labor Force*, Appendix X, Volume II (Washington: US Government Printing Office, 1979).
56. A. Sinfield, *What Unemployment Means* (Oxford: Martin Robertson, 1981).
57. G. A. Akerlof and B. G. M. Main, 'Unemployment spells and unemployment experience', *American Economic Review*, December 1980.
58. K. B. Clark and L. H. Summers, 'Labour market dynamics and unemployment: A reconsideration', *Brookings Papers on Economic Activity*, 1, 1979.
59. Ibid.
60. Brian G. M. Main, 'The length of employment and unemployment in Great Britain', *Scottish Journal of Political Economy*, Vol.28, No.2, June 1981.
61. *Ministry of Labour Gazette*, April 1962.
62. *Department of Employment Gazette*, March 1974.
63. R. Disney, 'Recurrent spells and the concentration of unemployment in Britain', *Economic Journal*, March 1979.
64. *Employment Gazette*, August 1982.
65. D. Metcalf and S. J. Nickell, 'The plain man's guide to the out-of-work', Discussion Paper No.6, Centre for Labour Economics, LSE. Subsequently published in the evidence in the low income reference of the Royal Commission on the Distribution of Income and Wealth.
66. W. W. Daniel, *A National Survey of The Unemployed (PEP, 1974)*.

8.   High-Incidence Groups

INTRODUCTION

In the UK, females experience lower unemployment rates than males, while teenagers and the elderly experience higher rates than the national average. Furthermore, while unemployment rates by colour and for different racial minorities are not published, such evidence as there is suggests that unemployment is higher among racial minorities, and that they are particularly vulnerable to rising unemployment. In the US, unemployment among teenagers, blacks and women has received special study because these are high-incidence groups, with unemployment rates that exceed the average by differing degrees.

In this chapter we focus on various aspects of the unemployment of these high-incidence groups. First, we present data on the rates for the different groups, comparing them with the average or with low-incidence groups. Next, we look at the mechanistic causes and time characteristics of this unemployment. In particular, we are concerned with the flows into unemployment from quitting or losing jobs on the one hand, and from labour force entry and re-entry on the other. Are high unemployment rates associated with differential rates of flow, or with longer, or more frequent spells of unemployment? In this section we also touch upon measurement issues.

The next section deals with the more fundamental economic explanations of high unemployment among blacks, as contrasted with the quantitative aspects of the previous section. In the final section we consider the important issue of the effect of demographic changes on unemployment. This issue is very relevant to the study of high-incidence groups, since these groups have experienced an increase in their labour force share. The question therefore arises: How much of the rising trend of unemployment can be attributed to this demographic shift? Attempts have been made to measure the shift effect, and in this last section we take a critical view of these efforts.

Before we proceed further, however, a few words of explanation are required concerning terminology. First, when comparing the unemployment rate of a particular group with the overall rate, we refer to this as the relativity of that group. Thus the unemployment rate of teenagers relative to the overall rate is the teenage relativity. When comparing the rates of two sub-groups, we refer to this as the differential. Thus the ratio of the female to male rate is the female–male differential. Second, we distinguish between the average relativity, or differential, and the *incremental* relativity or differential. Whereas the former measure refers to the ratio of one average rate to another, the incremental measure refers to the change in one rate between two points in time relative to the change in another over the same time period.

For example, if the overall rate at a given point in time is 5 per cent while the teenage rate is 10 per cent, then the teenage relativity is 2.0. If the overall and teenage rates rise to 8 per cent and 15 per cent, respectively, the teenage relativity falls to 1.9 per cent (=15/8), indicating a relative improvement in teenage unemployment. However teenage unemployment has increased by 5 percentage points and total unemployment by only 3. The incremental change in the relativity is therefore 1.7 (= 5/3), which means that for every 3 workers per 100 of the labor force who become unemployed between the two observation points, 5 teenagers per 100 of the teenage labor force become unemployed. Thus, where the incremental relativity is greater than 1, the teenage base is more adversely affected than the labor force generally during a recession, even though there is an improvement (i.e. decline) in its relative rate.

The opposite will be true in a period of general unemployment reduction, namely, that if the incremental relativity is greater than 1 then more teenagers per 100 of the teenage labour force will leave the unemployment register than is the case for workers generally. This would suggest an improvement in the teenage unemployment situation, but if the incremental relativity is less than the average relativity the latter would rise, suggesting a deterioration. Clearly, movements in average relativities and differentials need to be interpreted in conjunction with incremental changes for a fuller understanding of labour market changes.

DIFFERENTIAL UNEMPLOYMENT RATES IN THE UK

Female-Male Differential

For the UK the registered unemployment rate for males has been greater than the female rate throughout the post-second world war period, with the exception of 1951-2 when the female rate was greater, and 1955 when the rates were equal. Table 8.1 summarises the sex differential by expressing the female rate as a fraction of the male rate. This stood at 0.67 in 1948 and increased to 1.0 in 1955. Thereafter it declined, gradually until the mid-1960s, and dramatically in the late 1960s. During the early 1970s the female rate was less than one-third of the male rate, but after 1974 the unemployment situation deteriorated rapidly for females so that by 1980 the ratio was back to its 1948 level. During 1981-2 total unemployment increased rapidly and, although there was a relative improvement in the female rate, the ratio of female

to male unemployment was still almost twice as high in the early 1980s
as it had been a decade earlier.

For the period 1977-8 the incremental differential was actually
negative, reflecting a marginal deterioration in the female rate that
was actually accompanied by a marginal improvement in the male
rate.

Another method of comparing the differential impact of unemployment on males and females is to compare changes in the sex
composition of total unemployment with similar changes in the
composition of the labour force, as shown in columns 2 and 3 of Table
8.1. At the beginning of the period female unemployment accounted
for about one-quarter of all unemployment in the UK. Although this

Table 8.1: *Female Employment and Unemployment, UK*

Year	Ratio of female to male unemployment rate (1)	Females as a % of total labour force[1] (2)	Female unemployment as a % of total unemployment (3)
1948	0.67	33.5	24.7
1950	0.82	33.8	29.3
1955	1.00	35.1	35.9
1960	0.68	35.5	27.7
1965	0.56	36.3	24.2
1970	0.30	37.7	15.3
1974	0.32	39.5	17.0
1975	0.41	39.6	21.2
1979	0.64	41.0	30.7
1980	0.66	41.1	31.3
1981	0.59	40.6	28.9
1982	0.59	40.9	28.9

Note: [1] *Labour force* = total employees (both employed and unemployed) at mid-year.
Source: Department of Employment, *Employment Gazette*, various issues.

share increased until 1955, thereafter it declined and during the period
1968-74 accounted for only 16-17 per cent. There was a marked
increase in the female share in 1975 and this continued until 1980 when
females accounted for about 31 per cent of the total, although this
share declined a couple of percentage points over the next two years.
Taking the period as a whole, the female share of total unemployment
increased by 4-5 per cent compared with a 7 per cent shift in the
composition of the labour force in favour of females. However, over the
shorter period 1974 to 1981, the female share of total unemployment
increased from 17 per cent to about 29 per cent compared with only a 1
percentage point change in the composition of the labour force.

Therefore, although there has been a dramatic increase in female
unemployment since the mid-1970s, the rate in 1982 was still only two-
thirds that of males. Furthermore, despite the not inconsiderable

growth in the female labour force, in 1981–2 females accounted for the same proportion of total unemployment as they did in 1950, though this was somewhat smaller than what it had been in 1955.

Age Differentials

Unemployment rates by age are not available for years prior to 1975 because data on employment by age have not been available.[1] However, Table 8.2 shows rates by age for January and July for Great Britain for the period 1975–82. Two points stand out clearly from this table. First, as age increases, unemployment rates decline for all groups down to, and including, the 45–54 group. For the two oldest groups shown rates increase, particularly for those over 60. Second, although the rate for the under 18 age group is much higher than the overall rate, the rate for the under 18s rises dramatically in July of each year. This is caused by the flow of school leavers into the stock of unemployed each summer, and can be seen more clearly in Table 8.3 which shows unemployment age relativities for selected groups. For example, over the seven-year period 1976–82 the relative rate for the under 18s more than doubled between January and July in three years, and almost doubled in another two. However, despite the large seasonal increase in July of each year, the January rate for the under 18 group has shown no tendency to increase relative to the overall rate; if anything it has exhibited a relative decline. Thus the high rates of teenage unemployment since 1978 would seem to be attributable to the increase in the overall rate.

For the period as a whole, the under 18 unemployment rate was more than twice the overall rate, while the relativity for the 45–54 age group was only 0.5–0.6. That for the over 60s showed greater variability, ranging from 1.1–1.5.

Concentration on relative rates, and changes in these, can be misleading. As mentioned above, Table 8.3 suggests that there has not been a relative deterioration in the under 18 rate since the mid-1970s. However, between 1976 and 1982 the incremental teenage relativity, measured from January to January, was greater than one in five of the six years, and in four of those years unemployment was increasing. Thus, although teenagers continued to take a disproportionately large share of increases in unemployment, this share was below its average share, and the latter declined.

Minority Unemployment

The DE publishes a quarterly count of unemployment among racial minorities, but does not publish minority rates because the size of the minority labour force is not known. However, according to Smith,[2] in the early 1960s the minority unemployment rate was three to four times as high as the white rate, but thereafter declined as newly-arrived immigrants became absorbed into the labour force. At the time of the 1971 Census, the male minority rate was 6.8 per cent compared

Table 8.2: *Unemployment Rates By Age, Great Britain, 1975–82*

Age group	1975 July	1976 Jan.	1976 July	1977 Jan.	1977 July	1978 Jan.	1978 July	1979 Jan.	1979 July	1980 Jan.	1980 July	1981 Jan.	1981 July	1982 Jan.	1982 July
Under 18	12.2	12.1	26.3	13.5	29.0	14.4	27.1	11.3	23.4	11.0	31.5	19.2	30.8	22.6	33.4
18–19	8.0	9.7	9.9	10.3	11.1	11.2	11.3	10.4	10.1	10.5	13.4	17.2	19.7	22.9	24.1
20–24	5.2	8.0	7.9	8.8	8.7	9.4	8.1	8.6	7.5	8.9	10.1	15.0	16.4	18.8	18.3
25–34	3.8	5.2	5.0	5.7	5.5	6.1	5.2	5.7	4.7	5.7	6.2	9.7	10.8	12.5	12.0
35–44	2.7	3.7	3.6	4.1	3.9	4.2	3.6	3.8	3.2	3.8	4.2	6.6	7.4	8.6	8.5
45–54	2.4	3.3	3.2	3.6	3.5	3.8	3.5	3.7	3.3	3.7	4.1	6.2	7.0	8.0	8.0
55–59	3.0	3.8	3.8	4.2	4.2	4.4	4.2	4.4	4.2	4.7	5.0	7.2	8.4	9.7	9.9
60 and over	5.4	6.8	6.8	7.4	6.9	8.1	7.6	8.9	8.1	8.7	9.2	12.2	13.8	15.0	14.8
All ages	4.5	5.3	6.0	5.9	6.6	6.3	6.4	5.9	5.9	6.0	7.7	10.0	11.8	12.7	13.2

Source: Department of Employment, *Employment Gazette*, January 1983, Table 2.15. and earlier issues.

Table 8.3: *Unemployment-Age Relativities, Great Britain, 1975–82*

Age group	1975 July	1976 Jan.	1976 July	1977 Jan.	1977 July	1978 Jan.	1978 July	1979 Jan.	1979 July	1980 Jan.	1980 July	1981 Jan.	1981 July	1982 Jan.	1982 July
Under 18	2.71	2.28	4.44	2.23	4.51	2.29	4.23	1.92	3.97	1.83	4.09	1.92	2.61	1.78	2.53
18–19	1.78	1.83	1.68	1.73	1.71	1.78	1.77	1.76	1.71	1.75	1.74	1.72	1.67	1.80	1.83
45–54	0.53	0.62	0.64	0.60	0.54	0.60	0.55	0.63	0.56	0.62	0.53	0.62	0.59	0.63	0.61
60 and over	1.20	1.28	1.15	1.23	1.06	1.29	1.19	1.51	1.37	1.45	1.19	1.22	1.17	1.18	1.12

Source: Derived from Table 8.2.

with 5.4 per cent for all men. For women the differential was much greater,—9.1 per cent compared with 4.9 per cent. Similarly, minority youths experienced much higher rates,—the rate for West Indian male youths being 20 per cent compared with only 9 per cent for their white counterparts. The National Dwelling and Housing Survey estimated the minority rate to be 9.6 per cent in the Autumn of 1977, when the rate for the working population at large stood at 5.2 per cent. Although this survey is not directly comparable with the Census, minorities clearly suffered a substantial relative increase in unemployment between 1971 and 1977, a trend confirmed by the quarterly figures of the DE which show that minority unemployment increased its share of total unemployment from 2.1 per cent in May 1971 to 3.7 per cent in November 1977.

Analysis of the DE figures since 1970 shows that during periods of rising unemployment the increase in minority unemployment is greater than the increase in total unemployment. For example, although total unemployment more than doubled between May 1975 and August 1976, minority unemployment quadrupled, increasing as a percentage of total unemployment, and in August 1982 it stood at 4.2 per cent.

DIFFERENTIAL UNEMPLOYMENT RATES IN THE US

Table 8.4 summarises the experience of high incidence groups over the period 1952–82.

The Female–Male Differential

In direct contrast to the UK, the female rate has been above the male rate in all years but two, 1958 and 1982. In the former year the rates were equal; in the latter the traditional differential was reversed. This was the final outcome of a gradual trend decline in the differential from the late 1960s, exacerbated by the deep recession of 1980–2. This narrowing of the sex differential in recent years contrasts markedly with the movement in the UK which has been in the opposite direction; its causes are discussed below.

Teenage Unemployment

Although there is a cyclical tendency for teenage unemployment to fall relative to total unemployment as the latter rises, and vice versa, there has also been a trend increase in the teenage relativity. Furthermore, although it is not shown, there have only been five years in the 30-year period covered by the table in which the incremental relativity has been less than one, or negative.

Relatively speaking, teenage unemployment is higher in the US than in the UK, and, as in the UK, there has been an improvement in the relativity in the post-1979 economic downturn. However, taking the

Table 8.4: *US Unemployment Rates for High-Incidence Groups, and Comparable Low-Incidence Groups, 1952–82*

Year	Overall rate	Teenage rate (16–19)	Teenage relativity	Male rate	Female rate	Ratio Female to male rate	White rate	Black rate	Ratio Black to white rate
1952	3.0	8.5	2.8	2.8	3.6	1.3	2.8	5.4	1.9
1953	2.9	7.6	2.6	2.8	3.3	1.2	2.7	4.5	1.7
1954	5.5	11.8	2.1	5.3	6.0	1.1	5.0	9.9	2.0
1955	4.4	11.0	2.5	4.2	4.9	1.2	3.9	8.7	2.2
1956	4.1	11.1	2.7	3.8	4.8	1.3	3.6	8.3	2.3
1957	4.3	11.6	2.7	4.1	4.7	1.1	3.8	7.9	2.1
1958	6.8	15.9	2.3	6.8	6.8	1.0	6.1	12.6	2.1
1959	5.5	14.6	2.7	5.2	5.9	1.1	4.8	10.7	2.2
1960	5.5	14.7	2.7	5.4	5.9	1.1	4.9	10.2	2.1
1961	6.7	16.8	2.5	6.4	7.2	1.1	6.0	12.4	2.1
1962	5.5	14.6	2.7	5.2	6.2	1.2	4.9	10.9	2.2
1963	5.7	17.2	3.0	5.2	6.5	1.3	5.0	10.8	2.2
1964	5.2	16.2	3.1	4.6	6.2	1.3	4.6	9.6	2.1
1965	4.5	15.3	3.4	4.0	5.5	1.4	4.1	8.1	2.0
1966	3.8	12.7	3.3	3.2	4.8	1.5	3.3	7.3	2.2
1967	3.8	12.9	3.4	3.1	5.2	1.7	3.4	7.4	2.2
1968	3.6	12.7	3.5	2.9	4.8	1.7	3.2	6.7	2.1
1969	3.5	12.2	3.5	2.8	4.7	1.7	3.1	6.4	2.1
1970	4.9	15.3	3.1	4.4	5.9	1.3	4.5	8.2	1.8
1971	5.9	15.9	2.7	5.3	6.9	1.3	5.4	9.9	1.8
1972	5.6	16.2	2.9	5.0	6.6	1.3	5.0	10.0	2.0
1973	4.9	14.5	3.0	4.2	6.0	1.4	4.3	9.0	2.1
1974	5.6	16.0	2.9	4.9	6.7	1.4	5.0	9.9	2.0
1975	8.5	19.9	2.3	7.9	9.3	1.2	7.8	13.8	1.8
1976	7.7	19.0	2.5	7.1	8.6	1.2	7.0	13.1	1.9
1977	7.0	17.7	2.5	6.3	8.2	1.3	6.2	13.1	2.1
1978	6.0	16.3	2.7	5.3	7.2	1.4	5.2	11.9	2.3
1979	6.8	16.1	2.8	5.1	6.8	1.3	5.1	11.3	2.2
1980	7.1	20.0	2.8	6.9	7.4	1.1	6.3	13.1	2.1
1981	7.6	19.6	2.6	7.4	7.9	1.1	6.7	14.2	2.1
1982	9.7	23.2	2.4	9.9	9.4	0.9	8.6	17.5*	2.0

*The black rate is for August 1982.

Sources: For data up to 1981, the annual *Employment and Training Report of the President*; for 1982, various issues of *Monthly Labor Review*, and *Employment and Earnings*.

period 1979–82 as a whole, the incremental relativity was 1.8, indicating that during the latest recession the teenage labour force continued to suffer disproportionately from the increase in unemployment.

Black-White Differential
Much has been written about the stubborn stability of the black unemployment rate at about twice the white level. The last column of Table 8.4 bears out this stability. While it is also generally believed that bad times are especially difficult for blacks, the simple black–white ratio contradicts this view. Since 1971 the only time the ratio dipped below 2.0 was in the recession years 1975–76; in 1982 the ratio was 0.2 points below that of 1979, the last year of relatively low unemployment.

Gilroy[3] explains this contradiction by reference to the incremental black–white unemployment differential. In only five of the thirty years of changing rates was the incremental differential less than one, and in four of those years it was negative, indicating that the black and white rates moved in opposite directions.

UNEMPLOYMENT FLOWS

Flows into and out of unemployment provide us with descriptive explanations of the high unemployment rate for particular groups. The labour market phenomena (e.g. quits, new entries, withdrawals, etc.) that give rise to these flows were discussed briefly in Chapter 1, and summarised in Figure 1.1. Clearly the magnitude and direction of these flows between the three different labour market states, employment (E), unemployment (U), and not in the labour force (N), will affect the level and rate of unemployment (u). Figure 8.1 depicts these flows schematically.

If the members of a particular group are more prone to change their labour force (L) status, this will be reflected in the flows themselves. It might also lead to an increase in the frequency of unemployment spells for members of that group. Likewise, changes in the rates of flow into and out of unemployment might be associated with changes in the average duration of unemployment. Therefore, in this section we not only look at the direction (and magnitude) of flows for the high incidence groups, we also examine whether there are any marked differences between these groups in the frequency and duration of unemployment spells.

Direction of Flows
The flows depicted in Figure 8.1 exhaust the possibility of unemployment flows. But note that two of these flows, although they do not pass through unemployment, nevertheless affect the unemployment rate. These are the flows from N direct to E, and vice versa.

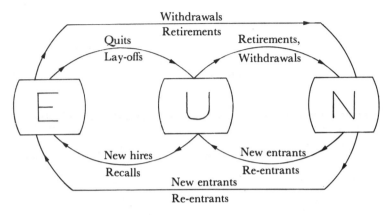

Figure 8.1: *Flows Affecting Unemployment*

The effects of the flows involving unemployment on the unemployment rate, U/L, are obvious, since they affect the numerator and/or denominator of the fraction directly. Thus a movement from employment to unemployment raises the numerator, and a movement from N to U, indicating that a non-working individual satisfies the conditions of unemployment by becoming ready, willing, able and actively in search of work, raises the numerator and denominator by the same absolute amount, thereby also raising the unemployment rate (u). Similarly, a movement from U to E lowers the numerator, and a flow from U to N reduces numerator and denominator equally, both movements lowering the unemployment rate, the decline being smaller in the latter case.

But the effect on the unemployment rate of the two flows that bypass unemployment are a little less obvious. The unemployment rate, u, is given by:

$$u = \frac{U}{L}$$

which can be re-written

$$u = 1 - \frac{E}{L}$$

When written in this form we see that a movement from N to E raises both the numerator and denominator of the fraction, E/L, by the same amount, causing the fraction to increase and the unemployment rate to fall. Similarly, a movement from E to N lowers both E and L by the same amount, reduces the fraction E/L, and causes u to rise. Thus movements from E to N, and vice versa, even though they leave U unchanged, exert an influence on u through their effect on L. Of course, if such movements do not bypass U, but also result in a period of time spent in unemployment, then the effect on the rate will be reinforced in the case of movements out of the labour force, and more than offset in the case of movements into the labour force.

In normal times, when the labour market is in some sort of equilibrium, with neither cyclical expansion nor contraction, a higher than average rate of female flow from employment to non-labour force status, coupled with a higher return flow, can help explain the relatively higher female unemployment rate in the US. With the demands of home competing with those of the labour market, women—and particularly married women—often leave jobs and directly assume home duties. As our flow discussion indicates, this outward movement will, in itself, raise the unemployment rate. But in an equilibrium situation this outflow will be matched by a similar inflow, cancelling out the unemployment rate effect. However, even when the inflow into employment just completely offsets the outflow those returning to the labour force will probably spend some time unemployed and searching for a job before they actually find one. Thus, other things being equal, females will experience a higher rate of unemployment than males.

Although this movement between employment and home can help explain the sex differential in the US, it cannot do so for the UK. The reason for this is quite simple. Those females who return to the labour force in the US, and whose employment is preceded by a period of search, will be included in the survey approach to the measurement of unemployment, but not necessarily in the registration approach. Indeed, given the operation of the National Insurance system in the UK, which prior to 1977 allowed married women to opt out of paying the full contribution—and forgo any entitlement to unemployment benefit—it is unlikely that such women would register: instead they would constitute part of the unregistered unemployed.

Before women began entering the labour force in large numbers at the beginning of the post-war period, their labour force behaviour was like that of older (US) workers today. If they were not at work they tended not to be in the labour force, a behaviour pattern which leads to a very low unemployment rate. (In the US the unemployment rate for men over 65 in August 1982, for example, was 3.9 per cent). The typical married woman in pre-war days did not look for work, she went straight from home to work if a job suited her. Similarly, when she lost or voluntarily left her job she stayed at home without experiencing much unemployment. In other words, the unemployment base for women was low, and the swings in the rate were less than if they had passed into and out of unemployment. All of this has changed over the years as the participation rate for married females has risen, and they have become more strongly attached to the labour force.

During a cyclical recession, those women who are least strongly attached will 'return home' on losing their jobs. Since during a recession this outflow will tend to be greater than the inflow of re-entrants, the female rate will tend to rise. But this increase in the female rate will not be as great as for men who, when they lose their jobs, are more likely to continue to search for others from within the labour force. Thus the movement of women in recession from E to N instead of from E to U, as is generally the case for men, compresses the sex differential.[4] Even in the most severe recession, this narrowing will occur unless the flow of *additional* females into the labour force, in response to the loss of jobs by husbands, is sufficient to offset the flow of *discouraged* females. Once the economy strengthens again, the differential will tend to widen as women leave home and engage in job search before becoming absorbed back into employment.

The negative features of labour force flows for teenagers and for blacks are even more pronounced than for women, as one might expect considering their much higher unemployment rates. Among teenagers, as among women, there is a strong movement from employment to non-participation, and back again. But even more serious, in terms of its effect on unemployment, is the marked tendency of teenagers to lose or quit their jobs.[5] Black teenagers, in addition to possessing these negative labour force characteristics, face the added problem of not being able to find jobs as easily as their white counterparts. Thus they suffer from a relatively sluggish flow from unemployment into employment. For blacks in general, the principal source of their high unemployment is their weak hold on jobs which is reflected in a higher rate of flow from employment to unemployment. For example, in a 1979 survey of racial minorities in the UK Smith[6] found that whereas 31 per cent of male West Indians and 29 per cent of male Asians (excluding Pakistanis) had been dismissed from their last job, the corresponding proportion for white males was only 19 per cent.

FREQUENCY AND DURATION OF SPELLS

The measured unemployment rate is a function of the duration of spells of unemployment and the frequency of these spells. The longer the duration of a particular spell the greater the probability that the unemployed worker will be included in the count, because the more likely he is to be unemployed on the day or during the week of the count. Certainly, the adverse social and political impact of unemployment will depend to some degree on the extent to which it is the result of long duration or frequent spells. For example, with a labour force of 120 million workers, the same 8.3 per cent unemployment would be recorded if 10 million people were out of work for the whole year, or if 10 million different workers were unemployed each month. In the latter situation the whole workforce would share the burden of unemployment equally, each experiencing an average spell lasting one month. Most people would agree that such a situation, in which all workers experience a relatively short period of unemployment, constitutes a less serious social problem than a situation in which a small proportion of workers experience long duration unemployment.

In Table 8.5 are some fragmentary data on duration and number of spells for the high-incidence groups in the US. Although the data for spells and duration are for different periods, the corresponding rate is given for each period. The pattern is clear—except for blacks, unemployment for high-incidence groups is characterised by high labour force turnover, with frequent short spells of unemployment. In fact, the average duration of unemployment tends to be inversely related to the unemployment rate.

Table 8.5: *US Unemployment Rate, Duration and Spells White Males and High-Incidence Groups*

Group	Unemployment[1] Rate (August 1982)	Mean Duration[2] in Weeks (August 1982)	Number of[3] Spells per Year (1975)	Unemployment[4] Rate (1975)
White males 35–44	6.4	21.6	0.24	4.5
Females	9.5	12.9	0.35	9.3
Teenagers	23.8	10.0	0.96	19.9
Blacks	19.1	17.2	0.45	13.8
Whites	8.7	15.2	0.30	7.8

Sources: [1] *Monthly Labor Review.*

[2] *Employment and Earnings*, September 1982.

[3] Derived from Ingrid Rima, *Labor Markets, Wages and Employment* (New York: Norton, 1981), p. 252, Table 13-15.

[4] *Monthly Labor Review.*

For white males, a very low-incidence group, there is a bias towards relatively few people being unemployed for a very long time. For females and teenagers, the pattern is for relatively short duration coupled with a high frequency of spells. When compared with whites, blacks suffer both a higher duration and a greater frequency of spells. This high frequency of spells creates an independent source of high unemployment for blacks. Betsey[7] finds that a prior spell of unemployment among blacks lengthens the duration of future unemployment for them. Similarly, Osterman[8] finds that for black teenagers there is a pronounced effect of unemployment spells in one period increasing the probability of unemployment in a later period. It is not surprising that this effect is much stronger among black adults than white adults since relatively more black adult workers will be in the same unskilled occupational class as they were in when they were teenagers.

As for the important issue of the hardship of unemployment, the data do not yield conclusive results. For the low-incidence groups, the period of unemployment is long, but not many people are involved.

For the high-incidence groups, the problems of unemployment would not be so serious if the turnovers were of different people. That is, if the higher rates are the result of relatively large numbers of different people experiencing short periods of unemployment.

CAUSES OF HIGH UNEMPLOYMENT AMONG BLACKS IN US

In the previous section we examined the sources of high-incidence unemployment from a mechanistic point of view, tracing the dominant labour market flows which result in high rates for particular groups. In this section we study the more fundamental economic causes of this high unemployment. Our focus will be on the high rate for blacks. There are two reasons for this emphasis: first their unemployment, compared with other high-incidence groups, imposes a more serious hardship on them; secondly, we have touched upon the underlying causes of the high unemployment of women and teenagers without regard to race, the former in the previous section on labour market flows, and the latter in Chapter 5 on minimum wages.

It is usually argued that high black unemployment poses the most serious unemployment problem of all. This is not because the black rate is the highest—the teenage rate is higher—but because black unemployment has the greatest impact on family income.[9] Before discussing the cause of high black unemployment in general, we first analyse the basis of the high black teenage unemployment rate.

Unemployment among Black Teenagers
Regardless of race, the teenage unemployment rate is very high, but the black rate, at 47.4 per cent in August 1982,[10] was 2.3 times as high as the white teenage rate of 20.6 per cent. This ratio is somewhat above the customary overall black-white unemployment ratio of 2.0, but not that much above it as to warrant special consideration of high black teenage unemployment.

The big difference between teenagers and the work force as a whole lies in their skill composition. An important element in the overall racial difference is the heavier concentration of blacks in the unskilled categories which have high unemployment rates. In August 1982, non-farm labourers formed 7.6 per cent of the black labour force and 4.7 per cent of the white; the corresponding percentages for service workers were 23.3 and 12.7 per cent, respectively. The unemployment rate for these labourers was 14.7 per cent, while that for service workers was 11.2 per cent. But teenage workers tend to be predominantly unskilled for both blacks and whites. In fact, we argued in Chapter 5 that we could treat them all as unskilled with little distortion of reality. Thus skill composition has little influence on the higher black teenage rate.

What then is the reason for the higher black teenage rate? We noted that the principal flow difference between the races for young workers is the longer period black youths are unemployed before becoming employed. Thus, as Ehrenberg and Smith[11] point out in their analytical text, the basic question is why blacks experience greater difficulty finding jobs than whites, and they provide a comprehensive list of conventional explanations of this phenomenon. First, they offer explanations based on job search methods—white teenagers are more likely to have more personal contacts who can help them find jobs located in areas outside of central cities, where more casual jobs are located. This admittedly contributes to higher black unemployment but, as Ehrenberg and Smith note, it does not explain much of the inter-racial difference.

Next, they offer what they call supply and demand factors. For example, there is the better education that whites receive. But if, as we have argued, all teenage employment tends to be unskilled, educational attainment should not have any effect unless it is used as a screening device. The growth of income maintenance programmes is also cited as a factor contributing to the relatively high black teenage rate. However, it is not obvious why this should be since the same welfare alternative to low-paid work is available to whites, and in any case the alternative of non-work income would reduce both labour force and unemployment for both groups if the movement is from unemployment rather than from employment to non-participation.

Increases in the minimum wage are also cited as a cause of relatively high unemployment for black teenagers, and this might well be true. But, as we argued in Chapter 5, if a (high) minimum affects black teenagers more adversely than whites, this points to discrimination as the basis of higher unemployment for blacks, especially teenagers. If a lower rate is required for the competitive employment of blacks, with the same productivity as whites, we have nothing more than an application of Becker's[12] basic discrimination model, in which employers' negative attitudes towards employing blacks can only be offset by a reduction in the black wage.

Similarly, if differential population growth and population shifts are a cause of the higher black teenage rate, they reflect the presence of labour market discrimination. If there were no discrimination, the relative growth in the black teenage population should have no effect on relative rates; at any time the rates should be equal regardless of their size. An example will serve to illustrate this. If the teenage labour force consists of 300 white workers and there are 270 jobs available, the unemployment rate would be 10 per cent if the problems associated with search, etc. are ignored. If, instead, the labour force consists of 200 blacks and 100 whites, the unemployment rate for each group would still be 10 per cent assuming that there are 270 jobs available and that each worker is equally productive and there is no discrimination in employment. If the size of the labour force doubles, then both rates would still be 10 per cent, assuming that the number of jobs also doubles and the productivity and discrimination assumptions still hold. If discrimination occurs in favour of whites, then more white workers would be employed and fewer blacks, and as a consequence the white unemployment rate would fall below 10 per cent and the black rate rise above it. But as long as the white rate is above its frictional–structural level, discrimination does not raise the overall rate, it merely causes unemployment to be redistributed.

Similarly, a reduction in the armed forces, with a larger percentage of black teenagers than whites flowing from the services into the labour force, has the same effect as does relative growth in the black population on the supply of black teenagers. But again, if there is no discrimination, this relative increase in black labour supply should not be a factor in raising the relative rate of black teenage unemployment.

The long-term movement of black youths from marginal farm labour in the South, where they were counted as employed even if they were in disguised unemployment—their marginal contribution to output being zero—to the North is, however, a factor raising the unemployment rate for black youths.[13] But if there was no racial discrimination in the unemployment of teenagers before this migration, the overall black teenage rate would have been lower, because of their over-reliance on employment in agriculture, a sector with little measured unemployment. The migration of black youths to the North would then raise the black teenage unemployment rate to the white level; without discrimination there is no reason for the flow of blacks into the non-farm North to raise the black rate *above* the white level.

In summary, except for the job search advantages of whites, and the fact that more jobs are usually held by teenagers in areas relatively more populated by whites, both of which contribute only marginally to the lower unemployment rate for whites, discrimination is the main source of higher black teenage unemployment. Demographic changes and shifts which have increased the relative number of black youths in the unskilled labour market would not, in themselves, contribute to higher black unemployment in the absence of employment discrimination. The policy implication for reducing this inter-racial difference is not better training for blacks, although training for adult employment certainly has its merits, but stricter application of anti-discrimination laws, which in the past have been more rigorously applied to those jobs employing educated and trained manpower to the neglect and disadvantage of unskilled black youths.

Black Unemployment in General

The main difference between the factors that influence the higher unemployment of blacks in general, or adult blacks, from those that affect teenage blacks lies in the lower skill-mix of the black workforce compared to that of the white. While we have assumed that all teenage labour is unskilled, for adults we must recognise that this is certainly not the case. Since unemployment rates for the unskilled are substantially higher than for the skilled, especially during recessions, the path of causation runs from the higher rate for the unskilled, to the lower skill-mix of blacks, to their higher unemployment rates.

While the lower skill-mix for blacks is an important factor, we do not mean to imply that it is the only cause of higher black rates. In August 1982, when the overall unemployment rate was 9.8 per cent, the rate for operatives was 16.7 per cent; and for transport operatives 12.3 per cent; for non-farm labourers 14.7 per cent, and for service workers 11.2 per cent. Recall that the overall black rate was 17.5 per cent. Thus, while the heavy concentration of blacks in these lesser skilled jobs (48.4 per cent of the black workforce compared with 32.2 per cent of the white) can partly explain their higher unemployment rate, there must be other factors since, as these rates indicate, if all blacks were in lower skilled jobs, and concentration was the sole explanation of the higher black rate, the rate would have been lower than that actually observed, even though higher than the white rate.

Before looking into these other causes, we should at least note the reasons for the higher rates for unskilled workers, regardless of race. Reder[14] attributes the widening between the unskilled–skilled rate during recessions mainly to the downward occupational flexibility of skilled workers, while Oi[15] uses the human capital approach in arguing that employers tend to retain their skilled workers, in whose training they have invested. In a similar vein, and in an argument which explains the tendency for the unskilled unemployment rate to be higher in all phases of the cycle, Taylor[16] points to the tendency for firms to hoard skilled workers. With reference to the theory of implicit contracts, Azariadis[17] claims that higher-wage workers are likely to enter into implicit wage contracts that will increase the likelihood of their job security.

Related to the inter-racial skill differences, some analysts claim that the higher rates for blacks result from their lower level of education.[18] Apart from quality differences which are difficult to measure, this argument is weakened by the trend towards equality in schooling levels. While in 1952, median years of school completed for whites in the labour force was 12.2 years, and for blacks only 9.6 years, by 1980 the gap had narrowed considerably, with whites completing 12.7 years of schooling and blacks 12.4 years.

Another explanation of the higher black unemployment rate relates to the dual labour market theory and the presence of relatively large numbers of blacks in the secondary labour market. According to the dualist argument, the dual market forms what Wachter[19] calls a new type of structural unemployment. Forced into unsatisfactory jobs on a more or less permanent basis, with no opportunity to qualify for the better ones despite their ability to perform the duties attached to these jobs, or to develop the skills to do so, workers develop negative work attitudes which raise even higher the barriers that keep them in the secondary market. A churning effect arises in which the workers in the secondary market obtain, but then quit or lose, unsatisfactory jobs. Thus turnover rises as a result of both job leaving and job losing, as workers become dissatisfied with jobs which offer little prospect of advancement and are often of a temporary or casual nature.

Structural unemployment conventionally refers to the inability of unemployed workers to fill job openings because of inadequate skill development. The pattern has unfilled high-level job openings and unemployed untrained workers. But in Wachter's 'new structuralism', which is a consequence of the dual labour market, low-level jobs are open, or frequently available. Workers trained beyond the low-level skill requirements of these jobs, but who are excluded from the primary market, choose not to take them, or remain in them, as evidenced by high turnover rates. In fact, as was pointed out in Chapter 3, the official criterion of unemployment status legitimates this refusal to hold inferior jobs. Those workers who do not accept available jobs that are below their skill qualifications and their previous employment experience are classified as unemployed.

High turnover rates for blacks are an important contributory factor to their high unemployment, and their strong participation in secondary-market type jobs, in which turnover is high, provides the link between high turnover and high unemployment for this group.

In recent years there have been many studies testing the presence of dual, separated labour markets.[20] At one extreme, denying market segmentation, Marston[21] argues that worker characteristics, and not job composition, relegate workers to the lower end of the occupational hierarchy. At the other extreme, Rumberger and Carnoy[22] find little job mobility between occupational sectors, with education an ineffective element in upward mobility. They find this pattern stronger for blacks.

The issue of whether there is or is not a segmented labour market really relates to the policy question of how to reduce black unemployment, rather than to the cause of their high unemployment rate. Put simply, if labour markets are not truly segmented, then the strong presence of black workers in bad jobs could be reduced by providing them with more education and training, while if there is a dual labour market the policy prescription is for the development of more of the better jobs. But in the latter case, discrimination must play an important part in the relatively large number of blacks in secondary jobs, otherwise why are they at the end of the queue for the primary ones? Furthermore, the movement towards equality in inter-racial educational levels makes discrimination a prime cause of black occupancy of unstable jobs.

Discrimination again appears as the basis for Gilman's[23] well-known study of inter-regional differences in racial unemployment patterns. Considering that racial discrimination is usually thought to be stronger in the South, at least back in 1965 when Gilman was writing, it might seem surprising that he found less differences in unemployment by race in the South than in the North. He attributes this finding to the greater wage flexibility in the South. In other words, Gilman's argument is exactly analogous to the view that a higher minimum wage leads to higher unemployment since the wage rigidity that it introduces does not allow the downward movement in black wages which, according to Becker's discrimination model, is necessary if black employment is to be increased. We are not suggesting that either Becker or Gilman recommended the policy prescription of lower wages for blacks to accommodate discrimination which handicaps their employment opportunities; they were merely describing a discriminatory situation. What is needed to reduce black unemployment is an improvement in education and training, the development of a greater demand for primary jobs—if segmentation is a realistic description of the labour market—and most of all, more rigorous application of anti-discrimination laws and practices for all jobs, those well down the occupational ladder as well as those at the top rungs where this policy is currently focused.

COMPARING UNEMPLOYMENT RATES IN RECESSIONS[24]

There is a tendency when the unemployment rate is high to minimise its significance, particularly by arguing that the rising rate between cyclical troughs is attributable to the demographic shifts in the labour force to high-incidence groups.[25] This argument holds that if the shift had not occurred unemployment would be lower, the impact of shift being measured by standardising the demographic distribution, by sex, age or race, for the same point in different cycles.

Although the basis of the argument, that there has been a demographic shift to high-incidence groups, is sound, its logic is weak, and its method of measurement faulty. For example, in the US the teenage labour force grew from 7.3 per cent of the overall labour force in 1960, to 9.0 per cent in August 1982, an increase of 23 per cent in the teenage share of the working population. By standardising the demographic distribution—that is, by calculating what the unemployment rate would have been had there been no demographic shift—the conventional method of measuring the effect of a demographic shift does take into account rising rates for higher incidence groups and, correctly, does not attribute the increase in these rates to the demographic shift itself.[26] But by attributing all of the remaining difference between the actual rate and the standardised rate to the shift, it exaggerates the impact of the shift on the overall unemployment rate.

This overstatement of the impact of the demographic shift on overall unemployment arises because the demand-deficient component of unemployment is ignored. To demonstrate this shortcoming, consider the extreme case in which the unemployment rate for each demographic group remains constant, but from one cycle trough to another there is a labour force shift to a high-incidence group—say, teenagers. Then, the conventional method of measuring the impact of the shift on the unemployment rate would attribute all of the increase in unemployment to the relative increase in the labour force share of teenagers, ignoring the possibility of a differential impact of demand-deficient unemployment on this group.

A simple numerical example will illuminate this point. Assume that the unemployment rate for teenagers is constant at 20 per cent in both periods, that a constant unemployment rate of 10 per cent holds for the rest of the population, and that teenagers comprise 5 per cent of the labour force at the first cyclical trough, and 10 per cent at the second. Overall unemployment would rise from 10.5 to 11.0 per cent, and the conventional method of measuring the impact of differential shift on the unemployment rate would attribute all of the 0.5 per cent increase to the shift towards teenagers. But if the 10 per cent rate for the rest of the population is above the frictional-structural level for this 'all others' group,[27] and if a higher teenage frictional-structural rate is ruled out, we can conclude that none of the higher unemployment rate is attributable to the demographic shift. The argument is similar to that advanced above in the discussion on higher rates for black teenagers.

Expressed strongly, if there are no teenagers at all, the overall unemployment rate would be just as high as is actually recorded in the second period, again abstracting from demographic differentials in frictional-structural unemployment rates. This conclusion follows since, with the unemployment rate above the frictional-structural level for the 'all others' group, any increase in their number would simply add to their demand-deficient unemployment. Alternatively, if there is no demographic shift, total unemployment would be the same in the second period as is actually reported. In effect, the conventional method does more than omit the demand-deficient component of unemployment in its calculations; it implicitly denies its presence.

Of course, if the frictional-structural component of the teenage group is relatively high, then the shift will be a factor in raising the overall unemployment rate. But the deeper the recession's trough, the less likely are frictional-structural elements to be a relatively important component of unemployment, and in any case, the main point here is that the conventional method of adjusting for the demographic shift yields an inadequate measure of its impact on unemployment.

SUMMARY

In the UK, female unemployment has increased relative to male unemployment since about 1970, while in the US the trend has been in the opposite direction. However, in the UK the female-male differential was still only about 0.6 in 1982 compared with 0.9 in the US—although the ratios would be much closer together if UK unemployment included the unregistered unemployed.

The high teenage unemployment rate in the UK over the last decade is a reflection of the general unemployment problem, although the teenage relativity declined somewhat after 1978. Nevertheless teenage unemployment in the UK in 1982 was not such a serious problem as in the US, despite the marked decline in the teenage relativity that occurred in the US after the late 1960s. As noted earlier (Chapter 7), the high teenage rates recorded in the US reflect, in part, the greater movement between school or college and the labour force.

Unemployment *rates* by colour and racial minorities are not available for the UK but the data on *numbers* unemployed shows that the proportion of unemployment accounted for by racial minorities doubled between the early 1970s and early 1980s. In the US, the black-white unemployment differential is about 2:1, and even higher for black teenagers. Thus to be teenage and black during the summer of 1982 meant that one had no more than a 50 per cent chance of being employed.

It is difficult to escape the conclusion that discrimination plays a large part in explaining the high unemployment rates experienced by blacks in the US, though this is clearly reinforced by the existence of segmented labour markets and inferior training opportunities for black workers.

NOTES AND REFERENCES

1. 'Unemployment rates by age', *Department of Employment Gazette*, July 1977, pp.718–19.
2. David J. Smith, *Unemployment and Racial Minorities*, Policy Studies Institute, No. 594, February 1981. The information in this section draws heavily on Smith, pp.2–6.
3. Curtis Gilroy, 'Black and white unemployment: the dynamics of the differential', *Monthly Labor Review*, 97, February 1974, pp.36–47.
4. R. Christopher Lingle and Ethel B. Jones, 'Women's increasing unemployment: a cross-sectional view', *American Economic Review*, 65, May 1978, pp.84–9, find a strong effect of recession in compressing the female-male unemployment rate difference. They also note that the prime cause of the compression is the tendency we have cited for women to leave the labour force when they lose jobs, which they describe as 'masking the problem of the effect of economic fluctuations upon the continuity of women's labour market experience'.

5. The strong movement of teenagers from E to N stems from a basically similar reason for women's parallel movement—the presence of a competitive activity for market work—housework for women and school for teenagers. In fact, the movement of teenagers from jobs to school in recession, instead of into unemployment, has the same dampening effect on teenage unemployment in recessions. But this effect is weaker for teenagers since even larger numbers move from E to U.

 The presence of a socially acceptable alternative to work, i.e. school, certainly eases the psychological blow that results from job loss for teenagers. On this point see Sue Berryman, 'Youth unemployment and career education', *Public Policy* 26, Winter 1978, p.45.

6. Smith, *op. cit.*, p.155.

7. Charles Betsey, 'Difference in unemployment experience between blacks and whites', *American Economic Review*, 68, May 1978, pp.192-7.

8. Paul Osterman, 'Racial differentials in male youth unemployment', US Department of Labor, *Conference Report on Youth Unemployment: Its Measurement and Meaning* (Washington: US Government Printing Office, 1978), pp.145-79.

9. Unemployed, unmarried white women would, of course, also contribute significantly to their household income, but in August 1982 the rate for widowed, separated and divorced white women was 8.9 per cent, and for single white women 10.5 per cent. Both of these rates were much lower than the corresponding black rate.

10. The actual black teenage rate of 32.2 per cent was a little lower than the 'blacks and others' rate used in this chapter, but close enough to it to justify our interchangeable use of the two groups.

11. Ronald Ehrenberg and Robert Smith, *Modern Labor Economics* (Glencoe, Ill.: Scott, Foresman, Glenview, 1982), pp.444-5.

12. Gary Becker, *Economics of Discrimination* (Chicago: University of Chicago Press, 1971). Leigh and Rawlins express this discrimination as follows, 'Since there is not perfect substitution between white and black teenagers *in the eyes of employers*, black teenagers would be expected to be particularly adversely affected by rising minimum wages.' Duane Leigh and V. Lane Rawlins, 'On the stability of relative black-white unemployment', *Monthly Labor Review*, 96, May 1973, p.31. (Emphasis added.)

13. John Cogan, 'The decline in black teenage employment: 1950-1970', *American Economic Review*, 72, September 1982, pp.621-38, views this movement as a result of the decline in demand for unskilled farm labour and considers it a significant but by no means comprehensive determinant of the relative rise in black teenage unemployment.

14. Melvin Reder, 'The theory of occupational wage differentials,' *American Economic Review*, 65, December 1955, pp.883-52.

15. Walter Oi, 'Labour as a quasi-fixed factor', *Journal of Political Economy*, 70, December 1962, pp.538-53.

16. Jim Taylor, 'Hidden unemployment, hoarded labor, and the Phillips curve', *Southern Economic Journal* 27, July 1970, pp.1-16.

17. Costas Azariadis, 'On the incidence of unemployment', *Review of Economic Studies*, 43, February 1976, pp.113-25.

18. Curtis Gilroy, 'Investment in human capital and black-white unemployment,' *Monthly Labor Review*, 98, July 1975, pp.13-21, finds lower quality and quantity of black education a strong determinant of their concentration in cyclically sensitive (unskilled) jobs and consequently a cause of

their high unemployment. He also finds a strong link between education and on-the-job training which reinforces the tendency for blacks to receive less opportunity for skilled jobs.

19. Michael Wachter, 'Primary and secondary labor markets: a critique of the dual approach,' *Brookings Papers on Economic Activity*, 3, 1974, pp.637–80.

20. For a review of this literature, see Glen Cain, 'The challenge of segmented labor market theories to orthodox theory: a survey', *Journal of Economic Literature* XIV, December 1976, pp.1215–57.

21. Stephen Marston, 'Employment instability and high unemployment rates', *Brookings Papers on Economic Activity* 1, 1976, pp.169–203. One of his important worker characteristics determining unemployment and presence in secondary jobs is the level of education.

22. Russell Rumberger and Martin Carnoy, 'Segmentation in the US labour market: its effect on the mobility and earning of whites and blacks', *Cambridge Journal of Economics 4*, 1981, pp.117–32.

23. Harry Gilman, 'Economic discrimination and unemployment,' *American Economic Review*, 55, December 1965, pp.1077–96.

24. Much of the analysis of this section appears in James J. Hughes and Richard Perlman, 'On the comparison between current and past rates of unemployment,' *Journal of Post-Keynesian Economics*, V, Fall 1982, pp.78–88.

25. George Perry, 'Changing labor markets and inflation,' *Brookings Papers on Economic Activity*, 1970, No. 3, examines the impact of this shift on a different phenomenon, namely on the Phillips curve relationship between inflation and unemployment. Perry's argument on this subject is treated in Chapter 4.

26. The conventional method is used in the well-known study of Paul Flaim, 'The effect of demographic changes on the nation's unemployment rate,' *Monthly Labor Review*, March 1979.

27. We should note that our example considers only one high-incidence group; thus to be precise the 'all others' group refers only to those with relatively low unemployment rates.

9. The Costs of Unemployment

Whenever resources are idle there is a loss of potential output. However, in the case of labour, the costs of unemployment, particularly prolonged unemployment, are more far-reaching. Here, we analyse the costs of unemployment under five different headings: (1) the costs borne by the individual unemployed, i.e. the private costs; (2) the financial costs incurred by government, i.e. the exchequer costs; (3) the macroeconomic costs measured in terms of lost output; (4) the wider costs to society at large, i.e. the social costs; and (5) the political costs facing governments that preside over high levels of unemployment.

PRIVATE COSTS

Monetary Costs

The costs borne by an individual who becomes unemployed will be of both a monetary and non-monetary kind. The private monetary costs consist of the loss of income that the individual suffers while he is unemployed. These costs will vary according to individual circumstances, and for any one individual they are also likely to vary according to the duration of the unemployment spell.

The individual will usually receive some form of welfare benefits when unemployed; in addition low-paid workers may also be eligible for certain benefits even though working (e.g. in the UK, family income supplement (FIS), rent and rate rebates; in the US, food stamps). Thus, the monetary cost of unemployment to the individual is the difference between the income that he would have received if in work, including welfare benefits, and the income support that he receives while out of work. If this cost, on a weekly basis, is denoted by C, it will be given by

$$C = EE - UB - WB - T$$

where EE = net weekly earnings from employment plus benefits received while in employment, UB = weekly unemployment benefit, WB = weekly value of all other welfare benefits, T = weekly tax rebate. Clearly, for there to be a cost, C must be positive and this will require that $EE > (UB + WB + T)$. When $(UB + WB + T)$ is expressed as a fraction of EE, it is referred to as the replacement ratio. The closer this ratio is to 1, the lower is the monetary cost of unemployment.

The timing of the tax rebate, T, is important here. Although it will theoretically reduce the cost of unemployment whenever it is received, in practice it might only be regarded as an offset if it is rebated immediately, or at least during the period of unemployment itself. For this reason the Minister for Social Security in the UK argued, in October 1976, that

> it is not realistic to regard tax refunds as part of the regular weekly income of an unemployed person since he does not automatically receive these refunds, and when payments are made, they usually occur at monthly intervals. Moreover the payment of tax refunds will depend not only on the point of time in a tax year but also on the number of weeks of employment during the tax year.[1]

Nevertheless, the interaction of the tax and benefit system might be such as to cause a considerable divergence between marginal replacement ratios and average replacement ratios. And, for someone who is already unemployed, it is the marginal replacement ratio rather than the average replacement ratio which determines the cost of remaining unemployed for a further week.

In the UK, where an earnings related supplement (ERS) to unemployment benefit was payable from 1966 until 1982,[2] C might be fairly small for low-paid workers (i.e. the replacement ratio might be close to 1), at least for short spells of unemployment. Indeed, low-paid workers with large family commitments, C might even be negative (i.e. the replacement ratio is greater than 1), implying that the individual is financially better-off out of work than at work. However, this is not the experience of the vast majority of the unemployed, particularly the long-term unemployed. A survey carried out by the DE in 1973 showed that only 1 per cent of the registered claimants were drawing benefits in excess of what they might have reasonably expected to earn if in employment, while another 6 per cent were drawing benefits in the same range as their likely earnings from employment.[3] This fact, that only a small proportion of the unemployed are better-off out of work than in work, is confirmed by Atkinson and Flemming,[4] who in 1978 estimated that *at most* only 2 per cent of male-headed households had potential replacement ratios greater than 1 in the first 28 weeks of unemployment, and that the actual number with such high ratios would be even smaller. In fact, the bulk of the evidence for the UK suggests the link between unemployment and poverty has not been broken, despite myths to the contrary. In his classic study of poverty in the UK, Townsend[5] found that nearly 40 per cent of households in which the head had been unemployed for 10 or more weeks were, according to the government's poverty criteria, in or on the margin of poverty. This has been corroborated by other studies.

Atkinson and Flemming have calculated hypothetical replacement ratios for different earnings levels, family types and unemployment durations for November 1977. These are reproduced in Table 9.1,

Table 9.1: *Replacement Ratios, Earnings, Family Type and Unemployment Duration: November 1977 (total income support[1] as % of that when working)*

Family type	Duration (weeks)	Weekly gross earnings at work (£)							% of male NI beneficiaries[3]
		25	35	45	55	65	75	85	
Single person	3–28	107	97	83	70	61	54	49	52 (including
	29–52	88	72	59	48	40	34	30	married men not
	53–	87[2]	71[2]	59[2]	47[2]	39[2]	34[2]	30[2]	claiming for dependent wives)
Claimant with dependent wife	3–28	110	96	101	92	80	71	64	
	29–52	110	90	79	70	59	52	46	14
	53–	109[2]	89[2]	79[2]	69[2]	59[2]	51[2]	45[2]	
Couple with 1 child (age 3)	3–28	115	99	99	98	89	79	71	7 (with 1 child)
	29–52	91	86	86	79	70	61	54	
	53–	89[2]	84[2]	84[2]	77[2]	69[2]	60[2]	53[2]	
Couple and 2 children (age 4 and 6)	3–28	120	102	97	101	95	88	79	13 (with 2 or 3 children)
	29–52	95	86	88	84	77	70	62	
	53–	95[2]	86[2]	87[2]	83[2]	77[2]	70[2]	62[2]	
Couple and 4 children (age 3, 8, 11 and 16)	3–28	130	110	98[2]	99[2]	98	95	93	4 (with 4 or more children)
	29–52	118[2]	102[2]	98[2]	99[2]	93[2]	88[2]	86[2]	
	53–	118[2]	102[2]	98[2]	99[2]	93[2]	88[2]	86[2]	
% of full-time adult males earning less than amount shown at top of column[4]		0.2	1.1	5.5	18.2	36.6	54.6	69.0	

Notes: [1] Total income support is defined as gross earnings or benefit, plus child benefit, FIS, value of free school meals and free welfare milk, less tax, NI contributions, work expenses and net rates and rent (after rebate). It is assumed that ERS is calculated on the basis of 'reckonable' earnings equal to 80 per cent of current gross earnings. It is assumed that wives are not at work nor in receipt of benefit income. The take-up of means tested benefits is assumed to be 100 per cent. Where payable in employment, FIS is assumed to continue for 6 months into unemployment. Tax refunds are not included. Gross rent is assumed to range from £4.70 (single person) to £6.30 (couple with 4 children), and gross rates from £1.85 to £2.50.
[2] Includes supplementary benefit.
[3] Data supplied by DHSS for May 1977. The balance consists of men with dependent children but not dependent wives.
[4] *New Earnings Survey*, April 1977.

Source: A. B. Atkinson and J. S. Flemming, 'Unemployment, social security and incentives', *Midland Bank Review*, Autumn 1978.

which shows that for all family types the replacement ratio falls as gross weekly earnings increase. Furthermore, the replacement ratios fall dramatically after the first 28 weeks of unemployment once entitlement to the ERS has been exhausted. Atkinson and Flemming also calculated a less extensive measure of the replacement ratio—one that excludes means tested benefits among other things—and this is shown in Table 9.2. After 1971 it can be seen that the ratio declined quite markedly, particularly when ERS is included, and Kay and Morris[6] report a continued decline in the average replacement ratio after 1978.

Table 9.2: *Comparison of Benefits and Average Earnings, 1965–77*

Year (October)	Benefits as % of net income					
	Single person		Married couple with no children		Married couple with two children	
	excl. ERS	incl. ERS	excl. ERS	incl. ERS	excl. ERS	incl. ERS.
	%	%	%	%	%	%
1965	27.0	27.0	41.2	41.2	49.3	49.3
1966	26.2	50.8	40.1	63.2	48.0	68.6
1967	28.3	53.9	43.4	67.5	51.8	73.2
1968	26.6	52.9	40.8	65.7	50.5	72.8
1969	24.8	52.1	38.2	64.1	47.6	71.0
1970	25.0	52.3	38.4	65.2	48.3	72.7
1971	27.1	57.5	41.8	70.8	51.8	77.9
1972	25.7	52.3	39.8	65.4	50.4	73.7
1973	24.8	48.4	38.7	61.5	49.5	70.6
1974	25.6	48.6	39.5	61.6	50.2	70.3
1975	24.5	45.9	38.0	58.4	48.3	67.0
1976	24.9	46.7	38.3	59.1	48.4	67.3
1977	25.6	47.6	38.9	59.6	49.5	68.4

Source: Atkinson and Flemming, *op. cit.*

However, it cannot be stressed too strongly that the calculations of replacement ratios contained in these two tables are hypothetical and will often exaggerate the income received by the unemployed. They will therefore tend to understate the true cost of unemployment. The reasons for this are twofold: first, those who appear in the statistics as having been unemployed for less than 28 weeks might have exhausted their entitlement to ERS because they had already experienced previous spells of unemployment during the qualifying period (this point is relevant to both tables); second, the calculations in Table 9.1 assume that all families claim all of the means tested benefits for which they are eligible, and this is not usually the case.

Table 9.3 shows that in November 1980 only about half of the registered unemployed were in receipt of National Insurance benefit,

Table 9.3: *Claimants to Unemployment Benefit According to Benefit Entitlement, 13 November 1980 (000s)*

	Males		Females		Total	
Entitlement to FRUB[1]						
	%		%		%	
FRUB only	233	(17.1)	148	(27.9)	381	(20.1)
FRUB + ERS[2]	301	(22.1)	96	(18.1)	397	(20.9)
FRUB + ERS + SB	43	(3.2)	4	(0.8)	47	(2.5)
FRUB + SB	101	(7.4)	13	(2.4)	114	(6.0)
Total	678	(49.7)	262	(49.3)	940	(49.6)
Entitlement to SB[3] *only*						
Total	487	(35.7)	177	(33.3)	664	(35.0)
No entitlement to FRUB or SB						
Total	198	(14.5)	93	(17.5)	291	(15.4)
Total claimants	1364	(100.0)	531	(100.0)	1895	(100.0)

Notes: [1] FRUB = Flate rate unemployment benefit

[2] ERS = Earnings related supplement to unemployment benefit

[3] SB = Supplementary benefit

Source: Social Security Statistics 1981 (DHSS, HMSO 1981) Table 1:36, p.16.

with only about a quarter in receipt of the ERS. On the question of benefit take up firm evidence is hard to come by, but for 1972 Sinfield[7] has estimated that for every two unemployed individuals receiving supplementary benefit there was one other person who was eligible for benefits but did not take them up. This can only be explained by ignorance on the part of a large proportion of the unemployed as to their entitlement, or their unwillingness to subject themselves to a means test.

Thus, the conclusion that emerges from all of this is that while the provisions of the welfare state protect individuals from the full costs of unemployment, the costs that do have to be borne by the unemployed are nevertheless quite considerable, particularly for the higher paid and the long-term unemployed. Daniel's[8] national survey of the unemployed underlines the difficulties that they experience. He found that in October 1973, when unemployment stood at about 500,000, almost three-quarters of the unemployed described their experience of unemployment to have been 'very bad', or 'quite bad', with the lack of money being the major cause of concern. The variation in the degree of concern across different age groups was closely correlated with the degree of financial difficulty experienced. Over half the respondents in his sample had been unable to meet at least one financial commitment, and over half of those who had previously socialised with friends had been forced to give this up as a result of their unemployment.

An additional source of relief for some unemployed workers in the UK is the receipt of statutory redundancy payments. However, the majority of those who become unemployed fail to qualify under the 1965 Redundancy Payments Act, as amended by further legislation in 1978. In 1980, about 491,000 of the 3.85 million workers who became unemployed (i.e. 12.8 per cent of the total) received statutory payments that averaged almost £1000. The number of redundancies is sensitive to changes in the level of unemployment and, given the increase in unemployment that occurred between 1980 and 1981, the number qualifying for statutory payments in 1981 increased to almost 810,000 (i.e. about 20 per cent of the flow of workers onto the unemployment register in that year). On average, each of these received a lump sum payment of about £1160. While such payments certainly cushion individuals from loss of income during unemployment, their main purpose is not income maintenance but compensation for job loss. Thus, they are best seen as capital payments for the property rights individuals lose when they lose their jobs, rather than income to tide them over their period of unemployment.

Recent evidence on private costs for the US is more difficult to come by. However, the interaction of the tax and unemployment benefit system produces similar results to those reported for the UK. In a 1974 study that was concerned with the disincentive effects of the unemployment benefit system, Feldstein[9] suggested that unemployment compensation could be regarded 'as imposing a very high rate of tax on the income that an individual would earn if he were not unemployed'. The tax analogy arises because the amount of prospective income that remains after the 'tax' has been paid shows the extent to which an individual is better-off as a result of being employed, rather than unemployed, given the existence of unemployment benefits. The net tax rate is the ratio of unemployment compensation to prospective net earnings. Clearly, it is a limited version of the replacement ratio discussed above, measuring the extent to which unemployment compensation replaces prospective earnings. The gross rate of tax is the ratio of unemployment compensation plus taxes (i.e. federal plus state plus social security taxes) to potential gross earnings. Thus the gross tax rate measures 'the wedge between the individual's marginal social product and the additional net income he would receive if he worked'. The estimates of net and gross tax rates for thirteen different types of unemployed worker are shown in Table 9.4. Since the extent of unemployment compensation varies from state to state, these rates would vary across states for each hypothetical case. Thus the minimum and maximum estimates, as well as the unweighted national average, are given for each rate.

For single men the range for the net rate is from 40 to 84 per cent, while that for the gross rate is from 56 to 90 per cent. For married men whose wives are not working, both rates are below those for single men. For median male earnings the average net rate is 60 per cent, while the

Table 9.4: Effects of Taxing Unemployment Compensation

| Family type and beneficiary | Earnings % of median by sex | Net tax rate (net unemployment compensation as % of net earnings¹) | | | | | | Gross tax rate (net unemployment compensation plus taxes as % of gross earnings¹) | | | | | |
| | | Unemployment compensation not taxed | | | Unemployment compensation taxed | | | Unemployment compensation not taxed | | | Unemployment compensation taxed | | |
		mean	min.	max.	mean	min.	max.	mean	min.	max.	mean	min.	max.
Single man	M = 100	63	40	84	46	29	61	74	56	90	63	49	74
Married man	M = 100	60	43	81	48	34	67	70	57	85	61	50	74
	M = 70	69	59	87	57	48	70	76	68	90	67	60	77
	M = 130	46	31	61	36	24	49	59	46	69	51	41	59
Working couple, Man unemployed	M = 100 F = 100	62	41	83	47	32	67	73	55	87	62	48	75
Single woman	F = 100	72	64	95	56	50	71	79	73	96	68	63	80
Working couple, Woman unemployed	M = 100 F = 100	77	64	109	59	50	82	84	74	106	71	63	87
	M = 100 F = 70	78	64	119	60	50	93	84	73	114	71	63	95
	M = 100 F = 130	77	64	102	58	50	72	83	73	101	70	63	82

¹Net unemployment compensation is now the same as gross unemployment compensation. For the alternative 'Unemployment compensation taxed', the net unemployment compensation is net of federal and state income tax at the individual's current marginal rate.

Source: Martin Feldstein, 'Unemployment compensation: adverse incentives and distributional amonolies', National Tax Journal, Vol.XXVII, 1974, pp.231–44, Table 4.

corresponding gross rate is about 70 per cent. The rates for lower-paid males are higher than this, while those for higher-paid males are lower. In the case of unemployed men with wives who work, the rates are generally higher since wives' earnings tend to raise marginal tax rates. The rates are generally higher for women than for men, and for unemployed married women with husbands in employment, with median earnings, both net and gross rates exceed 100 per cent for certain types of beneficiary in the most generous states. This suggests that the cost of unemployment for women in such states is negative. However, for married females the average net rate is around 77 per cent, while the average gross rate is around 84 per cent.

Although these estimates relate to the year 1970, Feldstein[10] still argued in 1977—when more than half the unemployment spells in the US lasted less than four weeks—that the private costs of unemployment were relatively low. Certainly his 1977 estimate of the replacement ratio for a hypothetical Massachusetts man is in line with the estimates contained in Table 9.4.

Non-Monetary Costs

Non-monetary private costs of unemployment arise because the unemployed are more prone to psychological pressure and ill health. Although the unemployed of today do not suffer physical deprivation and malnutrition on a scale that was often experienced by the unemployed during the inter-war period, the statistical evidence suggests that the unemployed still suffer physical deprivation and malnutrition. For example, in Northern Ireland, where infant mortality is higher than in other parts of the UK, it is at its highest among unemployed families. While firm conclusions cannot be drawn, the evidence is at least suggestive that the loss of income that accompanies unemployment is associated with lower levels of nutrition which have detrimental effects on newborn babies.[11]

A study[12] carried out in the US in the 1960s on redundancy among blue-collar workers found pathological and psychological changes that were sufficient to increase the likelihood of gout, hypertension and coronary heart disease. A more recent study in the UK by Fagin[13] also found that unemployed workers and their families tend to suffer greater health problems.

In a survey of the psychological impact of unemployment, Jahoda[14] mentions demoralisation and loss of self-respect among the unemployed as important effects. Furthermore, she stresses that the children of the unemployed do not escape; they become resigned to a life of limited opportunities and suffer a restriction of ambition and desires. According to Jahoda, the psychological costs of unemployment arise because of a breakdown in the latent functions of employment. For example, she stresses that in addition to the activity that it enforces, employment 'imposes a time structure on the working day', gives rise to shared experiences and contacts outside of the immediate family, links an individual to 'goals and purposes which transcend his own', and confers personal status and identity. When employment gives way to unemployment there is a breakdown in the time structure of the working day, a reduction in shared experiences and a severing of the individual's links with the wider goals of society. As a consequence of all this he suffers not only a loss of status and personal identity, but a feeling of social isolation, and often a sense of uselessness.

The increased leisure and free time that unemployment confers will, of course, offset the private costs of unemployment, provided that the leisure confers some net utility. For example, Feldstein[15] has argued that in 1977 a Massachusetts man, with a working wife and two children, he earning $140 and she $100 per week, would incur no private cost of unemployment if he valued his leisure and non-market work activities at only 50c an hour. Of course, even at 1977 prices, $140 a week is not a princely sum and, therefore, the breakeven price for someone on average earnings would be much greater than 50c an hour. At the other extreme Jahoda, drawing on her experiences gained from an inter-war study of an Austrian village, has argued that 'being unemployed is something very different from having leisure time'.

The difference between these two writers is one of time perspective. While Feldstein is thinking in terms of a fairly short period of unemployment, Jahoda's comments refer to the impact of much longer-term unemployment. Thus, while it might be reasonable for a period of short-term unemployment to assume that the increased leisure, albeit enforced, offsets some of the private costs of unemployment, such an assumption is less realistic for long spells of unemployment. This is because the ability to enjoy leisure usually requires income, and in a period of prolonged unemployment any departure from what might be termed permanent income will seriously undermine this ability. In other words, even though individuals might not require an ever-increasing income in order to be able to take advantage of leisure opportunities, it seems unlikely that such opportunities can be anything like fully exploited if they are associated with declining incomes. Furthermore, while the notion that unemployment will confer greater welfare if it is used to search for a better job might be valid during a short spell of unemployment,[16] when the individual has every prospect of securing another job quickly, it would not seem to be valid in a situation in which there are millions unemployed and very few jobs for them to fill.

An additional cost that falls on most US workers who become unemployed, but on relatively few UK workers, is the loss of health care insurance. In the US, where the private market in health care predominates, most workers obtain coverage through their employment. Loss of job therefore results in loss of coverage for the unemployed and his family. Thus the unemployed have to incur the cost of insurance themselves—unless they happen to be covered by a working spouse—or rely on Medicaid, the medical assistance programme for poor people. Where the health insurance premiums are paid by the unemployed the cost is obvious. In other instances the costs will arise as a result of a decline in coverage or in deterioration in treatment and care. In the UK the provision of private health insurance as a fringe benefit of employment is nothing like as widespread as in the US, and where it does arise it tends to be concentrated on those categories of workers who are better paid, and less prone to unemployment.

EXCHEQUER COSTS

The fact that individuals do not bear the full monetary cost of their unemployment implies that the additional cost is borne by other members of society, through the system of taxation and transfer payments operated by government. During the financial year 1978-9, when unemployment in the UK averaged about 1.5 million, the government paid out £657 million in unemployment benefits. In the US the total value of regular and extended benefits was $14 billion in the 1980 fiscal year. Large though these sums are, they grossly understate the true financial costs of unemployment to government because they exclude other benefits that the unemployed receive. Also, they exclude the direct tax payments that would have been made by the unemployed, and their employers, had they been gainfully employed. Finally, they exclude the indirect tax revenues that the unemployed would have contributed out of higher employment incomes. Clearly, any estimate of the financial cost to government must include these benefits and loss of tax revenues as well as the actual payments of unemployment benefit.

In the UK the Treasury,[17] using its macroeconomic model, estimated the direct exchequer costs of an increase of 100,000 in private sector unemployment above the level prevailing in 1980-1 (over 2 million) to be £340 million; that is almost £3500 per additional unemployed person. The breakdown of these figures is given in Table 9.5 which shows that the costs arising from the loss of current receipts exceeds the costs arising from the payment of unemployment and other benefits. The calculation embodied in the table represents a single estimate from a possible range. The exact cost is difficult to arrive at because complete information on the characteristics of the unemployed is not available (e.g. concerning their benefit entitlement, the income they would have earned, and the tax they would have paid had they been at work). Assumptions therefore have to be made, and some of these are made explicit in the notes at the bottom of the table. The other main assumptions on which the calculation is based are (i) that 75 per cent of a given change in employment is reflected in the change in registered unemployment; and (ii) that the unemployed would have earned 80 per cent of average earnings had they been in employment.

Table 9.5: *Direct Exchequer Costs of an Increase of 100,000 in Registered Unemployment (excluding school-leavers), 1980–81 (1980–1 outturn prices.)*

	Exchequer costs for 1980–1 (£m)
Current receipts	
Income tax[1]	115
National Insurance contributions[2]	75
National Insurance surcharge	15
Total current receipts	205
Current expenditure[3]	
National Insurance benefits (incl. ERS)	65
Other social security benefits	55
Rent and rate rebates	5
Administrative costs	10
Total current expenditure	135
Exchequer cost	340

Notes: [1] The fall income tax is assumed to be 23 per cent of the fall in wages and salaries. A six-week accruals lag has been allowed for.

[2] Employee and employer contributions, including payments to the National Health Service, Redundancy, and Maternity Pay Funds. The fall in accruals of National Insurance contributions before allowing for employees who would be contracted out is £100 million at unchanged contribution rates. The estimate given here allows for an accruals adjustment and assumes that 30 per cent of the employees would have been contracted out of the state pension scheme.

[3] Totals are the rounded sum of unrounded components.

Source: Economic Progress Report No.130, February 1981.

The estimate relates only to the cost of unemployment in the private sector. Where workers in the public sector become unemployed, the cost to the government is much less because of savings on pay, superannuation and National Insurance, etc. Indeed, it is likely that, on average, the savings to the exchequer exceed the costs when public sector unemployment increases. Furthermore, the estimate relates only to the first-year costs of additional unemployment since the cost in subsequent years is likely to be lower if, as a result of the initial increase in unemployment, contributions are raised in future years in order to maintain some sort of balance in the National Insurance fund. Finally, it would be unrealistic to gross up the estimate to obtain total costs of total unemployment for 1980–1 because the assumptions on which it is based would not be applicable to the total stock of unemployment.

Although the estimate needs to be treated with caution, the

exclusion of redundancy payments from the calculation means that it is biased downwards. The exchequer's cost of redundancy payments during 1980-1 was about £300 million, which amounts to about £150 per member of the unemployed stock in 1980-1. However, these are once-and-for-all costs which would not be repeated during subsequent years. Since the Treasury estimate only purports to capture direct costs, it would be wrong to criticise it on the grounds that it does not include such indirect costs as those resulting from changes in corporation tax receipts and nationalised industry surpluses, not to mention such second round effects as the loss of indirect tax receipts and changes in debt interest payment. However, the fact that these indirect costs occur will mean that the total cost, as reflected in the public sector borrowing requirement (PSBR), will be greater than the Treasury estimate.

In contrast to the Treasury approach, Dilnot and Morris[18] adopted a microeconomic approach to estimate total exchequer costs in fiscal year 1977-8. Their analysis is based upon 936 households which had at least one unemployed individual, drawn from the 1977 *Family Expenditure Survey*. Taking account of direct and indirect tax revenue losses, they calculated the total cost of unemployment to the exchequer to be £3429 million in 1977-8. Their estimates for subsequent years, based on the assumption that the structure of unemployment in these years would be similar to that prevailing in 1977-78, are given in Table 9.6, line 2. If in subsequent years the structure of unemployment is not the same as in 1977-8 because, say, an increase in the level of unemployment means that increasingly productive workers are laid off, then the Dilnot-Morris estimate will be on the low side. For

Table 9.6: *The Exchequer Cost of Unemployment 1977-8 to 1981-2 (current prices)*

	1977/8	1978/9	1979/80	1980/1	1981/2
1. Average unemployment	1.51m	1.46m	1.40m	2.04m	2.88m
2. Overall cost	£3.429b	£3.807b	£4.243b	£7.807b	£12.947b
3. PSBR	£5.597b	£9.198b	£9.913b	£13.184b	£10.500b
4. GDP[1] (at factor cost and current prices)	£126.900b	£145.800b	£167.500b	£193.500b	£209.900b[2]
5. Overall cost as % of PSBR	61	41	43	59	123
6. Overall cost as % of GDP	2.7	2.6	2.5	4.0	6.2

Notes: [1] GDP data relate to the calendar years 1977 to 1981.

[2] The figure for 1981 is based on the estimate derived from income data only. For all other years the figure is an average of the income and expenditure estimates.

Sources: Dilnot and Morris, *op. cit.*, for lines 1, 2 and 3 except for line 3 (1981/2). Treasury, *Progress Report*, line 3 (1981/2); *Economic Trends*, September 1982 line 4.

illustrative purposes, the PSBR and GDP at factor cost, both expressed in current prices, are also given, and the exchequer cost is expressed as a percentage of each. In none of the years under review was the total exchequer cost less than 40 per cent of the PSBR. Between 1980-1 and 1981-2, unemployment increased by almost 1 million and the impact that this had on the PSBR is clearly seen, with the exchequer cost increasing from less than 60 per cent of PSBR to over 120 per cent. In terms of GDP, total exchequer cost increased from around 4 per cent in 1980 to over 6 per cent in 1981. During 1981-2 the cost to the exchequer for every single person on the unemployment register was about £4500 (i.e. about £87 per week). This compares with average earnings during the year of about £125 per week for adult males, and £76 per week for adult females. Given that the assumption Dilnot and Morris made about the composition of unemployment remaining constant between 1977-8 and 1981-2 is unlikely to have been realised because of the large increase in unemployment, and the fact that they ignored the net costs to the exchequer of redundancy payments,[19] their estimate is likely to be on the low side.

It can be argued that even these estimates understate the true exchequer costs of rising unemployment because they do not capture the increased administrative costs associated with making benefit payments to the unemployed. Some writers[20] go even further and mistakenly suggest that the cost of special employment measures ought to be included. Government outlays on such measures[21] usually increase in times of high and rising unemployment, but they should not be included in estimates of the exchequer costs of unemployment because, to the extent that they are successful, such expenditures reduce unemployment—or at least prevent it from rising still further. Thus the benefit that stems from this expenditure is really the increase in unemployment that is not observed. Also, since many of the outlays on special programmes lead to savings elsewhere, they should not be included in the cost of unemployment. It is sufficient to note that during 1982-3 it is estimated that the outlay on special employment measures to combat rising unemployment was about £1.5 billion in the UK.[22]

For the US, information on exchequer costs is less readily available, but as for the UK UI benefits constitute only a fraction of these costs. In 1980 the Congressional Budget Office estimated that for every 1 per cent increase in the unemployment rate the federal budget deficit increased by about $25 billion.[23]

MACROECONOMIC COSTS

The macroeconomic cost of unemployment is the lost output that results whenever workers are unemployed rather than employed. However, deviations in the unemployment rate from the full-

employment rate will understate the cost of operating the economy
below its full potential because such deviations fail to capture changes
in the participation rate, changes in part-time working, reductions in
overtime working, and under-employment on the job. Taking all of
these factors into account, Okun[24] estimated that for the US economy
in 1962 a 1 per cent fall in the unemployment rate would be
accompanied by a 3 per cent increase in national output, and vice
versa. During the second half of the 1970s the relationship changed
and, according to Gordon and Hall,[25] a 1 per cent fall in unemployment
was then associated with only a $2\frac{1}{4}$ per cent increase in national
output. Indeed, Gordon and Hall reckon that the relationship between
output and unemployment has always been closer to 2:1 rather than
3:1, as suggested by Okun. In 1975, when the unemployment rate
averaged 8.5 per cent, the output gap—that is the difference between
actual and potential GNP expressed as a percentage of the potential—
was estimated to be 12.4 per cent.[26]

For the UK, Thirlwall[27] found that a given change in unemployment was associated with an even greater output loss than for the US.
For the period 1950-67 he estimated that a 1 per cent increase in
unemployment was associated with a 4 per cent decline in national
output. One explanation of the relative insensitivity of changes in
unemployment to changes in national output in the UK during this
period is that employment was less responsive to changes in aggregate
demand as a result of greater variations in the degree of labour
hoarding. An alternative explanation is that changes in employment
gave rise to smaller changes in the official measure of unemployment as
a result of greater cyclical variations in labour force participation and
hidden unemployment. Although Taylor[28] found that for the 1950s
and 1960s both the average rate of labour hoarding and the average
level of hidden unemployment were higher in the US than in the UK,
such findings are not necessarily inconsistent with there being greater
cyclical variation in both in the UK.

Burghes and Field,[29] adopting a peak-to-peak approach similar to
that used by Taylor, estimated that the output gap for the UK in 1976
was 7 per cent. In 1977 the NIESR[30] estimated that to reduce
unemployment from 1.4 million to a full-employment level of 0.5
million would require an increase in GDP of 9 per cent. This estimate
is based on the assumption that the elasticity of employment with
respect to output during the cycle is about 0.7, and that every third
worker hired during a period of cyclical expansion would not be
on the unemployment register, but would be drawn into the labour
force.

All of the foregoing estimates of the output gap implicitly assume a
full employment level of unemployment. Okun's original estimate for
the US was based upon the projection of a 4 per cent trend in
productivity growth and the assumption that 1955, a year in which
actual and trend GNP coincided, was a year in which full employment

was attained. Since the unemployment rate stood at 4 per cent in 1955, this became the full employment target, although by 1978 the Council of Economic Advisers[31] had revised the target to over 5 per cent. In the Burghes and Field study, the choice of beginning and end years (1960 and 1973) implicitly confers full-employment status on those years. Although both were cyclical peaks, the unemployment rate was 1.6 per cent in 1960 and 2.7 per cent in 1973. Thus for 1976—the year for which the gap was estimated—the full-employment rate is implicitly assumed to be close to 2.7 per cent.

Less sophisticated calculations based upon assumptions about the marginal product of the unemployed come up with similar estimates. For example, Cohen[32] estimates that in 1981 if the 2.6 million unemployed could have been reduced to 0.8 million, then GNP could have been increased by anything from 6 to 8 per cent, assuming that the social marginal product of the unemployed in that year was equal to average earnings. Clearly Cohen is assuming a higher full employment level of unemployment for 1981 than NIESR assumed for 1977 (0.8 million compared with 0.5 million), and his calculation does not take account of increased participation, increased overtime working or reductions in short-time working as the economy expands towards full employment. Nevertheless, it confirms that the output losses associated with the 1981 level of unemployment were considerable. Indeed, with unemployment in the US passing the 10 per cent mark in the autumn of 1982, and having reached almost 14 per cent in the UK, the output losses involved will have been even greater than indicated by the above estimates. Such losses cannot be recouped, they are gone forever. When cumulated over a number of years they reach gigantic proportions,[33] and it is no exaggeration to say that, at 1982 levels of unemployment, the equivalent of a whole year's GNP would be lost in less than a decade in both the US and the UK.

There is one respect in which all of the calculations and estimates of output losses associated with unemployment will understate the real losses that actually result from a period of prolonged unemployment. This is that the individuals who experience long-term unemployment will suffer a deterioration in their skills and a decline in their productivity. Thus, on re-employment the productivity of those who have suffered a prolonged period of unemployment will be lower than what it would have been had they continued in employment. For most it will take some time to regain their former productivity level, and therefore output losses will continue even after re-employment. In addition, retraining costs might be incurred in order to bring them back to experienced worker standard. Others may never regain their former levels of efficiency. But probably more important than the erosion of skills and productivity that results from the under-utilisation of those skills is the permanent loss of labour force efficiency that results from the lower level of on-the-job training which is a consequence of the higher level of unemployment. This loss of skill augmentation to the labour force means that productivity will be permanently lower than it otherwise would have been. Clearly, the long-term costs arising from this skill loss will be greater the more concentrated the unemployment is among the younger age groups, and the greater its average duration.

SOCIAL COSTS

Here terminology is important. By social costs we mean all of those costs borne by society, both economic and non-economic. The macroeconomic costs discussed above will, of course, constitute a large part of total social costs. But there is also evidence that non-economic costs are important, even though they are difficult to quantify. Under the discussion of private costs it was noted that individuals who become unemployed, and their families, might be prone to greater illness and stress. It is not surprising, therefore, that macro studies show the existence of correlation, albeit after a time-lag, between increases in unemployment and indicators of ill health, and between increases in unemployment and an increase in the population mortality rate. There is also statistical evidence of an association between unemployment and crime. Presumably the reduction in money income associated with prolonged unemployment will sharpen the incentive for potential criminals to engage in crime, while the increase in free time available to them will provide greater opportunities to do so. Furthermore, in a recent report,[34] unemployment among young males—both black and white—is seen as a contributory factor to the UK civil disorders and riots of 1981. Lord Scarman,[35] after his inquiry into the Brixton riots, also concluded that unemployment was one of the manifestations of racial disadvantage, which itself was one of the causes of the riots.

Brenner[36] has been a pioneer in the attempt to quantify the impact of unemployment upon health and mortality. His hypothesis is that economic instability and insecurity increase the likelihood that people will lead more unhealthy life-styles, thereby leading to an increase in ill health and that this, together with the stress that is associated with unemployment, will lead to higher mortality rates. Analysing time series data for the US over several decades, Brenner found a strong statistical relationship between unemployment and such stress indicators as suicide, mental hospital admissions, prison admissions, homicide, sclerosis of the liver mortality, cardiovascular mortality and total mortality. He estimated that a 1 per cent increase in the US unemployment rate has been associated with approximately 36,900 extra deaths, and over 4200 extra admissions to mental hospitals; and that the 1.4 per cent increase in unemployment that occurred during 1970 cost $7 billion in lost income due to illness, mortality and increased prison and mental hospital admissions.[37]

On the assumption that similar statistical relationships as Brenner found for the US hold for the UK, Rowthorn and Ward[38] have estimated that an increase in UK unemployment of 1 million, sustained over a five-year period, would lead to 50,000 more deaths, 60,000 additional cases of mental illness, and 14,000 more prison sentences. Furthermore, they estimate that over a five-year period this would give rise to additional public expenditure of £280 million on law and order, with a further £280 million on health and community services. Since these calculations were made, Brenner[39] has tested his US model on data for England and Wales for the period 1936-76 and finds that it supports the hypothesis that an increase in the aggregate unemployment rate has an adverse effect on mortality rates. However, this conclusion has been challenged by Gravelle, Hutchinson and Stern,[40] who argue that Brenner's model is incorrectly specified, omitting relevant variables. They also criticise the data used by Brenner on the grounds of consistency and reliability, and when they test his model using more reliable data, they find that unemployment has no significant effect on mortality for the period 1922-76, or for the shorter post-war period, 1952-76. They therefore conclude that though it is plausible that unemployment does have adverse effects on health and mortality, as yet there is 'no evidence which can be used to estimate their magnitude, timing, and form'.

Despite the reservations of Gravelle, Hutchinson and Stern, the House of Lords Select Committee, after surveying the evidence available to it, concluded that unemployment *is* one of the causes of ill health and mortality, as well as increased crime and civil disorder. As a consequence it increases the demands on the National Health Service, the social services, the police and the judicial system, giving rise to additional exchequer costs of 'at least hundreds of pounds for every person unemployed'. Thus, if the cost is only £300 per unemployed person, the level of unemployment prevailing in the UK in 1982 would imply additional exchequer costs of about £1 billion.

POLITICAL COSTS

It is always assumed that high unemployment involves political costs (i.e. loss of electoral support) for the government that presides over it. This assumption is not based simply on the belief that potential supporters of the government who have become unemployed will cast their vote in favour of another party, but also on the fact that the aggregate unemployment rate stands as a proxy for the state of the economy. Thus, even those who remain in employment might suffer because they find themselves not as well off as they would have been, and therefore switch their political allegiance. It has also been suggested that if the unemployed are perceived as being 'scroungers', getting something for nothing, the employed might regard themselves as 'victims' of a system that does not reward effort sufficiently and, accordingly, cast their vote against the government.[41]

Of course, linking changes in electoral support to changes in unemployment is somewhat simplistic because it assumes that, even within an economic context, changes in unemployment have a greater effect on electoral support for the government than success or failure in attaining any of the other macroeconomic goals that the government sets for itself—or rather, that the electorate expects the government to achieve. This might not always be the case. Since the simultaneous attainment of these goals (i.e. full employment, balance of payments equilibrium, stable prices, and economic growth) has proved elusive, governments often have to choose between them, trading off one against the other. Also, as opinion polls show, the electorate's perceptions concerning the most important problems faced by government change through time.

Nevertheless, despite the above qualifications, full employment was the primary goal of successive UK governments in the post-war period, at least until the mid-1960s. And, as Butler and Stokes[42] have commented, as a result of the wartime experience, and because the Keynesian message had been absorbed by those responsible for determining policy, a government's record over unemployment 'probably provided the leading test of its handling of the economy'. Thus, in the UK it came to be expected by all that governments would take effective action against unemployment when it occurred. In the US, such primacy was not given to the full-employment goal until the late 1950s because the application of Keynesian principles to the management of the economy was delayed.[43]

For the period 1959–64 Butler and Stokes found a marked correlation between changes in unemployment in the UK and the Labour Party's lead over the Conservative government in the polls. However, in the late 1960s variations in Party support were less explicable in terms of changes in unemployment. Since during this period the government was at great pains to convince the electorate that the balance of payments was the principal problem, and, therefore, the primary objective of policy, it is tempting to conclude that it was successful in distracting attention from the increase in unemployment that occurred between 1966 and 1970. However, Labour were defeated at the 1970 election by the Conservatives.

During the period 1970–4 unemployment increased to a new post-war peak and according to a former minister the government were 'dominated by fear of unemployment'.[44] As a direct consequence of this many believe that the government were 'frightened' into adopting reflationary policies which only served to exacerbate the problem of inflation. Although the central issue of the 1974 election was not unemployment, but the unions' challenge to government, it remains a fact that the Heath government of 1970–4 presided over a higher average level of unemployment than did its predecessor.

During the 1970s the rate of inflation accelerated and its control became top priority for the Labour government. By the late 1970s high unemployment became 'tolerable, even acceptable, to many politicians, economists and voters'.[45] As a consequence, even though unemployment had reached 1.5 million, and was still around 1.25 million at the time of the 1979 election, the issue of unemployment did not dominate the election as it would have done during the first two post-war decades. But once again a government whose unemployment record was worse than that of its predecessor lost the election.

In addition to the concern over inflation, the changed attitude towards unemployment has, according to Deacon, arisen because much unemployment is now seen as voluntary—induced by higher benefits in conjunction with high tax rates on low employment income. This disincentive effect to work has been strengthened by the increased opportunities to participate in the hidden economy, while still drawing tax-free benefits. Thus, unemployment does not give rise to the discontent that it once did. Indeed, Deacon argues that the highlighting of individual cases of benefit abuse in the press, whipped up into campaigns against 'spongers', has caused the employed, rather than the unemployed, to see themselves as victims of the system. As a consequence the employed have developed a 'deep-rooted hostility towards the unemployed' and this has become more intense as unemployment has increased.

Until 1979 British governments certainly could not become too complacent about unemployment. Between 1966 and 1979 there were three different governments, and during the period of each (i.e. 1966-70, 1970-4, 1974-9) there was an increase in unemployment and the governing party was not returned for a second term. The 1983 election, however, has changed this pattern of alternation between government and opposition. Although the Labour Party tried to make unemployment the key election issue, the outcome of the election would tend to suggest that the changed attitudes towards unemployment, and perhaps the changed perceptions about what constitutes the full-employment level of unemployment, have become deeply ingrained. In that sense the mould of British politics may well have been truly broken. But few would have foreseen such an outcome only three years ago. Writing in 1980, Hayek[46]—one of Mrs Thatcher's mentors—doubted 'whether any government could persist for two or three years in a policy which meant 10 per cent unemployment for most of that period.'

The Thatcher government has not only persisted with its policies, it won a vote of confidence for another five years. It will be interesting to see whether this outcome affects the policies of the Reagan administration in the US, making it more determined to pursue anti-inflationary policies rather than policies to reduce unemployment. Furthermore, the outcome of the 1984 elections in the US will be even more eagerly awaited, given that President Reagan has pursued similar policies to

Mrs Thatcher, and like her has presided over record post-war levels of unemployment.

SUMMARY

The costs of unemployment differ according to whether they are viewed from the standpoint of the individual, the government, or society at large. Although an individual does not bear the full monetary cost of his unemployment, replacement ratios are typically less than unity and, in the UK at least, have declined in recent years. But the non-monetary costs of prolonged unemployment can be considerable and should not be ignored. For the government the costs are both financial and political. The financial or exchequer costs are much greater than the total UI benefits paid out and include other benefit payments to the unemployed, redundancy payments, the loss of tax revenue and the cost of administering the unemployment benefit and placement services. The political cost is, of course, the potential loss of support for the government presiding over a high level of unemployment. From the point of view of society at large the costs of unemployment include not only those arising from the loss of output, but also the wider social costs that are reflected in a higher incidence of illness (and even mortality), as well as in increased crime and anti-social behaviour.

NOTES AND REFERENCES

1. *Hansard*, 1976i. Col. 245.
2. The earnings related supplement to unemployment benefit was phased out in 1982.
3. 'Characteristics of the unemployed: sample survey June 1973', *Department of Employment Gazette*, March 1974, pp.211-21.
4. A. B. Atkinson and J. S. Flemming, 'Unemployment, social security and incentives', *Midland Bank Review*, Autumn 1978, pp.6-16.
5. Peter Townsend, *Poverty in the United Kingdom* (London: Allen Lane, 1979).
6. J. A. Kay and C. N. Morris, 'The IFS position on unemployment benefits: a reply', *Fiscal Studies*, Vol.4, No.1, March 1983.
7. Adrian Sinfield, 'Low take-up of supplementary allowances by the unemployed', cited in Frank Field, 'Unemployment and poverty', in Frank Field (ed.), *The Conscript Army* (London: Routledge & Kegan Paul, 1977).
8. W. W. Daniel, *A National Survey of the Unemployed* (London: PEP, 1974).
9. Martin Feldstein, 'Unemployment compensation: adverse incentives and distributional anomalies', *National Tax Journal*, Vol.27, June 1974, pp.231-44.

10. Martin Feldstein, 'The private and social costs of unemployment', *American Economic Review*, Supplement, May 1978, pp.155–8.

11. *Report from the Select Committee of the House of Lords on Unemployment*, Vol.1 (London: HMSO, 1982).

12. S. Cobb and S. V. Kasl, 'Blood pressure changes in men undergoing job loss: a preliminary report', *Psychosomatic Medicine*, Vol.32, 1970, pp.19–38, cited in *Report From the Select Committee op.cit.*

13. L. Fagin, 'Unemployment and health in families', DHSS, cited in *Report from The Select Committee, op.cit.*

14. M. Jahoda, 'The impact of unemployment in the 1930s and 1970s', *Bulletin of The British Psychological Society*, Vol.32. 1979, pp.309–14.

15. Feldstein (1978), *op.cit.*

16. It might also be valid for someone on lay-off who, because of seniority, is certain of being recalled after a given period of time.

17. Treasury, *Economic Progress Report*, No.130, February 1981.

18. A. W. Dilnot and C. N. Morris, 'The exchequer costs of unemployment', *Fiscal Studies*, Vol.2, No.3, November 1981, pp.10–19.

19. The government's gross payments into the Redundancy Payments Fund will need to be reduced by the tax payable on them when disbursed in order to arrive at the exchequer cost.

20. e.g. Brian Showler, 'Political economy and unemployment', in Brian Showler and Adrian Sinfield (eds), *The Workless State* (Oxford: Martin Robertson, 1981).

21. e.g. the Temporary Employment Subsidy (TES) and the Youth Opportunities Programme YOP).

22. Department of Employment, *Employment Gazette*, April 1982, p.174.

23. *Wall Street Journal*, 13 November 1980.

24. A. Okun, 'Potential GNP: its measurement and significance', *Proceedings of the Business and Economics Statistics Section of the American Statistical Association*, 1962.

25. R. J. Gordon and R. E. Hall, 'Arthur M. Okun 1928–1980', *Brookings Papers on Economics Activity*, 1, 1980, pp.1–5.

26. Joint Economic Committee, Congress of the US. *The 1976 Joint Economic Report*, cited in E. J. Burtt, *Labour in the American Economy* (London: Macmillan, 1980).

27. A. P. Thirlwall, 'Okun's law and the natural rate of growth', *The Southern Economic Journal*, Vol.XXXVI, July 1969, pp.87–9.

28. Jim Taylor, *Unemployment and Wage Inflation: With Special Reference to Britain and the USA* (Harlow: Longman, 1974).

29. Louie Burghes and Frank Field, 'The cost of unemployment', in Field (ed.), *The Conscript Army, op.cit.*

30. *National Institute Economic Review*, No.79, February 1977.

31. *Economic Report of the President*, 1978.

32. C. D. Cohen, 'Employment policy', in C. D. Cohen (ed.), *Agenda for Britain 2: Macro Policy Choices for the 80s* (London: Philip Allan, 1982).

33. e.g. Leon Keyserling argues that in the US the deliberate creation of unemployment to combat inflation over the period 1953–80 resulted in an aggregate loss of 8 trillion dollars of GNP (at 1979 prices). This loss is equivalent to the loss of 83 million years of civilian employment opportunity. Thus had policies of deliberate unemployment creation not been pursued, Keyserling's figures suggest that, taking the period as a whole, average employment would have been 4.5 million higher than

what it actually was. See Leon Keyserling, 'The Humphrey–Hawkins Act since its 1978 enactment', in David C. Colander (ed.), *Solutions to Unemployment* (New York: Harcourt, Brace, Jovanovich, 1981).

34. *Report from the Select Committee, op.cit.*
35. Cmnd 8427 (London: HMSO, 1982).
36. M. Harvey Brenner, 'Mortality and the national economy: a review, and the experience of England and Wales, 1936–76', *The Lancet*, 15 September 1979, pp.568–73. This article develops and explains Brenner's basic model, before applying it to data for England and Wales.
37. M. Harvey Brenner, *Estimating the Social Cost of National Economic Policy* (Washington: US Government Printing Office, 1976), Paper No.5, cited in Jennie Popay, 'Unemployment: a threat to public health', in Louie Burghes and Ruth Lister (eds), *Unemployment: Who Pays the Price?* (London: Child Poverty Action Group, 1981).
38. Bob Rowthorn and Terry Ward, 'How to run a company and run down an economy: the effects of closing down steel-making in Corby', *Cambridge Journal of Economics*, Vol.3, No.4, December 1979, pp.327–40.
39. Brenner, *The Lancet, op.cit.*
40. H. S. Gravelle, G. Hutchinson and J. Stern, 'Mortality and unemployment: a critique of Brenner's time series analysis', *The Lancet*, 26 September 1981.
41. This view of the employed, rather than the unemployed, as victim has been put forward by Hugo Young in *The Sunday Times* 29 October 1977. See Alan Deacon, 'Unemployment and politics in Britain since 1945', in Showler and Sinfield, *op.cit.*
42. David Butler and Donald Stokes, *Political Change in Britain: The Evolution of Electoral Choice* (London: Macmillan, 1974, 2nd edn).
43. J. K. Galbraith, 'How Keynes came to America', *New York Times Book Review*, May 1965. Reprinted in Paul A. Samuelson, *Readings in Economics*, (New York: McGraw-Hill, 1970, 6th edn).
44. Sir Keith Joseph made this point in a speech delivered at Preston on 5 September 1974. This is reproduced in *Reversing the Trend* (Barry Rose, 1975).
45. Deacon, *op.cit.*
46. F. A. Hayek, *1980s Unemployment and the Unions*, Hobart Paper 87 (London: Institute of Economic Affairs, 1980).

10. The Path to Full Employment

The Keynesian–natural rate controversy has not only raised uncertainties as to the voluntary–involuntary nature of unemployment above the frictional–structural base, it has also made the policies for reaching that base debatable. For example, do we need demand stimulation, or more labour market information? In addition, it has also called into question the meaning of full employment itself.

The simplistic definition, which requires everyone who wants a job to have one, no longer holds—if it ever did. Apart from frictional-structural elements, we need to specify equality between labour demand and supply at the market wage, and that wage is certainly an elusive concept, one which is at the centre of contention between Keynesians and the microeconomists. The definition of full employment as the rate at which inflation would result if it were any lower also has operational problems. Both Phillips curve and natural rate adherents agree that inflation is likely at relatively high unemployment rates. But even if this were not so, the experience of stagflation would make such a definition unrealistic.

As Lucas[1] points out, 'neither of these approaches [whether based on an absence of involuntary unemployment or the threshold level toward unacceptable inflation] leads to an operational definition of full employment.' Nevertheless, despite the inability to formulate a precise definition of full employment, or even to agree on a precise unemployment rate goal, there is usually some sort of consensus when the unemployment rate is 'too high' and when policy should be directed to reducing it.

Specific policies for reducing unemployment have not been agreed, and even though the experience of the Great Depression led to the belief that the attainment of a low unemployment rate was a responsibility of government, we have been reluctant to specify the tools for meeting the goal. In the US, the Employment Act 1946 was little more than an expression of a belief in the responsibility of government for a low unemployment rate, and 32 years later the Humphrey–Hawkins Act 1978 did little more than restate that belief, despite the earlier intentions of specific goals and procedures contained in the original Bill. In the UK, where the departure from full employment has been even more marked than in the US, the government which presided over an unemployment rate in excess of 13 per cent steadfastly refused to promise when a return to normalcy could be expected, but despite this was returned to office in 1983 with a much stronger electoral mandate to sort out the nation's economic ills.

During the first two post-war decades economic management in the UK amounted to the management of aggregate demand. Although there was a greater emphasis placed on incomes policies from the mid-1960s onwards, demand management continued to play a central role until the mid-1970s. Thereafter it suffered a partial eclipse as the control of inflation became the overriding policy goal of the Labour government. That eclipse was completed after 1979 with the election of a Conservative government which pursued a vigorous monetarist policy in conjunction with a tight fiscal policy.

In the US, Keynesian demand management was not much in evidence during the 1950s, but in the early 1960s when unemployment was high demand management followed the traditional Keynesian pattern of personal income tax cuts, increased government expenditures and easy monetary policy. Incomes policy in the form of wage–price guideposts, basically another Keynesian measure, were called on to stem the inflation that would be stimulated by these measures. Early in 1969, shortly after assuming office, President Nixon was able to declare: 'We are all Keynesians now.'

In the 1980s 'Reaganomics' represents a diluted form of demand management, being a blend of Keynesianism and monetarism. A policy of tight monetary and loose fiscal policy might have seemed patently inconsistent before monetarist theory was developed, but the restrictive monetary policy is designed to curb inflation—with the hope that consequent high interest rates will not create real barriers to investment—while tax cuts for business and high-income savers will increase both the demand for, and supply of, investment funds. Thus, through controlling inflation, the private sector is provided with a favourable background for expansion rather than the government participating directly in stimulating spending programmes. Of course, monetary policy cannot be insulated permanently from budget deficits; either interest rates are driven up further, or money supply expands. In either case it might be difficult to achieve just the right degree of monetary tightness.

Given their reluctance, since the mid-1970s, to apply traditional Keynesian techniques of demand management, both governments have increasingly come to rely upon a pattern of special employment measures, including employment subsidies, training schemes and public sector employment programmes. In the next section we look specifically at public employment programmes, and we use this term to include what is referred to as public service employment in the US and job creation schemes in the UK. In the section that follows we look at two potential supply-side solutions to reduce unemployment directly; the introduction of early retirement and a reduction in hours of work.

Since neither special public sector employment programmes nor supply-side solutions offer much hope of successfully combating a chronic deficiency in aggregate demand, we conclude that the return to full employment is dependent upon the adoption of an expansionary demand policy. However, since this carries with it the accompanying risk of inflation we argue that this approach needs to be backed up with a renewed attempt to secure a workable incomes policy. It also needs to be backed up by a programme of manpower training and retraining to ensure that adaptation to structural change is not impeded by labour bottlenecks.

PUBLIC EMPLOYMENT PROGRAMMES

Here we do not refer to normal public sector employment, but the conscious effort to have workers in make-work programmes designed specifically to combat unemployment as well as to provide much needed public services. Despite this laudable goal, the success of such programmes in reducing unemployment is limited.

At first view the effects might seem unequivocably positive. Create jobs for heavily unemployed secondary workers and each worker so employed reduces the number of unemployed by one. But the analysis of earlier chapters, especially Chapter 3 on search unemployment, Chapter 8 on labour force flows among high-incidence groups, and Chapter 5 on minimum wages, warn us against such a simplistic solution. We need to know what the effects of an expansion in public employment are likely to be on private sector employment, on labour force participation, and on wage aspirations. All these elements combine to make the unemployment effects somewhat less than the increase in employment under the programme, to say nothing of the possibility that specially-funded anti-recession programmes might employ at least some workers who would have been hired anyway.

Let us assume initially that a public service job market is created under the following conditions:

(1) The jobs created are for unskilled workers, or for work that has a counterpart in the private sector; thus workers are capable of filling similar jobs in either the public or private sector.
(2) Unemployment in the private sector consists of what Wachter calls the 'new structural unemployment' (see Chapter 8, p.197) for unskilled workers and conventional search unemployment for others. This means that there are vacancies in the private sector which many of the secondary workers will not fill; they are searching for better jobs. More trained workers are simply holding out for higher pay.
(3) For each type of job, the wage in the public sector (B) is set above the market clearing wage in the private sector (R) in order to attract workers into employment.

The initial position is described in figure 10.1, with the public sector wage, W_B, set above the wage, $W_{R(0)}$, in the private sector. Under a microeconomic approach, an excess supply of workers searching for jobs at a higher wage than $W_{R(0)}$ is not inconsistent with equilibrium. These workers, in keeping with the analysis of Chapter 3, will cease to search and drop out of the labour force once they realise that higher-paying jobs are unavailable. However, for the purpose of this analysis they are still in the labour force, searching for better paying jobs.

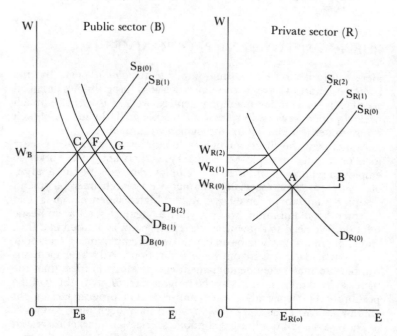

Figure 10.1: *Unemployment Effects of Public Employment Programmes*

To simplify the analysis, let us assume that this excess supply in the private sector is equal to AB, and that the individuals in it are holding out for W_B. Now if OE_B public service jobs are created, all of the AB workers will be absorbed, and full employment achieved, so long as $OE_B = AB$. But this felicitous result represents only the first round of adjustment to the new public service jobs. Up to this point of theoretical full employment in both sectors, there has been no reaction of employed workers in R to this situation. Since they can qualify for the new jobs in B, they will compete for these jobs alongside those previously holding out for higher wages in R. Just because they were willing to work for $W_{R(0)}$ before, there is no reason why they should not seek jobs that pay far more, especially when the uncertainties surrounding wage offers—which are the basis of search unemployment—have been removed. They know for certain that there are jobs paying W_B which they are capable of filling.

This shift of employed workers to B results in a shift in the supply schedule in R from $S_{R(0)}$ to $S_{R(1)}$, and a rise in wages to $W_{R(1)}$. Meanwhile, the influx to B shifts the supply curve, $S_{B(0)}$, to the right to $S_{B(1)}$, and excess supply, or unemployment, CF, arises in B. Labour market equilibrium in the traditional search model analysis might now be achieved in that the higher wage opportunity in B, compared to that in R, is balanced by the lower probability of finding a job at that wage in B. It is also reasonable to assume that CF is smaller than AB; that is, that there is a net reduction in unemployment even though unemployment arises in B. This follows since we can assume that, with rising wages in R, the number who will prefer unemployment in B to jobs in R will be fewer than the former number holding out in R at the lower wage $W_{R(0)}$. But, of course, new labour force entrants will be attracted into B to push out CF. Evidence of this labour force growth appears in the study by Cohen[2] who found that the growth in employment associated with four US manpower programmes was about 40 per cent greater than the decline in unemployment.

In any case, while a situation of equilibrium might be achieved with unemployment CF, after a sequence which somewhat parallels adjustments between covered and uncovered labour markets in response to a higher minimum wage, policy-makers may not be pleased because the unemployment reduction is too small. They might attempt to reach a full-employment equilibrium by increasing the number of jobs in B. By expanding demand to $D_{B(1)}$ they will absorb the CF workers, but this will not be the end of the adjustments towards a stable equilibrium. Now, with no unemployment in B, another disequilibrium situation arises as workers employed at wage $W_{R(1)}$ in R move to B, where the probability of getting a job has increased.

As long as a full-employment policy is pursued, a stable equilibrium with no unemployment and no further movement from R to B is reached only if wages in R rise to the level of W_B, and public sector employment pushes out to G. A large wage increase in R, such as is implied at the equilibrium, when $W_{R(2)} = W_B$, is the result of fewer workers being available for jobs in the private sector. Clearly such a solution is impractical, but it derives from the assumptions of the model.

The question that therefore arises is: Why should the public sector wage be set above the market clearing wage in the private sector? The only reason is to attract those working for a higher wage in R. However, if the unemployed in R (i.e. AB) do not simply consist of those searching, but includes, or consists largely of, people who are unemployed because of a deficiency in aggregate demand, then a higher wage is not necessary to attract them into B; the pull of job opportunities will be sufficient.

Thus, provided that there is demand-deficient unemployment in the private sector, the wage in the public sector need not be set above the private wage, and employment creation in the public sector will not be offset by employment losses in the private. Furthermore, the inflationary effects of the transfers need not arise.

In other words, the model described above is not really applicable to a situation in which unemployment arises largely because of a deficiency in aggregate demand, and when public sector jobs can be created at the same wage as comparable jobs in the private sector. The creation of public sector jobs on a temporary basis, therefore, remains an important part of the strategy to combat unemployment during recession. However, a problem that arises with the expansion of this sort of programme is that of displacement, and where this occurs the overall level of employment creation is reduced.

Whereas the central, or federal, government finances the programme of public sector jobs, these are often administered by state and local governments. Therefore, judged in terms of the unemployment objective, there can be a divergence between purpose and achievement. That is to say, while central or federal government allocates funds to state and local governments in the expectation that they will be used to further specific programme objectives, this does not always happen. Sometimes the funds might be used by state and local governments to finance expenditures on public employment which would have been undertaken anyway. When this happens there will be a displacement effect in public employment, those who find employment under the programme displacing workers who would have been employed in the absence of the programme. In some instances individuals currently employed might not be thrown out of work if the local government uses part of its existing workforce to meet the programme objectives, using central funds to pay their wages. Here current employees will be displacing the unemployed who are not taken on by local government. In a study of the net impact of public service jobs on employment, Johnson and Tomola[3] found that out of every 100 jobs funded, the net gain in jobs was only somewhere between 50 and 70, after displacement had been taken into account. Further, they found that the displacement effect became stronger the longer the duration of the programme, suggesting that employment gains tend to be shortlived.[4]

A final weakness of public service employment, which is not directly related to the above analysis, is that it is not always the case that the jobs created will be filled by secondary workers, those with the heaviest unemployment. And humanitarian considerations apart, money spent on lower-level jobs that are better suited to secondary workers would be more effective in reducing unemployment. This is because even if the unemployment rate for higher-skilled jobs is also above its frictional–structural base, as it is likely to be in the recessionary conditions under which public service employment programmes are implemented, a given amount of funding will create fewer high-wage jobs than low-wage jobs.

Baily and Tobin[5] present a strong argument for programmes to focus on unskilled jobs for this reason. Effective programmes to hire the unskilled would reverse the rightward shift in the Phillips curve, posited by Perry, caused by the compositional shift in unemployment towards lower skilled workers (see Chapter 4, p.81). But a contrary conclusion is reached by Johnson and Blakemore[6] who estimate that focusing on jobs for low-wage workers will have a negligible effect on their unemployment because of the increased labour supply of these workers in response to (higher wage) job opportunities.

Furthermore, if job creation programmes cater to the needs of the unskilled rather than those already possessing some skills, two beneficial consequences are likely to arise in the longer term. First, by providing more continuous employment, special programmes give the unskilled much needed experience in a work setting which will improve their job stability later on. This is especially true for younger workers, who are so numerous in the disadvantaged segment of the labour force, and who often constitute a target group for public service programmes. Secondly, such programmes often provide an element of training which will be beneficial to unskilled workers in enhancing their future prospects of securing steady employment in better jobs.

However, in practice, US public service employment programmes designed specifically to reduce unemployment during recessions have more often than not resulted in the employment of trained rather than unskilled workers. For example, Wiseman[7] finds that although employment is concentrated on minority groups, it is not the disadvantaged in these groups who benefit since there is little participation among poorly-educated workers. When CETA (the Comprehensive Employment and Training Act) incorporated PEP (the Public Employment Program 1971) in 1973 it continued the practice (for which PEP had been criticised) of employing workers in areas of public (state and local) job need rather than emphasising the employment needs of the unskilled.[8] But this situation changed somewhat after 1978 when focus shifted to the disadvantaged. Thus in fiscal year 1978, towards the end of the job programme, over 75 per cent of CETA job-holders could be classified as economically disadvantaged.[9]

The dominant pattern in the past of catering for public manpower needs rather than workers in greatest need (unemployed low-wage workers) is in keeping with the rationale of public service employment, which is to take advantage of the opportunity to finance worthwhile employment at the state–local level, while reducing high unemployment in the process. Public service employment is not to be confused with governmental job-of-last-resort programmes, which Wiseman[10] disparages as 'simply income maintenance with a work requirement'. This description emphasises the transfer aspects of the unemployment effects in the model of public service employment that was discussed above.

As described by Balkenhol,[11] public service job creation programmes 'are a palliative, a transitory measure that allows the unemployed to gain time until, it is hoped, overall economic prospects improve'. How weak a palliative it is can be gauged from the fact that in fiscal year 1981 it catered to only 118,000 first-time participants in the US,[12] that is something between 3–4 per cent of the average stock of unemployed during that period. In the UK, the Job Creation Programme (JCP) created about 140,000 jobs over its three-year life, 1975–8. While that also represented between 3–4 per cent of the average stock of unemployed during the period, Metcalf[13] has calculated that the annual average number of year-long jobs was only 29,000 during the three years. Thus, given some displacement, the average impact on unemployment would have been even less.

In both the US and the UK the number of workers benefiting from special labour market measures was much greater than the number affected by job creation programmes. For example, in fiscal year 1981 in the US, CETA provided training and temporary subsidised employment (in both public and private sectors) for 2.9 million workers. In the UK just over 300,000 were covered by special employment and training measures. Furthermore, in 1982 a new 21 billion Youth Training Scheme was announced in the UK, and it was intended that this would provide a programme of training, practical experience and further education for over 400,000 young people, by September 1983.

REDUCING THE LABOUR FORCE THROUGH EARLY RETIREMENT

In the UK there is a policy movement towards encouraging early retirement. Specifically, the Job Release Scheme (JRS) of 1977 compensates early retirees if their jobs are taken by an unemployed worker. The scheme is of limited application since it requires a close fit between the job status of the unemployed and that of older workers. Nevertheless, up to March 1982 about 130,000 had retired under the scheme. While schemes of this sort lead to a direct reduction in unemployment, the same would not necessarily be true of a general plan to encourage early retirement to make jobs available for unemployed workers. Although it might be thought that such a plan would also have a one-for-one effect on unemployment, with a much stronger effect on the unemployment rate than on the labour force participation rate, this would only be the case if there is a fixed amount of work to be done.

In the US, the normal age of retirement is 65 for both males and females, although the 1977 Age Discrimination in Employment Act allows individuals to postpone retirement to 70 if they so choose. In the UK, the normal retirement age for males is 65, but for females it is 60.

Ignoring the possible expansion in the labour force as job availability improves, there would be substantial initial effects in reducing unemployment if earlier retirement for all was introduced. But there are three long-run effects—all adverse—that may arise from this induced reduction in the labour force. The first relates to the reduced level of production at any stage of the cycle. While it is true that in a recession this reduction in output is potential rather than actual in that there will be a one-for-one replacement of unemployed workers for employed older ones, production potential during the next period of expansion will be limited by the reduced labour force. As the economy becomes stronger and unemployment declines there will be less than a one-for-one replacement and at the next cyclical peak output and employment will be less than they would have been had the early retirements not taken place. As a consequence the average standard of living is reduced. Expressing the effect on lifetime earnings, there will be a shorter work period to finance non-work consumption. The situation may call for more transfers to the aged, but this does not mitigate the loss in total output; it merely spreads the loss throughout the population rather than have it concentrated on non-producing, former older workers. To the extent that employers bear part of this cost they will try and recoup it through higher prices.

The second negative feature of general early retirement is—as Metcalf[14] has noted—that private firms will be pressured to lower the age of eligibility in their own occupational pension schemes. The effect would be to raise labour costs and weaken international market status.

The third adverse consequence is that the benefit of reduced unemployment will only occur during that recession in which the early retirement is introduced. In subsequent recessions of similar intensity, the unemployment rate will revert back to what it was prior to the early retirement, and could even rise. The reason for this is that recessions that occur after the retirement age is lowered will begin from a lower full-employment production base. A given percentage reduction in employer demand from this base will generate the same percentage reduction in employment as it would from a higher production base with the larger workforce that prevailed prior to early retirement. Thus, from the demand side, there is no reason to believe that the benefit of lower unemployment will persist during future recessions. However, supply-side considerations suggest that the rate could worsen, in the US at least. This is because many of those in the age range immediately above the official retiring age tend to be in the labour force only when they have jobs; in bad times if they are unable to find a job they tend to leave the labour force rather than become unemployed. The effect of this will be to cushion the rise in the unemployment rate. If some of this group are no longer in the labour force because they have taken early retirement, they will no longer be able to withdraw once the recession gets under way. And, given that the decision to leave the labour force will be a function of age *per se* as well as the official retiring age, the number who are willing to withdraw during recession will tend to decline as the official retiring age is reduced. Instead, the unemployment will fall on younger age groups who will tend not to withdraw.

Given these adverse consequences, and the fact that to reduce the normal age of retirement would be irreversible, it seems unwise to pursue this approach to combat recession unemployment. It is far better to tackle such unemployment by the introduction of selective retirement schemes such as JRS. Inducements to older workers to leave the labour force can always be withdrawn as the economy picks up again, thus ensuring that future expansion is not jeopardised. Of course, if unemployment on the scale experienced in the UK in 1982-3 becomes a permanent feature of the labour market, then the arguments against a general reduction in the normal retiring age are much weakened. The real output loss is the same irrespective of whether a given number of people are permanently unemployed or allowed to take early retirement. Furthermore, the increased financial costs of retirement would be offset by the reduction in unemployment benefit payment, although the costs of both are borne by those who remain in employment.

Although the recent trend in the US has been towards earlier retirement as a result of improved benefits, this trend is likely to be reversed by the 1983 Social Security Reform Act. This was introduced in order to assure the solvency of the Social Security system and under it the normal retirement age will be pushed up from 65 to 67 in the next century. To be more precise, a worker who was 23 years old in 1983 will have to go on working until he is 67 before he becomes eligible to draw his pension.

Although this extension in the normal age of retirement will be introduced gradually, its effect on unemployment will be reinforced if private pension plans also follow suit. If recession coincides with the age extension, there will be more older workers in the labour force and the unemployment rate will be higher. In subsequent recessions the full-employment production base will be higher and the same percentage cut back in employment demand will be associated with a lower unemployment rate, even though with retirement benefits deferred more older workers will tend to be locked into the labour force as unemployed job seekers, assuming that they wish to retain consumption standards.

Finally, the long-run effects on production and income would be opposite to those of early retirement. There would be greater full-employment production, a higher standard of living at that level, and less need for transfers to those under 65.

REDUCTION IN HOURS OF WORK

The object here is to reduce the number of hours of work supplied by a typical individual. There are several ways in which this might be achieved, including (i) a reduction in the length of the normal working week; (ii) a reduction in overtime working; (iii) an increase in holiday entitlement; and (iv) the splitting of full-time jobs into two or more part-time equivalents.

In the UK the trade union movement has for several years been pressing for the introduction of the 35-hour week.[15] Quite apart from the increase in leisure that would be enjoyed by those currently employed, trade union leaders argue that such a policy would reduce unemployment. However, the unions' demand is not just for a reduction in hours, but for weekly rates of pay to be maintained. If conceded, such a demand would imply an increase in hourly wage rates of 14.3 per cent, assuming a reduction in hours from 40 to 35. Such an increase would be inflationary unless it could be matched by a corresponding increase in productivity over and above the increase necessary to finance any annual improvement in wages that is also negotiated. It seems most unlikely that productivity could grow so quickly, even if the reduction is spread over several years, unless at the same time unions moderate their wage demands and accept lower increases in real wages. But, of course, to the extent that the reduction in hours can be compensated by an increase in productivity, there will be no need to increase employment in order to maintain output, and there will be no consequential reduction in unemployment.

Even when the reduction in hours is not offset by an increase in productivity, a reduction in unemployment is not inevitable. Since hourly wage rates will rise, employers will demand fewer hours in total and whether there is an increase in employment will depend on the elasticity of labour demand. There will be a critical value of demand elasticity and if the actual elasticity is greater than this the reduction in hours will not lead to an increase in employment, unless it is also accompanied by a reduction in weekly pay.[16] Just what this critical level of demand elasticity will be will depend on the number of hours reduction that is sought, and on the importance of fixed labour costs relative to wage costs. However, there is a further complication since a reduction in hours is likely to result in an increase in employers' demand for overtime hours, thereby enabling them to spread fixed costs, of both capital and labour, over a greater volume of output. Since many workers will also offer to work overtime it seems likely that greater overtime working will in fact result. Clearly, to the extent that there is increased overtime working, the reduction in hours will not contribute to a reduction in unemployment. Where employers are able to introduce shift working, or other patterns of work that enable a significant reduction in overhead costs to be secured, the chances of an expansion in employment are greatest.

The reduction in the normal working week is also likely to be accompanied by a reduction in output per worker (even though output per hour might increase); and unless this is compensated for by a sufficiently large increase in the number of workers employed, total output will fall. In the case of the UK, such a reduction in output, coupled with the inflationary consequences of the reduction in hours, would have an adverse effect on the UK's competitive position, unless, of course, foreign competitors experienced similar tendencies.

In the late 1970s the Department of Employment[17] estimated that the introduction of the 35-hour week would result in a reduction in unemployment of anything from 100,000 to 500,000, depending upon the extent to which output losses were made up by productivity growth and overtime working. It was estimated that labour costs would increase 6.0–8.5 per cent. Assuming that only 35 per cent of lost output would be made up by increased employment, the DE estimated the consequential reduction in unemployment to be about 350,000. But this represents only the initial impact effect; the final outcome would be less favourable than this as the adverse consequences on the foreign trade sector work themselves through.

In the UK, some trade union leaders[18] have also advocated a ban on overtime working as a means of reducing unemployment. Even during the fourth quarter of 1982, when unemployment exceeded 13 per cent, 31 per cent of all operatives in manufacturing industry in Great Britain were working over eight hours of overtime each week, giving a total of about 10 million hours. If these hours could be translated into jobs, at a rate of 40 hours per job, another 250,000 jobs would be created for manufacturing operatives alone. In practice, this would be extremely difficult to achieve simply because it pays both employers and employees to continue with overtime working. Even though overtime hours might be less productive than ordinary hours, and attract premium rates of pay, it might still make good economic sense for employers to rely on overtime working rather than take on more workers. This is most obvious when they are confronted by an unexpected increase in orders, or a predictable but temporary increase in demand. However, as noted above, even in normal times overtime working enables capital to be worked for longer hours and its cost to be spread over a greater volume of output. For any given level of output, overtime working might allow an employer to operate with a lower level of fixed capital. In short, it might help an employer to achieve a more optimal combination of capital and workers, and therefore he will be reluctant to abandon recourse to it. From the point of view of the individual worker, overtime working offers the means of earning a higher income, and he too might be very reluctant to give it up. Thus, despite the protestations from trade union leaders about the undesirability of high levels of overtime working co-existing with high levels of unemployment, there will be strong pressure from individual employers and individual workers to retain it.

Longer holidays could also lead to an increase in employment if employers took on more workers to compensate for the weeks lost. However, given that the demand from trade unions is for extra paid holidays, the effects would be similar to those resulting from a reduction in the length of the normal working week. The demand for total man hours would fall, output would decline, and industrial costs would rise. While in certain instances it might lead to an increase in employment, there would be a tendency for employers to try to rearrange work in such a way as to make do. Indeed, the problem here, as with any policy for reducing hours, is how the extra hours and weeks can be translated into job equivalents. In practice, the existing pattern of the working day, week or year will make this extremely difficult to achieve.

A novel approach to the reduction in hours was launched in the UK in July 1982 when the government announced financial incentives to firms willing to split a full-time job into two half-time jobs. In order to qualify for the cash payment of £750, the employer has to offer at least one of the jobs to someone who is unemployed, or will become so, in the near future. Although the scheme is unlikely to attract many takers, and is therefore unlikely to make a major dent on the unemployment figures, it is nevertheless sound in principle. It allows two people to work half-time rather than full-time or not at all. Since it is a voluntary scheme, everyone participating in it is presumably better-off as a result of it.

A general reduction in working hours does not therefore offer much scope for combating unemployment. While work sharing is fine in principle, to be successful it also needs to be accompanied by income sharing. But those who advocate a reduction in normal hours and more paid holidays do not accept that there should be some reduction in the real income of those affected. Only in the case of a ban on overtime working is this implicit in the proposal, but here opposition from individual workers and employers is likely to be so strong as to render such a policy ineffective. All of this is not to imply that there is anything sacrosanct about the current length of the normal working week, or about current levels of provision for paid holidays. Improvements in both will no doubt continue in the years ahead as a result of the conscious decisions of individual bargaining units to allow part of the fruits of economic progress to accrue in the form of greater leisure.

Temporary early retirement schemes, introduced during a cyclical recession, would seem to offer greater scope for unemployment reduction, and also have the advantage of being reversible when the economy picks up again.

THE NEED FOR DEMAND EXPANSION

Apart from temporary early retirement schemes, there does not therefore seem to be much scope for tackling unemployment from the supply side. And, although special public sector programmes of job creation are useful, the jobs they provide are temporary and quite often cause displacement. These displacement effects can be fairly large if the programmes are budgetary self-financing—i.e. the expenditure on the programme is offset by the reduction in benefits plus the increase in tax revenue generated by higher employment incomes.[19] The same is true if there is fiscal substitution, with state and local governments using centrally-committed funds to finance expenditure that they would have undertaken anyway. But displacement apart, if the public sector jobs are at higher rates of pay than similar jobs in the private sector, further problems arise and the unemployment reducing impact is not so great.

The inevitable conclusion that we are driven to in considering these alternatives is that if there is to be a return to full employment there will need to be an expansion in aggregate demand. This conclusion also follows from the analysis of Chapter 7, where, after taking account of the increase in the frictional–structural base, it is suggested that 40–50 per cent of US unemployment in 1982, and about 70 per cent of that in the UK, was attributable to a deficiency in aggregate demand. A prerequisite for the return to full employment in both countries is therefore an expansion in aggregate demand, particularly in the UK. It almost goes without saying that this expansion should be gradual, otherwise labour market bottlenecks and inflationary pressures will develop. Indeed, it is because of the fear of stimulating inflationary pressures that both governments are afraid of engineering an expansion in demand, preferring instead to wait until inflation has been conquered, and, under the natural order of things, the economy returns to something approaching full employment. But this could take a very long time. As Chapter 4 explains, the main consequence of relying exclusively upon monetary policy to deflate inflationary expectations is that unemployment in excess of the natural (i.e. frictional–structural) rate arises during the transitional period. Just how long this transitional period will be is not known. All that can be said is that if the economy behaves as the theory predicts, there will, in time, be a movement back to the natural rate.

This reluctance to expand is greater when the western world generally is suffering from recession. Any country that goes it alone and pursues expansionary demand policies under such conditions runs the risk of both an accelerating rate of inflation and a balance of payments problem. Given the importance of international trade to the UK, its economy would be particularly vulnerable to a domestically generated expansion.

Since no country—and in particular the UK—is likely to act as a locomotive, pulling itself and the world economy out of recession, there is an overwhelming need for expansionary demand policies to be agreed upon and coordinated at the international level. In other words, there needs to be a renewed attempt to develop a spirit of international Keynesianism, but this will need to be supplemented by domestic policies designed to curb the growth of money incomes, particularly wage incomes.

Many economists, both in the UK and the US, advocate incomes policy as an alternative to *restrictive* monetary policy. This is because it is capable—potentially at least—of reducing the rate of inflation without incurring the high economic and social costs of unemployment. However, it is wrong to regard monetary policy and incomes policy as strict alternatives to each other. The policies are complements rather than substitutes because, as Peston[20] has observed, 'the effects of the behaviour of money wages and the money supply are significantly inter-related, and . . . *together* have an impact on the inflation rate and the employment position.' Any attempt to reduce the full employment rate of inflation will have the same consequences for the growth in money supply as for the growth in money wages, and therefore 'the announcement of [say] a money supply target for the medium term is equivalent to the announcement of an incomes target, and vice versa.'[21] If the two diverge in the short run then employment must take the strain.

Although the emphasis in recent years has been on creating unemployment to dampen down wage inflation, it is by no means certain that such a policy will always command political support. Once inflation has been brought under control, or at least brought down to an acceptable level, the political will to tackle unemployment through expansionary demand policies might return. At that point there will be a need to reintroduce some form of incomes policy in combination with both monetary and fiscal policies. If policy-makers refuse to accept that these policies have to be 'rationally combined' then the suffering of the last few years may well prove to have been in vain.

A staunch advocate of this integrated approach to policy is James Meade. However, while still advocating reliance on a whole panoply of Keynesian financial policies to regulate aggregate demand, Meade[22] suggests that orthodox Keynesianism needs to be replaced by a new variety of Keynesianism. Whereas the old orthodoxy relies on the use of financial policies, including exchange rate policy, to achieve target levels of real effective demand and thus *real* levels of national income, the new variety would use the same financial policies 'to maintain a steady but moderate rate of growth of total monetary expenditures on domestically produced goods and services and so of the national *money* income.'[23] And whereas the orthodox Keynesian policy needs to be backed up by an incomes policy that concentrates on fixing money rates of pay in order to curb price inflation, the new orthodoxy would need to be accompanied by a reform in wage fixing designed 'to promote real output and employment in each sector of the economy'.

But even under the new orthodoxy, the need for international cooperation still arises because individual countries pursuing expansionary demand policies would still have to ensure that they achieve external balance. Any country expanding its way back to full employment that found itself in balance of payments difficulties would still be faced with the choice of abandoning its full employment goal, restricting imports, or depreciating its real exchange rate, unless international cooperation could be secured on policies relating to interest rates, exchange rates and the use of international reserves and liquidity. Thus Meade concludes that Keynesian full employment can only be secured if international financial institutions are suitably reformed as well as national wage fixing institutions. But, however desirable or essential economically, Meade accepts that both will be 'extremely difficult, if not impossible, to achieve politically'.

Even with sensible policies, however, the return to full employment in the UK is going to take several years to achieve. Writing in late 1982, Metcalf[24] estimated that even the modest goal of 2 million unemployed by 1986 would have required the creation of 1.7 million new jobs over the four-year period—i.e. the creation of new jobs at twice the fastest rate actually achieved in the post-war period.

Because we see incomes policy as playing an important role in facilitating non-inflationary demand expansion, it is discussed further below. But first we discuss active manpower policy, which is equally important.

ACTIVE MANPOWER POLICY

The return to full employment, and the achievement of a faster rate of economic growth that must underlie this, might well be accompanied by a faster rate of structural change. Many commentators argue that this has already been occurring with the advance of new technology, but that its full impact on unemployment has been masked by the depressed state of the labour market. Once demand picks up again, and unemployment generally begins to fall, the full extent of these structural changes will show through in greater labour market imbalance.

It is true that as the number of robots increases, and the use of the micro chip spreads, the displacement of labour from traditional occupations will increase, making it more difficult to attain full employment. But on the other side of the equation there will be the growth in new jobs generated by the new technology itself, and an expansion in job opportunities in the more labour-intensive sectors of the economy. Whether the growth of new jobs exceeds the disappearance of the old ones depends upon the rate at which total output is expanding relative to the pace of productivity growth, which in turn is related to technological progress and structural change. A faster rate of structural change need not lead to greater mismatch in the labour market and higher structural unemployment provided that sufficient emphasis is placed on labour market policies, particularly manpower policies. In the 1960s and early 1970s the OECD placed considerable emphasis on the need for active labour market policies, including manpower policy. High unemployment has tended to push such policies into the background in recent years, but the need for them will be as great as ever in a period of sustained demand expansion if that expansion is not to be impeded by skill shortages.

The objective of manpower policy is to achieve a better match between labour supply and demand in the different sub-sectors of the economy. This is achieved by increasing labour mobility generally, and in particular by mobilising marginal groups within the labour market (e.g. the unskilled, young workers, the handicapped, etc.). The main element in such a policy is the provision of adequate training and retraining facilities. While most industrial training is provided on the job by employers, during recession the amount of training carried out is greatly reduced, and even in good times the amount actually undertaken is often inadequate to meet the economy's needs—hence the need for government intervention. Also, since it is not absolutely clear where vocational education and counselling should end and industrial training begin, young school leavers often enter the labour market ill-equipped to make rational choices about jobs, training, etc. Thus it might be necessary for the government to devote resources to job counselling, particularly for school leavers.

It is therefore absolutely essential that demand expansion be coupled with a programme aimed at upgrading the skills of the labour force. While most of this will be carried out by industry itself, government must stand by ready to identify emerging needs and ensure that these are met. Sometimes this will necessitate the government, or its agencies, acting as provider of last resort.

The sort of training and retraining that is required will not be confined solely to the provision of traditional skills—although future needs in this area should not be underestimated. According to one authority,[25] the chances of a British school leaver finding an apprenticeship in 1981 was 25 times less than in Switzerland. As noted in Chapter 2, the need for government intervention will range from the provision of job orientation and job motivation programmes for the long-term unemployed, to the encouragement—and, perhaps, even provision—of higher-level skills.

The importance of active manpower policy cannot be stressed too strongly, particularly in the UK where the labour market has been depressed for so long that it is just not known at what level of demand shortages will begin to appear once expansion gets under way again. Like incomes policy—to be discussed next—manpower policy is complementary to aggregate demand policy and vital to its success.

INCOMES POLICY

According to Worswick,[26] the term 'incomes policy' embraces 'all devices designed to modify the system of wage and price determination so that, at any given level of employment, the economy will deliver a slower rate of increase in money wages and prices.' In the present context, the reference to a 'given level of employment' needs to be stressed because we are advocating incomes policy as a complementary policy to aggregate demand policy to secure full employment at a lower rate of inflation than would otherwise obtain.

Incomes policy has been tried more frequently in the UK than in the US where it is usually referred to as 'wage-price guidepost' policy. The object of such policies is to reduce cost-push inflationary pressures that tend to build up as the economy moves towards full employment. Their roots are essentially Keynesian in that they imply that inflation arises mainly from the operation of the wage-price system itself, rather than from monetary factors.

Traditional Incomes Policy Mechanisms

Productivity serves as the pivotal element in incomes policy. Under the traditional mechanism, a formula is established for tying wage and price changes to the average productivity growth for the economy. The basic relationship is quite simple: if wage increases are set equal to the rate of productivity growth price stability is achieved and, as a by-product of this sequence, factor shares remain constant, assuming that one starts from a position of zero inflation.

However, problems arise when different industries and sectors experience different rates of productivity growth. If a uniform wage increase is to apply, then the attainment of zero inflation and the maintenance of factor shares requires that prices fall in those sectors where productivity is rising relatively quickly, and rise in those sectors experiencing a relatively slow rate of productivity growth.

Incomes policies can be either voluntary or compulsory, with the full backing of the law. Irrespective of whether it is voluntary or compulsory, so long as it is rigidly observed a system of wage and price fixing develops 'that is almost indistinguishable from an economy in which wages and prices are directly fixed by government authority'.[27] Therefore, all that a rigidly adhered to incomes policy is, is simply a wage-price freeze adapted for productivity changes. Thus the criticisms against it are the same as the familiar ones against rigid wage-price controls.[28]

For example, it perpetuates wage differentials and causes labour market distortions because it does not allow shifts in labour supply and demand to work themselves out through relative wage changes.[29] In addition, it is likely to result in imbalances in the product market for, as Lancaster[30] has pointed out, even in the simplest two-sector model, only by the most fortuitous of coincidences would markets clear under price movements in the formula.

These microeconomic maladjustments that arise under incomes policy are identical to those that would be generated by wage–price controls and can be countered by adopting a more flexible policy, that is, one that departs from a simple wage–productivity formula. A more flexible approach would allow wages to rise faster than average productivity in fast-growing sectors, and in sectors experiencing labour shortages. Below-the-norm increases would be required in sectors with labour surpluses and slow-growing product demand. In practice, the major problem will be to strike the right balance between flexibility and tight control.

The most serious drawback to the successful implementation of incomes policy arises at the macroeconomic level. While it is true that productivity-related wage increases will not generate inflation, inflation can arise for reasons other than that wage increases outstrip productivity growth. Indeed, even when wage increases exceed productivity growth this does not necessarily imply that these increases are the cause of inflation. Price increases may be the initiating force in the wage–price relationship. If expansionary monetary policy, or effective demand stimulation, or exogenous supply-side shocks, trigger off an increase in prices, workers will require a wage increase that exceeds productivity growth if they are not to suffer a reduction in their share of income and a lower rate of real wage increase than they would otherwise have received. It has long been recognised that incomes policy will break down under demand–pull inflation, but in broader terms it will not be supported when inflation comes from sources other than wage pressures.

If at the time an incomes policy is introduced inflation is already under way, a formula that allows average wages to increase in line with average productivity, and at the same time confers full compensation for the previous period's price increases, will lead to a stable rate of inflation, ensure that real wages grow in line with productivity, and maintain factor shares. If the rate of inflation is to be brought down, it will be necessary not to compensate fully for the past price increases. However, this would imply a reduction in labour's share of national income, and a slower rate of growth in real wages than is justified on productivity grounds, and in the extreme case perhaps even a reduction in the real wage. Thus, once an inflation is under way, trade unions will tend to resist incomes policy, not only because it limits their freedom to bargain and enhance labour's relative position, but because if it is to be successful it must, by definition, have adverse consequences on labour's share of national income and on real wages.

All of this is not to deny that incomes policy can play its part in stemming supply-side inflation, but to stress that such a policy will require forceful unions and large firms to give up their wage and price-fixing powers and adhere to norms and guides that would leave them no better-off than they would be if perfect competition prevailed. It can be done, but it requires great discipline, and there will be lapses from time to time just as there are in all other areas of policy.

US Experience

In the US, voluntary guideposts were introduced in compliance with the recommendation of the Council of Economic Advisors in their 1962 Annual Report.[31] The productivity growth rate of 3.2 per cent at the time served as the guide for wage increases. The guidepost seemed to work for a while, despite a brief conflict between President Kennedy and the steel industry in late 1962 when he forced a roll-back in steel price increases in excess of the guidepost formula, a result which called into question the voluntary nature of the programme. In 1966, in response to inflationary pressures, the Council recommended a productivity guide that was lower than the prevailing rate of productivity growth.

On the surface, if the productivity guide is reduced below the actual productivity gain the risk of inflation recedes, but there is a danger in deliberately pitching the guide 'too low'. The danger lies in the fact that the growth in real wages is suppressed and workers' share of income reduced, thus making it less likely that organised labour will voluntarily accept the policy.

Even if the adjusted guideposts had not failed in the face of demand and exogenous supply-side inflationary pressures, worker resistance to them would have made them inoperable. By 1967 they were quietly discarded, only to be reintroduced in the Nixon administration's Phase II anti-inflationary programme in late 1971, after the brief wage–price freeze of Phase I. The new guideposts were a recognisable variant of the old, although they were never called guideposts, perhaps because of the failure of the former programme. Under Nixon they became compulsory, with wages administered by a Pay Board, and prices by a Price Commission. Further, the wage rise limit was set at 5.5 per cent in the expectation that prices would not increase by more than 2.5 per cent, with an implicit expected productivity growth of 3 per cent.

Since prices rose by only 3.3 per cent in 1972 compared with over 5 per cent in the year immediately preceding the initiation of the anti-inflationary policy, the policy seemed to work, at least for a while. But the Nixon administration's own pre-election expansionary policy, and the rise in food prices consequent to the large grain export deal with the USSR,[32] undermined the guidepost policy. Furthermore, by early 1973 labour chafed at the guidepost barrier which prevented bargained increases in line with incipient inflation, and as Phase II came to an end the policy was dropped.

The last attempt at guidepost policy was made by President Carter in 1979, but the programme was never implemented. However, it is interesting to note that the Carter formula proposed a wages limit of 7 per cent in the hope of limiting price increases to 6 per cent, with a realistic assumption of only 1 per cent productivity growth. Thus, whereas the original guideposts were geared for zero inflation and the Nixon programme for 2.5 per cent, the Carter formula assumed 6 per cent. This simply reflects the point made earlier, namely, that if inflation is already a fact of life when the policy is introduced, the wage-guide formula must take account of this. By implication, the higher the rate of inflation at the onset of the policy the higher the wage-guide must be set, and the longer it will take to bring the inflation under control.

UK Experience

While incomes policy has a longer history in the UK than in the US, we only discuss its application since the 1960s. Unlike guidepost policy in the US which was applied sporadically, in the UK incomes policy was almost continuous between 1965 and 1978, though varying in the intensity of application and the degree of compulsion. However, for the period 1960-77, Henry and Ormerod[33] find no evidence that incomes policy had any lasting success, although they do find evidence of short-run success in combating wage inflation. Of course, the accuracy of such tests of effectiveness is not foolproof, based as they are on comparisons of *actual* wage movements under the policy and *predicted* wage movements in the absence of the policy. While we do not fault the tests of Henry and Ormerod, their period of investigation ends in 1977 and does not therefore cover Stage 3 of the Labour government's Social Contract Mark II, which ran from 1975 to 1978.[34] Over this period inflation was reduced from a rate of over 25 per cent per annum to around 8 per cent.

Earlier, during the period 1965-70, the Labour government's incomes policy had a percentage norm but allowed exceptions on the grounds of low pay, higher productivity and manpower shortages. For most of the period the policy was presided overby the National Board for Prices and Incomes (NBPI), to which the government made selective references. The stress placed by the NBPI on the need to improve productivity gave stimulus to the development of productivity agreements. Unfortunately many of them turned out to be bogus, designed merely as a means of circumventing the policy and contributing nothing to productivity growth.

During the 1970s there were two distinct periods of incomes policy, each representing a different approach to the perennial problem of wage inflation. The first, modelled on the 1971 US wage-price guides, was introduced by the Conservative government under Mr Heath and covered the relatively short period from the end of 1972 to the beginning of 1974. This was a compulsory policy, extending to prices as well as wages, and it began with a complete freeze on both. Although it had the full backing of the law, the policy and the government were challenged by the miners during the winter of 1973-4. The outcome was a change of government and the abandonment of the policy.

Despite its short life, and its ignominious end, the policy had certain features which distinguished it from earlier attempts at incomes policy. It was enshrined in detailed pay and price codes and administered by two new agencies, the Pay Board and the Price Commission. Furthermore, the policy was innovative in that it introduced a flat rate element into the pay norm, thus benefiting the lower paid, and in its provision for threshold payments. Under the latter, workers were compensated over and above the norm for each full percentage increase in the rate of inflation in excess of the threshold level, which was fixed at 6 per cent.

The Pay Board also tried to get to grips with the problem of pay anomalies, caused by the introduction of the policy itself, and the wider question of pay relativities. On the latter it emphasised the need for policy to be sufficiently flexible to adapt to longer-term changes in economic circumstances as well as changes in perceptions about what is 'fair'. By implication this suggests that the policy was seen as something that 'ought' to last more than just a short period of time.

The tendency towards flat-rate pay increases continued under the Labour government's Social Contract. This was a voluntary policy that ran for three years. The government's attempt to secure a fourth year failed because it tried to 'impose' too low a norm on an unwilling trade union movement. Apart from its voluntary nature, and its success—in the short run at least—in combating inflation, the policy was significant for the fact that its Stage 2 was much tougher than Stage 1, although there was some relaxation between Stages 2 and 3. It was possible to secure a Stage 2 that was tougher than Stage 1 because of the Labour government's willingness to trade off tax concessions in return for trade union acceptance of a lower norm—that is, lower than what the unions were initially willing to agree to, but also lower than the norm that had prevailed in the preceding year.[35]

Thus, while geared to productivity, UK incomes policy has been more flexible than US policy in responding to price changes. Perhaps it is this flexibility, albeit within a framework of restraint that permits pay increases only grudgingly, that explains the greater reliance that has been placed on incomes policy in the UK, at least until 1979 when Mrs Thatcher introduced changes in both the style and the emphasis of economic management. Recent discussion in the US has suggested innovations in incomes policy that approximate more closely to the UK system in which wage–guides are adjusted for price changes to allow for greater continuity in the policy's application.

Guidepost Innovations: Tax-Based Incomes Policy (TIP)
In 1979 President Carter recommended a new type of incomes policy, TIP, the analytical framework for which had been constructed previously by Okun.[36] Basically, TIP calls for the taxing power of the federal government to be used to induce voluntary compliance with anti-inflationary incomes policy. Specifically, under the Carter plan,

wage increases were to be limited to 7 per cent, with the expectation that the inflation rate would be 6 per cent, implying a productivity growth of 1 per cent. Factor shares would have been maintained and real wages increased in line with productivity growth. The tax system came into play under the plan in that workers' real wages were to be protected by tax rebates on a one-for-one basis if the actual inflation rate exceeded 7 per cent, subject to a 3 per cent limit on rebates. The similarity with the UK threshold experiment of the early 1970s is thus apparent, even though the real wage protection offered under TIP would not have been as open-ended.

The difference between the TIP proposal and the UK threshold policy is that the latter allowed higher-than-expected price increases to be translated directly into wage increases, while the former proposed to do so only indirectly with redistributive effects. The UK policy was also backed up by a detailed Price Code which spelt out just when cost increases were allowed to be passed on.

The unions opposed Carter's TIP plan because, if implemented, it would have reduced their scope for bargaining. They were also concerned that the tax rebates were only to apply for one year, with no future promise of real wage protection. They were particularly opposed to the 3 per cent limit on rebates since, given the prevailing inflationary climate, there was no certainty that the inflation rate would be under 10 per cent.

The TIP proposal would probably have reduced the wage demands from those unions that would have pressed for money wage increases in the range 7–10 per cent on the grounds that they expected inflation to be somewhere within the same range. It is not so obvious that the proposal would have reduced the wage demand of a union that felt justified in demanding, or confident of receiving, a wage increase in excess of 10 per cent. However, with expected productivity growth of only 1 per cent, it seems highly likely that the proposal would have had a depressing effect overall on wage demands, assuming that the inflation rate was not expected to exceed 10 per cent.

Although a programme along the TIP lines would check cost–push inflation from the labour side, like any guidepost policy it would not be able to cope with demand–pull inflation. This will mean that in practice TIP threshold formulae for wages and prices will be close to anticipated levels resulting from demand forces and inflation in the preceding period. As You[37] points out, there will be a tendency to set targets at the current inflation rate to avoid the risk of demand–pull forces upsetting the programme. This will do nothing to reduce inflationary expectations, but it might help to prevent them from rising still further.

An alternative TIP proposal, designed by Wallich and Weintraub,[38] would operate directly on firms. Instead of tax rebates for workers, this plan would set tax penalties on firms granting wage increases above the target level. This would certainly strengthen the resistance of firms in that wage concessions above the target level would now cost them more. Obviously, unions would not welcome this added employer resistance to their wage demands.

There would also be administrative difficulties in monitoring compliance, especially from the millions of unincorporated businesses, and from non-profit and government employers. But these problems are no more serious than the problems encountered in administering conventional guidepost policies. At any rate they could be tackled by concentrating, in the first instance, on the largest employers.[39]

Although this TIP variant would reduce the probability of wage–push inflation, there would be no restraint on profits–push inflation. Firms might be encouraged to raise prices slightly above the level needed to maintain profit margins, while holding wages at the threshold level, or below. In order to counter this, a penalty would need to be imposed on firms that raise their prices above some specified target level. However, if rigidly applied, such a policy would be unfair to those firms which need to raise prices because of non-labour cost increases. The only way around this problem would seem to be the introduction of a detailed price code in which allowable cost increases are specified.

CONCLUDING COMMENTS

While no firm conclusions can be drawn from this brief survey of UK and US experiments with incomes policy, the future prospects for incomes policy are not as bleak as many commentators would have us believe. While the econometric evidence suggests that such policies have not resulted in a permanent reduction of the long-run rate of wage inflation, there is evidence of short-run successes. Also, it is important to stress that while they might not have had much success in reducing the long-run rate of wage inflation, incomes policies might well have prevented that rate from accelerating. Better designed policies that strike the right balance between flexibility and overall control might achieve greater success in the future,[40] particularly if they can be kept going for more than just a short period. The UK experience suggests that it is possible to introduce more sophisticated policies than inflexible wage guides and at the same time develop more effective mechanisms of control. The TIP proposals in the US reveal that there is no shortage of ideas; all that is required is the political will to implement some of them. Although this will require the absorption of manpower to administer such a policy, manpower is the one resource which the UK and US have in abundance at the moment.

Pay determination needs to be brought to the centre of economic policy-making and integrated with monetary and fiscal policy. One method of achieving this would be for economic ministers to discuss with trades unions and employers' associations the sort of tax packages that they would be prepared to trade for various levels of wage settlement. Given that the level of wage settlements in the year ahead is a vital factor in the determination of aggregate monetary demand, it is perhaps surprising that there has not been more effort to influence this level in pre-budget discussions between government and those responsible for determining it. Of course, agreement at the centre between government, employers' representatives and trade unions about the appropriate wage-guide does not itself amount to an incomes policy, but if it could be achieved it is an important first step. Although it would require trade unions to relinquish *some* of their bargaining power, that might be a price that they would now be prepared to pay if, in return, governments committed themselves to expansionary demand policies and the return to full employment. After all, with double digit unemployment, union bargaining power is greatly reduced anyway. Thus, in reality, there would be very little sacrifice.

On the other, hand, unless governments take an initiative of this sort they might find it necessary to create still further unemployment in order to prevent the rate of wage inflation from accelerating again. If trade unionists see that moderation in their wage demands does not have much impact on unemployment, they might abandon their moderation and press for higher settlements. Governments would still be faced with the same choices as they now have for dealing with this, but in exercising their choice they would be starting from a much higher unemployment base.

The time is ripe for another attempt at incomes policy in both the UK and the US. The allocative inefficiency that such policies give rise to is nothing compared to the output losses that result when 10 per cent and more of the labour force is out of work. If politicians and trade union leaders continue to shun incomes policy, it will be they who will be responsible for the continuation of mass unemployment.

NOTES AND REFERENCES

1. Robert Lucas Jr, 'Unemployment policy', *American Economic Review*, 68, May 1978, p.355.
2. Malcolm S. Cohen, 'The direct effects of federal manpower programs in reducing unemployment', *Journal of Human Resources*, 4, Fall 1969, pp.491–507.
3. George Johnson and James Tomola, 'The fiscal substitution effect of alternative approaches to public service employment policy', *Journal of Human Resources*, 12, Winter 1979, pp.3–26. But Michael Buros and Daniel Hamermesh, 'Estimating fiscal substitution by public service employment programs', *Journal of Human Resources*, 13, Fall 1978, pp.561–5, find that long-term results are even lower and unpredictable if the time-path of adjustment is not constrained as it is in the Johnson–Tomola model.
4. In another study, Alan Fechter, *Public Employment Programs* (American

Enterprise Institute for Public Policy Research, 1975), finds a long-run displacement of up to 75 per cent of expenditures on public service jobs from other potential employment.

5. Martin Baily and James Tobin, 'Macroeconomic effects of selective public employment and wage subsidies', *Brookings Papers on Economic Activity* (1977) pp.511-40.
6. George Johnson and Arthur Blakemore, 'The potential impact of employment policy and the unemployment rate consistent with non-accelerating inflation', *American Economic Review* 69, May 1979, pp.119-23.
7. Michael Wiseman, 'Public employment and fiscal policy', *Brookings Papers on Economic Activity*, 1976, pp.67-104.
8. Only 27 per cent of PEP participants had less than a high school education compared with almost half the unemployed. Sar Levitan and Robert Taggert (eds), *Emergency Employment and the PEP Generation* (Salt Lake City: Olympia, 1974).
9. Deborah Jamroz, 'Public service employment: its role in a changing economy', *Federal Reserve Bank of New York Review*, 4, 1979, pp.34-8.
10. Wiseman, *op. cit.*, p.68.
11. Bernard Balkenhol, 'Direct job creation in industrialized countries', *International Labor Review*, 120, July-August 1981, p.425. Data following are from pp.425-38.
12. *Employment and Training Report of the President*, 1982.
13. David Metcalf, *Alternatives to Unemployment: Special Employment Measures in Britain* (London: Policy Studies Institute, 1982), p.20.
14. Metcalf, *op. cit.*, p.43.
15. e.g. Jack Jones, *Target 35, The Case for the 35 Hour Week* (London: T&GWU, April 1976).
16. For a more detailed discussion of the effect of a reduction in hours of work on employers' demand for hours, see James J. Hughes, 'The reduction in the working week: a critical look at Target 35', *British Journal of Industrial Relations*, November 1980, pp.287-96.
17. Department of Employment, 'Measures to alleviate unemployment in the medium term: work-sharing', *Department of Employment Gazette*, April 1978, pp.400-2.
18. David Basnett, of the General and Municipal Workers, is one of the most outspoken leaders on this particular issue. See e.g. *GMW Journal* (September 1979), pp.4-5.
19. In such a situation there would be no net stimulus to aggregate demand and, therefore, in a Keynesian sense, no expansion in employment.
20. Maurice Peston, 'The integration of monetary, fiscal and incomes policy', *Lloyds Bank Review*, July 1981, pp.1-13.
21. Ibid.
22. James Meade, 'A new Keynesian approach to full employment', *Lloyds Bank Review*, October 1983, pp.1-18.
23. Ibid.
24. David Metcalf, 'Special employment measures: an analysis of wage subsidies, youth schemes and work-sharing', *Midland Bank Review*, Autumn/Winter 1982.
25. Wil Albeda, 'Reflections on the future of full employment' (Part II), *Labour and Society*, Vol. 8, No.1, January-March 1983, pp.57-71.
26. G. D. N. Worswick, 'The end of demand management', *Lloyds Bank Review*, January 1977, pp.1-18.

27. Arthus E. Burns, 'The effectiveness of wage and price guideposts', *Harvard Business Review*, 43, March–April 1965, p.59.

28. For a strong position against guideposts based on their similarity to outright controls, see Milton Friedman, 'What price guideposts?', *Guidelines, Informal Controls, and the Market Place*, ed. George Shultz and Robert Aliber (University of Chicago Press, 1966), pp.17–39.

29. This negative effect of incomes policies in perpetuating wage structures has beeen minimised by Fores who points out, at least for the UK, that over a long period in the labour market itself relative wages have tended to be very stable as workers shift about in response to job openings rather than in response to differential pay. Michael Fores, 'Job evaluation and Incomes Policy', *Lloyds Bank Review*, October 1974, pp.38–48. This argument denies Harberler's contention that incomes policy, by its nature, cannot be successfully applied for long periods because of the wage rigidity it creates. See Gottfried Harberler, 'Incomes policy and inflation: some further reflections', *American Economic Review*, May 1972, pp.234–41.

30. Kevin Lancaster, 'Productivity-geared wage policies', *Economica*, 55, August 1958, pp.199-212.

31. Council of Economic Advisers, *Annual Report* (Washington: Government Printing Office, 1962), pp.185-90.

32. Barry Bosworth, 'Phase II: the US experiment with an incomes policy', *Brookings Papers on Economic Activity* (1972), pp.343-48, claims that the rise in food prices played a major role in the breakdown of Phase II.

33. S. G. B. Henry and P. A. O. Ormerod, 'Incomes policy and wage inflation: empirical evidence for the UK 1961-1977', *National Institute for Economic Research*, 85, August 1978, pp.31-9.

34. The Social Contract was an agreement between the Labour Party and the trade union movement on a range of policy issues, including wages. On the issue of wages, it allowed for these to rise with the cost of living. When Labour was returned to office after the February 1974 election the Social Contract came into being. However, it did little to restrain wages and inflation, and therefore a new and tougher version was introduced in July 1975. It is the new version that we have referred to as Mark II. By implication, the Social Contract Mark I ran from early March 1974 to July 1975.

35. For a general discussion of this willingness to trade tax concessions against a lower norm, see James J. Hughes, 'Budgeting for a wage policy', *The Banker*, March 1977, pp.53-6. For a discussion of the economic impact of such a proposal, and the conditions under which it would be beneficial to workers, see Norman Blackwell and Anthony Santumero, 'Incomes policy and tax rates—an innovative policy attempt in the United Kingdom', *Economica*, 95, May 1978, pp.153-69.

36. Arthur Okun, 'The great stagflation swamp', *Challenge*, 20, December 1977, pp.6-13.

37. Jong You, 'Is tax-based incomes policy an answer?', *Canadian Public Policy*, 86, Winter 1982, pp.95-102.

38. Henry Wallich and Sidney Weintraub, 'A tax-based incomes policy', *Journal of Economic Issues*, 5, June 1971, pp.1-19.

39. Richard Slitor, 'Implementation and design of tax-based incomes policies', *American Economic Review*, 69, May 1979, pp.212-65, suggests that to avoid these problems the programme should be limited to the 2000 to 3000 largest corporations. This suggestion may be more practical than

equitable, but such a limitation was implied if not expressly stated in guidepost implementation.

40. Laurence Seidman, 'The case for a tax-based incomes policy', *Sloan Management Review*, 20, Winter 1979, pp.75–9, proposes a flexible approach through a TIP variant that has both tax rebates and penalties for wages set below and above threshold levels.

Index